ZOO STORY

ZOO STORY

Life in the
Garden of Captives

THOMAS FRENCH

HYPERION
·····
New York

Library of Congress Cataloging-in-Publication Data
has been applied for.

ISBN: 978-1-4013-2346-2

Hyperion books are available for special promotions and
premiums. For details contact the HarperCollins Special
Markets Department in the New York office at 212-207-7528,
fax 212-207-7222, or e-mail spsales@harpercollins.com.

Book design by Karen Minster

FIRST EDITION

10 9 8 7 6 5 4 3 2

THIS LABEL APPLIES TO TEXT STOCK

For the colt and the spider monkey

and the girl riding bareback in the sun

··· CONTENTS ···

This is a work of nonfiction, based on four years of reporting at Lowry Park Zoo in Tampa, along with additional reporting in Africa, Panama, and New York. The book follows the lives of both humans and animals, and all of the names and details describing them are real. Nothing has been invented. Though I witnessed many of the scenes and overheard much of the dialogue firsthand, some sections are reconstructed from interviews and research. My descriptions of some of the human characters' thoughts and feelings are based on what those subjects shared with me and on my years of shadowing them. Although it is impossible to fully understand the interior lives of animals, several sections in the book attempt to explore those landscapes, based on detailed reporting into the animals' histories, on interviews with the keepers and other humans who knew them best, on my own observations of them, and on readings from research on animal cognition, communication, and behavior. For specifics on how each chapter was reported, please see the endnotes.

"I know zoos are no longer in people's good graces.
Religion faces the same problem.
Certain illusions about freedom plague them both."

—

YANN MARTEL,
Life of Pi

ZOO STORY

The New World

Eleven elephants. One plane. Hurtling together across the sky.

The scene sounds like a dream conjured by Dalí. And yet there it was, playing out high above the Atlantic. Inside the belly of a Boeing 747, eleven young elephants were several hours into a marathon flight from South Africa to the United States. Nothing could have prepared them for what they were experiencing. These were not circus animals, accustomed to captivity. All of these elephants were wild, extracted at great expense and through staggering logistics from their herds inside game reserves in Swaziland. All were headed for zoos in San Diego and Tampa.

The date was August 21, 2003, a Thursday morning that stretched on and on. The elephants were confined in eleven metal crates inside the semidarkness of the freighter jet's cavernous hold. Before they were loaded into the plane, they had been sedated. Now they were woozy and not particularly hungry. Some lay on their sides, slumbering. A few stood and snaked their trunks toward a human who moved up and down the line of crates, replenishing their water, murmuring reassurance.

"Calm down," Mick Reilly told them. "It's not so bad."

Mick was thirty-two, with light brown hair and the permanent tan of someone who has grown up in the African bush. As usual, he was clad in his safari khakis and an air of quiet self-assurance. His arms and legs bore the faint scratches of acacia thorns. His weathered boots were powdered with the red dust of the veldt. Everything about him testified to a lifetime of wading through waist-high turpentine grass and thickets of aloe and leadwood trees, of tracking lions and buffalos and rhinos and carefully counting their young, of hunting poachers armed with AK-47s.

Mick and his father ran the two game reserves where the elephants had lived in Swaziland, a small landlocked kingdom nestled in the southern tip of Africa. Mick and these eleven elephants had come of age together in the parks. They recognized his scent and voice, the rhythms of his speech. He knew their names and histories and temperaments—which of them was excitable and which more serene, where each of them ranked in the hierarchies of their herds. Watching them in their crates, he could not help but wonder what they were thinking. Surely they could hear the thrum of the jet engines and feel the changes in altitude and air pressure. Through the pads of their feet, equipped with nerve endings highly attuned to seismic information, they would have had no trouble detecting the vibrations from the fuselage. But what could they decipher from this multitude of sensations? Did they have any notion that they were flying?

"It's OK," Mick told them. "You'll be fine."

Not everyone, he realized, agreed with his assessment. He was tired of the long and bitter debate that had raged on both sides of the Atlantic in the months before this flight. Tired of the petitions and the lawsuits and the denunciations from people who had never set foot in Swaziland, never seen for themselves what was happening inside the game reserves. There simply was not enough room for all of the elephants anymore, not without having the trees destroyed, the parks devastated, and other species threatened. Either some of the elephants had to be killed, or they could be sent to new homes in these two zoos. Mick saw no other way to save them. He had heard the protests from the animal-rights groups, insisting that for the elephants any fate would be preferable to a zoo, that it would be better for them to die free than live as captives.

Such logic made him shake his head. The righteous declarations. All this talk of freedom as if it were some pure and limitless river flowing through the wild, providing for every creature and allowing them all to live in harmony. On an overcrowded planet, where open land is disappearing and more species slip toward extinction every day, freedom is not so easily defined. Should one species—any species—have the right to multiply and consume at will, even as it nudges others toward oblivion?

As far as Mick could tell, nature cared about survival, not ideology. And on this plane, the elephants had been given a chance. Before his family had agreed to send them to the two zoos, he had visited the facilities where they would be housed and had talked with the keepers who would care for them. He was confident the elephants would be treated humanely and be given as much space to move as possible. Still, there was no telling how they would adjust to being taken from everything they knew. Wild elephants are accustomed to ranging through the bush for miles a day. They are intelligent, self-aware, emotional animals. They bond. They rage and grieve. True to their reputation, they remember.

How would the exiles react when they realized their days and nights were encircled as never before? When they understood, as much as they could, that they would not see Africa again? Either they had been rescued or enslaved. Or both.

The 747 raced westward, carrying its living cargo toward the new world.

The savanna, alive just after sunset. Anvil bats search for fruit in the falling light. A bush baby wails somewhere in the trees. Far off to the east, along the Mozambique border, the Lebombo Mountains stand shrouded in black velvet.

A fat moon, nearly full, shines down on a throng of elephants chewing their way through what's left of the umbrella acacias inside Mkhaya Game Reserve. A small patch of green in the center of Swaziland, Mkhaya is one of the parks the elephants on the 747 were taken from. This was their home. Before deciding what to think about the fate of the eleven headed for the zoos, it helps to see the wild place they came from. To know what their lives were like before they ended up on the plane and to understand the realities that pushed them toward that surreal journey.

An evening tour through Mkhaya is especially dramatic—climbing into a Land Rover at the end of a golden afternoon, then lurching along the park's winding dirt roads, searching for the elephants who remain. Mkhaya's herd is a good-sized group—sixteen in all, counting the calves—and even though they are the largest land mammals on earth, they are not always easy to find. Elephants, it turns out, are surprisingly stealthy.

As the sunlight fades, other species declare their presence. Throngs of zebras and wildebeests thunder by in the distance, trailing dust clouds. Cape buffalo snort and raise their horns and position themselves in front of their young. Giraffes stare over treetops, their huge brown eyes blinking, then lope away in seeming slow motion. But no elephants.

A couple of hours into the tour, the visitors begin to wonder if they will glimpse any of the hulking creatures tonight. Then suddenly the entire group seems to materialize from nowhere. The driver has unwittingly turned a corner into the center of the herd. On both sides of the road, elephants loom like great gray ghosts. They're in the middle of their evening feeding, knocking down trees, snapping branches and chewing on leaves and peeling bark with their tusks. As the Land Rover sputters to a stop in their midst, the elephants turn their massive heads toward the intruders. Two calves hurry toward their mothers and aunts. A towering bull, his tusks faintly glowing in the moonlight, moves from the shadows into a patch of red leopard grass only twenty feet away.

"Here's my big boy," says a woman in the back row of the vehicle. "Come over and say hello."

As if on cue, the bull steps into the road and lumbers toward the Land Rover. He doesn't appear angry. Just insistent. Behind the wheel, the tour guide quickly restarts the engine, then shifts into reverse. He's hurrying backward down the road when, in his mirror, he spies one of the females waiting beside a bushwillow. As the vehicle approaches, the cow bends the tree across the road and holds it there, directly in the humans' path. She makes it look easy.

Without slowing down, the guide spins the wheel, taking the Rover off the road—still in reverse—and maneuvering around both the elephant and her roadblock. He keeps his foot on the gas, tearing and bumping backward down a little hillside and across a dry riverbed until he's sure none of the herd is following.

The guests inside the Land Rover try to process what they've just witnessed. What was that elephant doing?

The guide smiles, shrugs. "She was just being naughty. They've got a sense of humor—more than people realize."

Naughty?

Another shrug. "She was definitely trying to block our way," says the guide. "It's just not good to drive through an elephant herd. They don't like you to drive through. They want you to listen to them."

Driving back to camp, he explains that elephants get irritated when they're not in control. He talks about how helicopter pilots, flying over herds, have seen elephants grab small trees and shake them, as if trying to swat the helicopters from the sky.

Here in Mkhaya, encounters between elephants and humans tend to be more relaxed. Every day, the herd indulges the curiosity of the tourists who approach in Land Rovers with their camcorders. Usually the elephants seem curious as well, walking within a few feet of the humans, calmly reaching forward with their trunks. Still, whenever the two species meet, anything can happen. Once, a park employee was bicycling to work when he accidentally pedaled into the middle of a herd. The rattling of his bike spooked a mother with her calf, and the cow attacked, chasing down the man and then picking him up and throwing him several times. He survived—barely.

In Swaziland, as in other parts of Africa, elephants have struggled to hold their own against humans. Americans tend to think of Africa as a continent of vast, unclaimed spaces, where species can roam to the horizon and beyond. In reality, humans have occupied so much of the continent that many animals are confined inside game parks. Although these parks are often huge—sometimes stretching across hundreds of miles—the animals increasingly find their movement restricted by human boundaries, human considerations, human priorities.

As our species paves over the planet, squeezing other species out of existence, we seek solace in the myth of unlimited freedom. Inside our subdivisions, we sit with our kids and watch *The Lion King*, singing along as Simba and Pumbaa and Timon parade across the endless veldt and majestically celebrate the circle of life. But the truth is, the circle of life is constantly shrinking. If you're going to see a lion, even in Africa, it will almost certainly be on a tour inside a fenced park.

The conflict unfolds in miniature inside Swaziland, a country smaller than New Jersey. Although elephants once thrived here, the only two places where they can be found today are inside Mkhaya and at another fenced reserve, Hlane Royal National Park. Compared with the mammoth game parks in South Africa and other neighboring countries, Mkhaya and Hlane are tiny. Only a few dozen elephants live inside the two parks.

Fifty years ago, not a single member of their species could be found in Swaziland. They had all long since died off or been killed by hunters. Then Ted Reilly, Mick's father, stepped in. Ted was born and raised in Swaziland and spent his childhood in the bush, watching antelope graze in the distance, studying how kingfishers bore holes into the dirt to make their nests. As a young man he left home to study conservation, working as a ranger in game reserves in nearby South Africa and Zimbabwe. When he returned to Swaziland in 1960 to help run his family's farm, he discovered that during his years away almost all of the country's wildlife had been wiped out. Traveling through regions that had once teemed with dozens of species, he found them all gone.

Reilly decided to bring the animals back. First he turned the family farm in Mlilwane into a wildlife sanctuary. He planted trees and savanna grasses, built dams to create wetlands, then stocked the new habitat with species he had imported from other countries or had captured himself. His adventures bestowed him with a larger-than-life reputation. He tore through the bush in an old jeep named Jezebel, pursuing impala and warthogs and any poachers foolish enough to venture inside the sanctuary. He scoured the Swazi countryside, gathering scorpions and frogs and lizards. He had a female hippo from a London zoo flown in, then ferried a male from the same zoo across the English Channel and had it flown in from Paris. His rangers captured a nine-foot crocodile on the banks of the Nkomati River, then drove the thrashing reptile to Mlilwane in a pickup truck.

One harrowing day, Reilly and a crew of thirty were transporting a white rhino that they'd tranquilized and then hoisted onto a flatbed truck. The men, seated around the sleeping prize, were startled when the rhino awoke enough to snap through his ropes and stand up beside them on the back of the moving vehicle. Their armored captive was groggy, but no less fearsome. Some of the men jumped off. Others yelled until the driver stopped and the rhino could be restrained again.

The campaign to restore the country's wildlife inevitably drew the attention of King Sobhuza II. The Swazi monarch, one of the last kings to reign over an African country, was famous for having fifty wives, some of whom he chose at the annual Reed Dance, a great tribal celebration where thousands of bare-breasted virgins undulated in public and paid homage to his majesty and the queen mother. As a national symbol of fertility, the king was expected to have many wives and produce many children. In nearby South Africa, where Swaziland was often viewed as a backwater, mention of the dance and the king's topless maidens prompted eye-rolling. The jibes of outsiders were of little consequence to Reilly. A royalist through and through, he dismissed these naysayers as ignorant of his country's ancient traditions. Besides, his battles against hunters and poachers had earned him more than a few foes in the Swazi parliament. If he was to prevail, he needed the king's support.

Sobhuza, who longed for the return of wild creatures, proved a dedicated ally. The sanctuary at Mlilwane was only the beginning. Working closely with the king and his successor, his son Mswati III, Reilly went on to create the country's first national park at Hlane and then opened Mkhaya, a reserve designated for the protection of endangered species such as black rhinos and Nguni cattle. A nonprofit trust was formed to operate the three parks. Reilly trained more rangers, including his son Mick, and stocked the land with more species—lions, sable antelopes, buffalos, cheetahs.

The elephants began to arrive in 1987, when Mick was still a teenager. From the start, they were controversial. There were a dozen of them, all trucked in from South Africa, all of them calves only a few years old. They were survivors of the annual culls carried out to control the country's elephant population. Though the calves had been spared, they had witnessed the slaughter of their families. Not everyone was sure it made sense to bring them into Swaziland. How would they survive without their mothers? Even if they did make it, would they be haunted by memories from the culls?

Ted Reilly brushed away the questions. He agreed that the calves would be happier roaming the bush beside their mothers. But their mothers were dead. Weren't they better off, Reilly said, starting new lives in Mkhaya and Hlane?

The elephants survived. They did so well, in fact, that within a few years of their arrival, they exceeded the parks' resources. Elephants are among the most beloved animals on the planet. But they are also voracious eaters that feed for up to eighteen hours a day. They have a remarkable ability, unrivalled by any species except for Homo sapiens, to alter their surrounding ecosystems. The elephants inside Mkhaya and Hlane were tearing the bark off so many trees and knocking down so many other trees that they were systematically deforesting entire sections. The destruction threatened the future of the eagles and owls and vultures that nested in those trees. It also posed a serious challenge for the black rhinos, one of Africa's most endangered species, which depended on similar vegetation for their diet.

In the months before the eleven elephants were loaded onto the plane, some animal-rights groups argued that there was plenty of room inside Mkhaya and Hlane, that the overcrowding had been exaggerated, that the Reillys had invented a crisis so they could justify selling the elephants to the zoos.

But the magnitude of the problem is obvious to anyone who tours the parks, even today. The devastation inside Mkhaya is striking. And in Hlane, it is catastrophic. Standing at one of the interior fences, looking toward a section of the park where there are no elephants, visitors see a lush expanse of green trees and bushes. If they turn their heads a few inches and look on the other side of the fence, toward the area where Hlane's elephants live, all that meets the eye are miles of dead trees. Many have been pushed to the ground. Hundreds of others stand like twisted silhouettes, their branches black and broken and bare.

Gazing across this moonscape, it seems impossible that the elephants have managed to survive, much less any other species.

• • • • • • • •

Above the waves and the clouds, the 747 soared on. Sunlight burned along the wings. A thin trail of exhaust tapered behind, etched across a canvas of perfect blue.

Inside the hold, some of the elephants drifted in and out of sleep. Others were more alert, the effects of their Azaperone and Acuphase injections slowly wearing off. Mick, beyond exhaustion by now, was still patrolling back and forth between them, talking softly in the human language they were most likely to recognize.

"*Kahle mfana,*" said Mick, speaking in siSwati, the native tongue of Swaziland. "*Kutwulunga.*"

Steady, boy. It will be OK.

A South African veterinarian named Chris Kingsley worked nearby, assessing the elephants. The vet watched their respiration patterns, checked to see if they responded to sounds, made sure that none were shivering or showing other signs of trauma.

Chris and Mick had been working for more than forty hours straight. They began their labors before dawn early that Wednesday morning, where the crew tranquilized the elephants inside the boma—a fenced corral where the animals had been kept in preparation for the journey— then lifted the animals via a conveyor belt and a crane onto flatbed trucks to be driven to Manzini, the nearest city with an airport. Loading them onto the trucks took all day, and then the drive to Manzini took most of the night. The airport didn't have a runway big enough for a 747, so the elephants were shifted onto a pair of Ilyushin IL-16s, and then when they flew into Johannesburg, they had to be unloaded from those two planes, with forklifts moving the crates, and reloaded into the hold of the 747. It was winter in that part of the world, and cold enough that night that Mick could see ice glinting on the tarmac. Despite the chill, there were formalities to be observed. They had to wait for customs officials to sign a stack of release forms. By the time the freighter jet accelerated down the runway, the sun was up, and it was Thursday morning.

Chartered for $700,000, the plane had more than enough thrust and weight capacity for the task at hand. A few more tons would have been no problem. Still, the pilots were not eager to cause their passengers any distress, so they eased their ascent, taking off at a gentle angle before heading across the tip of the continent toward the Atlantic.

As the 747 carried them across the equator and backward through eight time zones, the divide between morning and afternoon began to blur. Mick and Chris were enveloped in the hum of the engines and the breathing of the animals. Watering cans in hand, they checked on the elephants' progress, making sure that they had enough to drink and that the trays underneath their crates were not overflowing with urine. Elephant urine is so corrosive it can eat through metal.

All of the elephants were juveniles, between ten and fourteen years old. Four were headed for Tampa, and the other seven would travel on to San Diego. So far they seemed to be doing well. Early into the flight, Chris had been concerned about Mbali. Named after one of Mick's two daughters, she was the youngest and smallest of the group. After take-off, Mbali wasn't eating or drinking. She simply lay in her crate. The vet had the impression she was depressed. A few hours later, the young elephant seemed to have recovered. She was back on her feet, drinking water with her trunk, responding to the humans' voices. The other elephants were vocalizing too, sending out waves of rumblings that Mick and Chris could feel in their chests. The two of them were startled when one of the males trumpeted. The bulls were more restless than the cows. Already, some strained at their confinement. Mick could see them leaning against the interior of their crates, pushing with their feet, testing the strength of the walls. A sickening thought occurred to him: What if one broke out?

His mind fixed on the image. He visualized the male elephant charging toward the front of the plane. He saw it bulldozing into the cockpit, trampling over the pilots, then finally bursting through the nose.

The bull would plummet toward the waves far below. The shattered 747—no more pilots, no controls—would tumble close behind.

At first, when the Reilly family was trying to find an answer to the elephant problem, they did not even consider zoos. After decades of fighting to create open spaces for wildlife, the notion of constraining animals inside a zoo seemed appalling. Anne Reilly, Mick's sister, admits that when she originally heard that her father and brother were considering sending some of the parks' elephants to San Diego and Tampa, she was aghast.

"I thought, Isn't that why we have them here—to keep them out of zoos?"

Both Ted and Mick acknowledge that they, too, had difficulty contemplating the possibility. In his head, Mick pictured animals pacing in reeking cages.

"We would have personally preferred the animals to go into a wild situation," he says. "I never visited zoos much in my life, and my idea of zoos was the traditional sort of zoo that was around fifty years ago."

Neither contraception nor surgical neutering was an option. Trials were being conducted on elephants in the field, but no viable methods had been fully tested. An assortment of difficulties—the nature of the females' cycles, the length of time required to perform vasectomies on the males, the threat of violence from other elephants watching on—made it impossible to seriously consider such procedures. Besides, there were already too many elephants inside the parks.

The Reilly family searched neighboring South Africa for other parks that could take the elephants. But every time they thought they might have found a new home, the permits were denied. South Africa already had more than enough of its own elephants to contend with. The government, the Reillys say, would not allow any more to be brought in.

They considered other places in Africa. But almost everywhere they looked, the threat of poaching seemed too great. Some countries even sanctioned organized elephant hunts. In Botswana, where the elephant surplus is even greater than in South Africa, a wealthy American tourist can pay $50,000 to join a safari and shoot down an elephant bull, then climb atop his fallen corpse for a victory photo. The Reillys did not want Mkhaya's and Hlane's elephants to end up dead, their meat and tusks sold on the black market, their bodies treated as trophies. But if they could not find an alternative, Mick and his father concluded they would have no choice but to destroy some of the herd themselves. They already controlled the populations of warthogs and impala and other animals inside the parks with culls. They were prepared to do the same with the elephants, even though they recognized that no other species triggered quite the same depth of emotion among humans.

With their size and intelligence and emotional complexity, elephants were irresistible. People admired the tender attention with which they reared their young, the way the calves were raised not just by their mothers but by their aunts. Their extraordinary memory was cited as evidence of self-knowledge and an awareness of both the past and future; ethicists pondered whether these qualities proved that elephants achieved personhood and should be accorded a moral status and rights equivalent to those of humans. The social hierarchy of the herd—a matriarch directing their lives with almost no interference from adult bulls, who usually roamed the bush on their own or in smaller bachelor groups—appealed to feminist sensibilities. To many, elephants embodied modern notions of progress and benevolence. They were seen not just as awe-inspiring animals, but as nature's great vessels of enlightenment. For all of these reasons, the public identified with the species more intensely than with almost any other.

Even so, elephant culls had long been a reality in other African countries, especially after the ivory trade was banned in the second half of the twentieth century and elephant populations surged in the southern regions of the continent. From the 1960s to the mid-1990s, culls were used to thin herds inside Zambia, Namibia, Zimbabwe, and South Africa. One early method, pioneered in Uganda, required a team of hunters to quietly take position near a family of the animals, then deliberately signal their presence by coughing or breaking a stick. The startled elephants would circle around their young and bunch together, making it easier for the hunters to shoot them down. In Zimbabwe, where close to fifty thousand elephants were culled over the years, the techniques were more efficient. Low-flying planes drove the elephants toward a team waiting in the bush with automatic weapons. Bulls in breeding herds were usually shot first, and then the matriarch and other older females. Killing the matriarch early was standard protocol in many countries, since she anchored the rest of the herd. Without their leader's guidance, they would become confused and not know what to do or where to go. Sometimes, a gunman would scale the matriarch's body, wait for other elephants to venture close, then pick them off too.

The brutal choreography evolved inside South Africa's Kruger National Park, a massive reserve where more than fourteen thousand elephants were culled over the decades. Every year a quota was designated to keep the park's population within manageable limits. Helicopters buzzed over the targeted animals, pushing them toward a preselected kill zone. Sometimes the elephants would be forced to run for miles. The preferred sites were away from the eyes of tourists but close to patrol or firebreak roads so that cranes and trucks could clear away the massive carcasses. The helicopters would spook the elephants toward the killing ground, then circle overhead to keep them close together. Calves, struggling to stay with their mothers, would fall. The adults would roar and raise their tusks as the shadow of the helicopter swept across them.

For a time, the rangers darted the animals from the air with Scoline, a neuromuscular anesthetic used in human heart surgery. An armed ground crew—sometimes as many as sixty men—would then finish off the immobilized giants. But the practice was deemed inhumane after it was discovered that the darted elephants were paralyzed but fully conscious for several minutes and sometimes suffocated to death before the ground crews could shoot them. Eventually the use of Scoline was prohibited. Instead the marksmen leaned out of the helicopters with large-caliber rifles, waiting until they were positioned just above and behind the elephants, and would then fire through the backs of the elephants' necks and into their lower skulls. The elephants did not make for especially difficult targets. Usually they ran in a straight line, with a smooth gait and relatively little bobbing of their heads. When hit by a clean brain shot, the elephants would collapse in midstride, dropping so fast and hard that their tusks would plow into the ground.

The men aiming the rifles understood the logic behind the slaughter, the cold necessity of reducing the herds to save other animals and protect some of the park's most irreplaceable plant life. Kruger's elephants had grown so numerous that they were wiping out entire groves of baobab trees, some of which had towered over the savanna for four thousand years. Knowing these things did not make it easy to squeeze the trigger and watch a young calf tumble to the dirt beside his mother's carcass.

"Don't ask me if I enjoyed it," a game ranger warned a British reporter who witnessed a cull inside Kruger in the early '90s. That day, the ranger and his team had killed three hundred elephants.

"Elephants are beautiful creatures. Of all the animals in the Kruger Park, I respect the elephant most," he said. "We play God, but we are not God. Every time you cull, it takes something away from you. This is not a nice job, but it has to be done."

The aftermath was just as unsettling. Calves old enough to have been weaned and survive on their own were often spared to be sent to other game parks or sold to zoos in the United States or Europe. Sometimes, to prevent the calves from running away, they were tied to their mothers' bodies until they could be pushed or dragged toward transport crates. Around them, disposal teams dressed in overalls and white boots moved between the dead elephants, slitting their throats with pangas to bleed them and then preparing the carcasses for removal. Vultures flapped their wings in nearby trees. In the distance, hyenas waited.

The disposal teams cleaned the killing ground as thoroughly as possible. They didn't want other herds that had not been targeted to enter the area in days to come and stumble onto evidence of the massacre. After years of observing the species inside the park, the staff knew that elephants—unlike most animals—were aware of death and were drawn to the remains of their kin, sometimes burying them in branches and grass. Some researchers even believed that elephants could identify the fallen body of a cow or bull they had known in life. Once, after a cull in Uganda, park rangers had stored severed feet and other body parts of the fallen inside a shed. That night, other elephants pushed their way into the shed and then buried the body parts.

Kruger officials had no desire to instill lingering fear or hostility in surviving herds. They didn't want emotionally scarred elephants seeking revenge against the thousands of humans who tour the park every year. So the culling crews were instructed to remove every trace of the carnage. The cranes and trucks rolled forward onto the blood-soaked ground, and the bodies of the dead were lifted and then hauled away to Kruger's abattoirs. The ivory tusks were collected and stored in warehouses, away from poachers. The meat and hides were sold.

The dead were erased.

Despite these efforts, in Kruger and elsewhere, the other herds somehow seemed to realize that something terrible had occurred. After some culls, elephants would come from every direction, gravitating toward the kill zone. They would stay for a while—lingering at the scene as though they were investigating. Even more remarkably, the behavior of these surviving elephants suggested that they were aware of the threat even before the shooting stopped. In the middle of some culls, herds far from the site were observed to begin moving away from the helicopters and the gunfire. In Zimbabwe, elephants ninety miles from a cull apparently became so alarmed that they fled and hid. Later they were found in the far end of their game park, huddled together.

How did they know to be afraid? In some cases the wind could have carried the scent of blood to their extraordinarily sensitive nostrils. Or they might have heard the pulsing chop of the helicopter blades. Elephants are believed to be capable of hearing storms more than a hundred miles away. As researchers discovered more about the physiology and habits of the species, another answer emerged. The rattled herds, it turned out, were almost certainly responding to long-distance distress calls from the elephants under attack.

Elephants routinely communicate with one another through snorts, shrieks, roars, bellows, and trumpets. They also exchange information through low-frequency rumbles, most of which humans can't hear. Sometimes people in the vicinity of elephants can feel these rumbles; the vibrations have been described as "a throbbing in the air" similar to thunder. One researcher in Kenya, listening to the infrasonic calls on a specialized recorder that picked up low frequencies, reported that they sounded like soft purring. Elephants tune in to these rumbles not just with their ears, but also their feet. Through motion-sensitive cells in the soft pads of their feet, they can detect low-frequency sounds as they ripple in seismic vibrations along the ground. Elephants use these infrasonic signals to attract mates, to assert dominance, and to find and rescue calves who have fallen into watering holes or gotten into other trouble and are calling for help.

The trauma of the culls, then, could not be completely contained. As the targeted animals ran in vain from the helicopters, they would have been capable of sending out terrified warnings to other elephants beyond the horizon. It's easy to picture the distant herds freezing as the messages reached them. The elephants would have held completely still for a second or two, then turned their heads back and forth, ears stiffened and spread wide as they waited for more information.

Who knows how long the distress calls would have lasted. Maybe ten minutes. Maybe half an hour. The cries would cut off, one by one.

Swaziland's elephants had been born into this bloody history. They were among the hundreds of calves who had survived the Kruger culls. They had all run from the helicopters, heard the rifle shots, then watched as their families were butchered.

In the years since, this generation of orphans had wreaked havoc. In different parks around southern Africa, some of these elephants were displaying classic symptoms of post-traumatic stress disorder. They were easily startled and showed elevated levels of aggression. With no older bulls or cows to guide them as they matured, the young males became notorious for their rampages. They knocked down fences, pulled up pipes, trampled farmers' crops. They seemed to be attacking humans and other species with increasing frequency. In a startling display of aberrant behavior, some bulls sexually assaulted rhinos and then killed them.

The Reilly family had encountered these problems with their orphans too. Over the years, several of the males inside Mkhaya and Hlane had exhibited aggression toward the white rhinos. Four bulls had killed rhinos. One bull had fatally attacked three rhinos within twenty-four hours. Mick had shot and killed the aggressors himself. Luckily, these incidents were fairly rare. Most of the three dozen elephants living in the parks were females and seemed to have adjusted well to their new surroundings—too well, given their appetites and the destruction of the trees. By 2001, just seven years after some of the elephants arrived from Kruger, the devastation in Mkhaya and Hlane had reached the point where the Reillys felt they had no choice but to consider a cull of their own.

"We had run out of time," Mick says.

It was right about then that the two American zoos—first San Diego, then Tampa—suggested another possibility. Officials from both zoos flew to Swaziland to describe the new homes they could offer the elephants. San Diego already had a three-acre elephant exhibit. Tampa's Lowry Park Zoo was willing to build one of similar size. The zoos invited the Reillys to see the facilities for themselves. Mick flew to the United States, toured both zoos, and was impressed—not just with the exhibits but with the expertise of the staffs and the care they offered. The animal clinic at San Diego, Mick said, was more sophisticated than any hospital inside Swaziland. At Lowry Park, he was struck by the zoo's manatee hospital, where over the years dozens of injured or ailing manatees had been rehabilitated and then released back into the wild.

That was it. If there was no more room in the game parks, then San Diego and Lowry Park made sense.

"There are zoos," says Ted, "and there are zoos."

With the blessing of King Mswati III, the Reillys and the zoos began the long process of applying for the necessary permits. The zoos agreed to pay the game parks $12,000 for each elephant. The money, the Reillys said, would go to management of Mkhaya and Hlane, protection of the animals within, and the purchase of more park land. In their permit applications, Lowry Park and San Diego pointed out that the arrival of eleven wild elephants would benefit zoos around the United States. It had been more than fifteen years since any African elephants had been brought into the United States, and now the captive elephant population was aging and having trouble reproducing. Bringing in the wild elephants—all designated for breeding—would rejuvenate the genetic pool.

Mountains of paperwork awaited the lawyers and the bureaucrats. But even more was required of the zoos and the game parks. They had to figure out how to transport eleven elephants across an ocean and prepare for their care once they arrived. San Diego already had an African elephant exhibit, but still needed to ship some of its current occupants to other institutions to make room for the new arrivals. Lowry Park had not exhibited elephants in ten years, ever since 1993, when an Asian elephant killed one of the zoo's keepers. After the young woman's death, the zoo closed the exhibit and sent its two elephants to new homes. Now Lowry Park had to build new facilities, hire new elephant keepers, and adopt updated protocols to protect the staff.

In Swaziland, the Reillys had to figure out which elephants would be chosen, then move them temporarily into the boma and ready them for their journey. Working with the zoos, the Reillys designated thirteen elephants from two herds at Mkhaya and Hlane—the eleven elephants intended for the trip, plus two more in case any became unfit for the flight or died during the stress of the preparations. They didn't want any females with young calves or any that were in the third trimester of a pregnancy and at risk for a miscarriage from the stress of the long journey ahead. Elephant pregnancies, however, are difficult to judge without an internal exam. To be certain they weren't choosing any cows late in a pregnancy, the parks decided to bring in two veterinary specialists from Berlin, widely considered among the world's authorities on elephant reproduction.

There was another challenge. The Reillys worried that the elephants who were not chosen might be traumatized if they saw members of their group being tranquilized and taken away by ground crews. To their eyes, the mass removal to the boma could easily look like another cull. To avoid that shock and any resulting hostility toward the park's rangers and visitors, the Reillys decided on a different plan. In March 2003, when the thirteen were to be gathered, a helicopter crew darted every elephant in the two parks, knocking them all out so none would be awake to see the removal. The two German vets, flown in to assist, moved among the unconscious elephants and performed field sonograms on the selected females. Two of the females were pregnant, but neither had entered her third trimester. The elephants were loaded onto trucks and taken to the boma in Mkhaya. The Reilly family assumed the elephants would only have to stay there for a few weeks. But by then, a coalition of animal-rights groups, including Born Free and People for the Ethical Treatment of Animals (PETA), was protesting and organizing letter-writing campaigns and filing a lawsuit in federal court to block the importation of the elephants. "The Swazi Eleven," the activists were now calling them.

"If the elephants are euthanized," Katherine Meyer, a lawyer for the animal-rights groups, told a judge, "that would be a better outcome than to have these elephants put in crates, put on an airplane, brought over here, trained with bull hooks, put in cages, and live the rest of their lives in captivity."

In Swaziland, the Reilly family was denounced by members of parliament, the local newspapers, even other elephant experts. Nine researchers studying wild elephants in Kenya, including Cynthia Moss and Joyce Poole, renowned for their studies on elephant behavior and communication, released an open letter protesting the move, citing the intricacy of the emotional lives of the species and the damage to those lives in captivity. The researchers wrote:

> (W)e believe the time has come to consider them as sentient beings and not as so much money on the hoof to be captured and sold and displayed for our own use. We should be beyond the exploitation of animals as complex and magnificent as elephants.

PETA offered to pay for moving them to other parks in Africa. One politician accused the Reillys of attempting to smuggle the elephants out of Swaziland. Others suggested that the Reillys' talk of a cull was an empty threat, designed to pressure officials in the United States to approve the permits.

Mick and Ted were unprepared for the vitriol. They knew the reputation of Dr. Moss and the other researchers who had signed the letter of protest. But Kenya was not Swaziland. As for PETA's offer to bankroll another alternative to the culling, the Reillys were skeptical. They were sure the offer would come with too many strings. Besides, just because another park was willing to take their elephants didn't mean that the permits would be granted. The Reillys noted that there was no international outcry when they culled impalas or warthogs. Why didn't PETA or Born Free issue press releases and launch petition drives for them? In court and in the media, the coalition hammered away at how San Diego and Lowry Park were angling to buy the elephants because they were a so-called "flagship species," an animal so beloved that their presence in a zoo's collection was sure to increase profits. But the Reillys argued that it was the animal-rights groups who were guilty of exploitation, whipping up the outrage for their own gain, capitalizing on elephants as their own flagship species guaranteed to draw a flood of donations from horrified animal lovers around the world. If the coalition truly believed the crisis in Mkhaya and Hlane was a convenient fiction, why didn't they send someone to see the parks and all their dead trees? The smuggling charge made the Reillys laugh. How exactly, they asked, did one smuggle eleven elephants past customs?

By now it was August 2003, and the elephants had been in the boma for five months. The staff did what it could to keep them comfortable; sometimes their caretakers hand-fed them marula fruit, one of their favorites. Even so, the animals chafed at having their movements restricted. One day, several tried to break through the electrified fence, using another elephant as a battering ram. They chose Mbali—the small female named after Mick's daughter—and thronged together to push her through the fence, apparently so they wouldn't have to touch it themselves. When the current traveled through Mbali and shocked them, too, it put a quick end to their plan.

In Washington, the legal arguments went back and forth in federal court. The government permits had been approved, but now memoranda were being filed, injunctions requested, motions granted and denied and appealed. Finally, on August 15, two circuit judges on the U.S. Court of Appeals in Washington denied one last emergency motion from the animal-rights groups.

The Reillys heard the news and began the final preparations in the boma. It was time to get the elephants into the air.

The 747's engines droned on and on. Mick, still standing, had lost track of time. All he knew was that the sun had finally left the sky and that they were flying in darkness again. A little while ago, they had stopped in Barbados for refueling. Now they were headed for Florida.

The elephants appeared to be holding up well in their crates. Extra doses of Azaperone had calmed the bulls and soothed Mick's fears of disaster. Still, he knew the trip could not be easy for them. After all this time in the air, they had to be hungry.

"*Kunekudla lukunengi,*" he told them. *There's lots of food where you're going.*

Mbali, the little one, was quiet again. She had been sleeping, off and on. Was she dreaming? Did she still feel the jolt in the boma, when the other elephants pushed her into the electric fence? Did she see herself back in the park, wandering through the leopard grass and umbrella thorns?

Inside the hold, among the crates, there was a shift in equilibrium. The plane was descending through the clouds, toward a grid of shimmering light.

Tampa.

2

The Audacity of Creation

Dawn, and already the highway was overrun. A chorus of muttered curses rose from the great steel and chrome herd jammed, snout to tail, in the middle of another morning migration along Interstate 275 toward the towers of downtown Tampa.

Trapped inside their climate-controlled cars, alone with their cell phones and their iPods and their satellite mapping systems, the drivers fought back the urge to swerve onto the shoulder and break free. Instead they inched forward, thumping fists on steering wheels, snarling at other cars that drifted into their lane, allowing themselves a few controlled bursts of aggression even as they stayed in line.

Just off the Sligh Avenue exit, another chorus was sounding. The drivers couldn't hear it. But it was there.

At Lowry Park Zoo, the beasts were waking.

The Malayan tapirs whistled, calling to one another in the early morning light. The orangutans lounged in the rope netting of their exhibit and sighed their philosophical sighs. Through serrated teeth dripping with toxic saliva, the Komodo dragons hissed. From their hiding places under the rocks and logs, the clouded leopards—secretive and mysterious and nearly invisible in the shadows—panted and meowed. A raven cawed and flapped its black wings; a leopard gecko yowled, sounding almost like a cat. The hammerkops cackled; the New Guinea singing dogs barked; and the sloth bears snuffled and sniffed, their long, curved claws clicking on the rocks as they padded out into the sun. A fever of Southern stingrays, flying in slow-motion circles around their shallow pool, were silent except for the tiny splashes of their wing-tips cresting the surface.

High above them all, Cyrus and Nadir serenaded each other with another duet in the sky. The male and female siamangs—Asian gibbons, with long arms and thick black fur and big bulging throat sacs—swung from poles thirty feet in the air as they traded the exact same sequence of hoots and wails that they performed every day. Mated for life, the siamangs sang to seal their bond, to declare their shared history, to warn away intruders. Their duets carried to every corner of the zoo, cutting through the recorded jungle drums beating incessantly from the P.A. system.

Other songs joined the soundtrack. Cries of desire and hunger, protest and exultation. A multiplicity of voices from nearly every continent, at nearly every frequency, of almost infinite variation. Hearing them together on a bright, clear morning was to contemplate the audacity of creation. Not just God's audacity, but man's.

From the argus pheasants to the goliath bird-eating spiders, each of Lowry Park's sixteen hundred animals offered living proof of nature's endless gift for invention. In the curves of their skulls, in the muscles of their wings, in their blood and bones and the twisting nucleotides of their DNA, each carried millions of years of the planet's biological history. But their presence inside these walls also testified to the epic self-regard of the species that had seen fit to build the zoo and so many others like it around the world.

Taken together, the narratives of how the animals ended up at Lowry Park revealed as much about Homo sapiens as they revealed about the animals themselves. The precise details—how and where each was born, how they were separated from their mothers and taken into custody, all they had witnessed and experienced on their way to becoming the property of this particular zoo—could have filled an encyclopedia with insights into human behavior and psychology, human geopolitics and history and commerce. Lowry Park's very existence declared our presumption of supremacy, the ancient belief that we have been granted dominion over other creatures and have the right to do with them as we please. The zoo was a living catalogue of our fears and obsessions, the

ways we see animals and see ourselves, all the things we prefer not to
see at all. Every corner of the grounds revealed our appetite for amusement and diversion, no matter what the cost. Our longing for the wildness we have lost inside ourselves. Our instinct to both exalt nature and
control it. Our deepest wish to love and protect other species even as
we scorch their forests and poison their rivers and shove them toward
oblivion.

All of it was on display in the garden of captives.

By now the sun was climbing in the sky. The front gates weren't open
yet, but the staff was busy feeding the animals and raking the empty
exhibits and searching for any trash that might have blown or been
tossed into the enclosures. When they were done, they shifted the animals into the open air of their exhibits, ready for public viewing.

An Indian rhino, seeing his keeper, ran over and pressed against the
thick gate that separated them. Begging for attention, he whimpered
like a puppy.

"Hi, Naboo," said the keeper, scratching his snout through the
bars.

The rhino's official name, the name shared with the public, was Ar-
jun. But in private the staff called him Naboo, after a planet in *Star
Wars*. They loved bestowing the animals with *Star Wars* names. There
was an otter named Chewbacca and a camel who answered (or didn't) to
Leia. One of the young howler monkeys had been christened Anakin,
as in Anakin Skywalker, which was Darth Vader's name before he grew
up and went to the dark side. The name made sense, because howler
monkeys are born with tan fur and then turn black as they mature. It
was an inside joke. A keeper thing.

In the herps department, the section of the zoo reserved for snakes
and turtles and other cold-blooded creatures, the blue poison-dart frogs
were peeping, very softly, inside a small warm closet clouded with man-
made mist. The room was designed to replicate, as much as possible, the
atmosphere of a rain forest. The males planted their legs on the rocks
beneath them, the heart-shaped pads at the ends of their toes gripping
like tiny suction cups. Their bodies were so bright blue, they seemed

radioactive. Their calls to the females were so quiet, they were almost drowned out by the hum of the ventilation system.

Poison-dart frogs were vanishing from the wild. All over the globe, from the forests of Panama to the spray zones of waterfalls in Tanzania, frogs and toads were dying off. So many species were disappearing so quickly—disappearing much faster than the mass extinctions that had wiped out the dinosaurs—that there was no time to save even a sampling of them all for posterity. Many of these species would simply fade away. Others, selected for survival, would live out the rest of their time on Earth in aquariums and zoos, in small rooms like this one at Lowry Park.

At the zoo, every day was another lesson on living in a world where there were no more pure choices.

Inside the birds-of-prey building, the cement block walls echoed with screeches and caws and chittering mating calls. A parade of raptors—a bald eagle, a merlin falcon, a Eurasian eagle owl, and a pair of Harris hawks—stood at their perches, talons clasping tightly. In the wild they would have been swooping down on voles and rabbits and salmon. Bald eagles have been known to grab dogs and to attempt to lift small children into the air. Harris hawks are famed for hunting above the desert in coordinated teams. Now their dark eyes shined as they waited for someone to bring them another offering from a nearby freezer full of rodents. "Ratsicles," the staff called them.

A trainer extended her arm toward a black vulture named Smedley. Time for his daily weighing.

"What do you say, bubba?"

Smedley shuffled from foot to foot, considering the invitation. Then the trainer offered him a tidbit of dead quail and cued him with a little sound.

"Doop!" she said, and the vulture flew onto her arm to claim his treat.

The department worked with almost any bird brought to their door. They nursed baby screech owls that had tumbled from nests, peregrine falcons that had crashed into power lines, hawks and eagles with birth defects that would have led them to starve in the wild. Some of the birds had been born into captivity and were too dependent on humans to ever make it on their own. Others eventually recovered and were given a chance to fly away for good. The staff found it deeply satisfying to help the birds heal and then set them loose, watching them power toward the trees. But the transition was rarely simple, especially after the birds grew accustomed to the zoo's routine and to the presence of the humans and the steady diet of ratsicles. The keepers tried to ease their way back into the wild with a protocol known as "a soft release." Instead of simply abandoning the birds, they would let them go at the end of the day, but leave a supply of food for them in case they weren't ready to strike out on their own. Sometimes, after a few nights of experimenting with freedom, the birds would not be seen again. Sometimes they would find it too hard to break away and never leave.

Not long ago, the staff had tried a soft release with a young mourning dove named Myrtle. Someone had found her as a newborn squab, on the ground and away from her nest, and then brought her to Lowry Park. A ball of fluff, she weighed less than an ounce and still lacked most of her feathers. For weeks her handlers nursed her. They cradled her in their hands, listened to her coo, made a little home for her in a small enclosure outside the building, safely away from the bigger birds. Though it was impossible to avoid becoming attached, they knew it was time to let her go when she began experimenting with test flights, flitting and hopping. The wings of mourning doves tend to whistle, especially when they're taking off and landing, and it made her handlers happy to hear that explosion of musical fluttering as they said good-bye and watched her dart into the late-afternoon sky. But every morning, she came back. To thwart her homing instinct, the department supervisor took her to his house, fifty miles away, and tried another release in a big field out back. The first couple nights, Myrtle stayed close. Then one morning the supervisor couldn't hear her cooing anymore. At last she was on her own.

One night not long afterward, one of the other trainers dreamed about Myrtle. In the dream, the dove returned to Lowry Park yet again. This time, she didn't return to her roost outside. Instead she flew through an open door into the birds-of-prey building and landed near the red-tailed hawk. Always ready for another snack, the hawk seized and devoured her.

Days later, the dream still haunted the trainer. She wasn't sure how to interpret it. Was it a foreboding that something terrible had happened to Myrtle once she was back in the wild, vulnerable to predators? Perhaps it was a parable, bubbling up through the subconscious, on the difficulties of introducing new creatures into the garden, even with every intention of setting them free.

Across that long summer of 2003, Lowry Park waited for the elephants. In federal court the battle over the Swazi Eleven raged on. PETA and the rest of the animal-rights coalition hurled accusations and innuendoes. Wildlife lovers from around the world e-mailed fiery protests. Weary of the stress and drama, the staff at Lowry Park wondered when, if ever, the case would be over and the elephants would start toward their new lives in Florida and California.

The war kept escalating. Animal-rights protesters gathered in front of Lowry Park to wave signs that proclaimed SWAZI ELEPHANTS: BORN FREE, SOLD OUT. PETA, with its gift for macabre theatrics, staged a media event outside the San Diego Zoo, cheering as a man dressed in a fuzzy gray elephant costume parked a rented dump truck in front of one of the zoo's entrances and unloaded a large mound of horse manure onto the street. The elephant man would not leave the truck until the police summoned a locksmith and led him away in handcuffs. By then he had removed the head of his costume so that he could issue a statement to the news crews.

"I'm going to be in jail for a while," he said. "But those elephants are going to spend the rest of their lives behind bars."

While the fate of the Swazi Eleven remained in limbo, Lowry Park added to its collection with a stream of other animals. The northern section of the grounds, undeveloped until now, crawled with bulldozers and construction crews, all of them erecting acres of new exhibits designed to showcase African species. If the importation went forward, the elephants were to be the centerpiece—not just of the new wing, but of a completely new vision for the zoo.

Lowry Park was in a hurry to get bigger. Reinventing itself for a new century, the medium-sized zoo was deep into the most ambitious and most daring expansion of its history, a radical overhaul almost entirely dependent on the elephants. The potential gains for the zoo—increased profits, higher visibility—were almost as huge as the animals themselves. For years, Lowry Park had surveyed visitors on which species they most wanted the zoo to add to the collection, and every time, elephants were number one. But the risks inherent in the plan were also enormous.

Beloved as they were, elephants tested a zoo's limits. They were expensive to feed and house, they were extremely dangerous to work with, and their very nature—their independence and intelligence, their emotional sensitivity, their need to bond with other elephants and walk for miles a day—made it difficult to provide them with surroundings in which they would not lapse into misery. At a time when some American zoos were considering closing their elephant exhibits for good due to these ethical and logistical problems, it was striking for a zoo to consider adding any elephants at all, even those raised in captivity. To rip them from the wild and use them to crown an upgraded collection was incendiary. The plan had already catapulted Lowry Park into the public spotlight as never before. If anything went wrong, either during the flight or after the new arrivals settled in, the zoo would be cast into disgrace. Animal-rights organizations from around the world would point to any such failure as proof that elephants did not belong in zoos, period.

Until that summer, Lowry Park would have seemed an unlikely target for international furor. The place was too small, too low-profile—a respected zoo, accredited by the Association of Zoos and Aquariums (AZA) and known for its commitment to endangered Florida species, but not particularly flashy. With the move to bring in the wild elephants, the zoo was announcing that it was ready to step onto a bigger stage and embrace a whole new set of possibilities and challenges.

Lex Salisbury, Lowry Park's hard-charging CEO, was well aware of the risks. A tall man with light blond hair and the swagger of a silverback gorilla, Lex was gambling millions of dollars and his own reputation in a bid to transform his institution into one of the most dazzling zoos in the country. Lex was often hailed as a visionary, even by people who didn't like him, and of those there were plenty. He was living proof that visionaries can be hell on the minions who toil beneath them.

Depending on the circumstances, he could be inspiring or vengeful, seductive or tyrannical. He spoke of zoos and their mission with religious intensity—a passion so pure that it made audiences visibly swoon—but treated Lowry Park as his own fiefdom. He did not tolerate employees who challenged him. He had a beguiling smile, a taste for the kill, and a penchant for appearing in publicity photos and even the zoo's annual reports in bush khakis and a safari hat, as though he had just jetted in from the Serengeti. "Blond, blue-eyed, with chiseled good looks," a reporter once wrote, "he resembles the great white hunter portrayed by Robert Redford in *Out of Africa*."

Lex's reputation had been sealed a decade before, when he was the zoo's general curator, and one of the groundskeepers took to calling him "El Diablo Blanco." According to the legend, this groundskeeper had studied Lex's already volatile management style and pronounced, "One day, El Diablo Blanco will run this zoo." Among discontented members of the staff, both past and present, he was still known as "the White Devil."

Lex was aware of the nickname and did not let it trouble him. He enjoyed being larger than life and did not mind instilling a healthy fear in his employees if it helped him take Lowry Park to the next level. He had a talent for getting things done, no matter the cost. More than anyone else, he was the architect of the plan to import the elephants and create a new zoo around them. He had spent several years attending to all the details. He had traveled to Swaziland to see the elephants in the game parks and to help select the four who would be brought to Tampa. Negotiating the purchase, he had comported himself favorably in the exalted presence of the Swazi king, Mswati III. Back in Florida, he had lobbied the Tampa city council to grant the zoo more land for its expansion and for the funds to build the new facilities to house the elephants. He had personally insisted on implementing a protocol that would allow the keepers to work with the animals more safely. With the arrival of the wild elephants, he wanted to push Lowry Park into the forefront of defining what a zoo could be, all that it might accomplish. If such boldness courted the wrath of PETA, so be it.

Lex knew what could be accomplished if he had the support of the city. Fifteen years before, when he was hired at Lowry Park as a young assistant curator, he had witnessed another transformation. Lex had been brought to the zoo, in fact, as part of a larger team whose job it was to turn around an institution that had become a civic embarrassment.

The city's zoo had started in the 1930s as a tiny menagerie—a handful of raccoons and alligators, a few exotic birds—and then had slowly grown into a larger collection of lions and tigers and bears and even one elephant, a female Asian named Sheena who had been transported from India on a jet in 1961, making her the zoo's original flying elephant. The undisputed star in those early years, Sheena performed twice a day in a circus ring and then gave rides to children. Admission was free. The place was sometimes called "the Fairyland Zoo," because the animal attractions were merged with a panorama of storybook houses and scenes re-created from Mother Goose and other children's tales. Kids skipped across the Rainbow Bridge and darted among replicas of the Seven Dwarves, Humpty-Dumpty, and the Big Bad Wolf and the Three Little Pigs. They clambered onto a small train that chugged and curved across the grounds, and spun on the Tilt-a-Wheel, and threw food over a fence within reach of Sheena's trunk. Just north of the zoo stood Safety Village, a miniature replica of Tampa, with a shopping mall and a fire station and a tiny City Hall, where police officers tutored young citizens in how to recognize traffic signs and use crosswalks and repel the advances of molesters. Second-graders even got to ride small electric vehicles as they practiced braking at stoplights on Happy Drive and Polite Boulevard.

Nick Nuccio, the Tampa mayor who had started it all, called the zoo "a children's paradise." As the years passed, though, Lowry Park aged poorly. What was once quaint became dreadful. The train rusted, and two toddlers were injured when a kiddie roller coaster derailed, and Sheena the elephant was shipped off to Canada, where she died of a heart attack. Worst of all was the soul-killing collection of dilapidated cages where the animals kept dying from abuse. Years later, adults who had visited the old zoo as children still shuddered when they recalled the grimness of the place. The National Humane Society declared it one of the five worst zoos in America.

"It was a rat hole," one city councilman remembered.

In the 1980s, in response to widespread concerns about the appalling conditions, the old zoo had been torn down and a new zoo had been built. Today the cages were gone, replaced by more spacious enclosures where the animals were separated from the public not by bars, but by moats and raised walkways. In the section of the zoo devoted to Florida species, visitors wandered a boardwalk that led through stands of pine and palmetto, where black bears dug under logs for grubs and whooping cranes strutted their mating dance, and tiny Key deer darted in the shade. Waiting at the end of the boardwalk was a bunkerlike building where the guests descended into darkened subterranean chambers to gaze through picture windows into crystalline pools made to look like freshwater springs teeming with bass and snapping turtles and manatees who dived and spun and nibbled on romaine lettuce.

Around Tampa, Lowry Park was hailed as a jewel. More than a decade after the improved version was opened to the public, area residents remained so pleased—and so relieved by the abolishment of the forlorn cages—that they still referred to it proudly as "the new zoo." Mayors and city council members applauded the zoo's dedication to its endangered species and its long, steady climb from shame to redemption. At ribbon-cutting ceremonies for new exhibits, the politicians beamed for the news cameras and posed with massive scissors. Every year at budget time, they nodded in appreciation when Lex reminded them that the zoo was a paragon of fiscal caution. The zoo, Lex assured the city council repeatedly, was living within its means even as its capital construction projects blossomed.

A nonprofit organization, the zoo relied on Tampa's benevolence. Leasing its grounds from the recreation department, it occupied fifty-six acres of a city park that stretched along the western banks of the Hillsborough River. This was the place that had given Lowry Park its name, the same spot where the old zoo had once stood. The location was hardly prominent. The park was miles north of downtown, tucked inside a sleepy, slightly run-down neighborhood filled with bungalow houses that had long needed a fresh coat of paint and dusty streets that seemed frozen in time. Cats slunk under old cars covered in yellow blankets of pollen. Thick beards of Spanish moss, bleaching gray under the monstrous Florida sun, dangled from the branches of live oaks above forgotten yards where no one appeared to have lifted a rake since the Eisenhower administration. Some of the houses lined the zoo's exterior fence, their backyards scarcely fifty feet from some of the exhibits. On many mornings, the residents woke to the duets of the siamangs and the piercing cries of seramas.

For all its successes, the zoo lingered in the shadows of its competition. It was dwarfed by central Florida's other two major animal attractions—Busch Gardens of Tampa, a couple exits away on 275; and Disney's Animal Kingdom, located outside Orlando, barely more than an hour away. Both were gargantuan tourist meccas that combined roller coasters and other theme-park thrills with carefully scripted safari tours through counterfeit savannas that teemed with lions, zebras, hippos, giraffes, and Nile crocodiles. Busch Gardens had a Serengeti section so huge it single-handedly outstripped the size of all of Lowry Park's exhibits put together. Animal Kingdom, literally ten times bigger than the Tampa zoo, featured a 145-foot-tall replica of a baobab tree, with a tapestry of dolphins and baboons and hundreds of other animals carved into its massive trunk and a movie theater hidden inside the tree's maze of fake roots. As the theater darkened, swooning children donned special glasses to watch an animated 3-D short called *It's Tough to Be a Bug*, starring a host of adorable insects who danced in a chorus line and belted out show tunes that chronicled the travails and triumphs of cockroaches and dung beetles.

With its limited budget, Lowry Park had no hope of competing against Disney's armies of Imagineers or Busch Gardens's beer-drenched millions. It had no 3-D movies, no flumes, no rustic trains chugging through the jungle, no skycars that sent the guests soaring above the animals. By necessity, its charms were more intimate. The only ride in the entire zoo was a jungle carousel that offered children a spin on the galloping backs of handcrafted endangered animals. It was unclear if their endangered status rendered the ride any more meaningful than a typical merry-go-round. It didn't matter. Lex and the zoo's board of directors recognized that they could not duplicate the scale of Busch Gardens or Disney's Animal Kingdom. But they didn't have to. They were running a zoo, not a theme park. The entrance fees were lower, the expectations of the guests less grandiose. People didn't come to Lowry

Park hoping to twist upside-down on a screaming roller coaster or to laugh at an animated bug. They came to see real animals, and the zoo had plenty of those. In fact, the zoo's collection was not that much smaller than what awaited them at Busch Gardens or Disney.

Even before the elephants arrived, Lowry Park was blessed with an abundance of "charismatic megafauna"—zoo jargon for larger animals immensely popular with the public, such as the rhinos and the bears and the manatees. The most beloved species were typically mammals, because people identified with them more readily than with an emu or a moray eel and because they loved to watch the animals court and mate and nurse their babies. Humans found it easier to project their own lives and emotions and assumptions onto such creatures. They responded with special fervor when the mammals exhibited traits that were discernible, even across the barriers that separated them, and behaved in a way that declared their individual character. It made it easier not just to connect with the animals but to believe the animals were opening a window into their mysterious inner selves.

Out of all the charismatic megafauna, none had more personality or was more beloved than the king and queen of the zoo.

The alpha chimp crouched at his throne. Every morning, he claimed the same spot on the shelf of rocks beside the waterfall, a perfect vantage point from which to survey his domain. The rocks were replicas, airbrushed to look like a weathered canyon wall; the waterfall was an illusion, too, a stream pouring from a PVC pipe. But there was nothing fake about Herman. He had reigned at Lowry Park for three decades, longer than any other animal or any of the humans who worked here. He was the zoo's most famous resident, its living memory, the walking embodiment of its history. Each of the zoo's sixteen hundred animals was assigned a number. Herman's was 000001.

By now the years were catching up with him. His chin hairs had gone gray. He grew winded more easily than in the past. Still, he seemed to miss nothing. If one of the other chimps in his group was upset, he offered comfort. If a dispute erupted, he stepped in. Often, though, he held himself apart from the others and stayed at his stony perch. Tired of standing, he lay down on the rock shelf, studied the black nails of his fingers. His empty gaze suggested not just boredom but a deeper weariness. Who could blame him? He had never asked for the responsibilities of an alpha. This existence had been thrust upon him long ago. Several lifetimes ago. On another continent, in another century.

"See the big monkey?" a mother said to her child.

At the sound of the woman's voice and the sight of her blond hair, Herman jumped to his feet. Suddenly he was alert and energized, delighted to find someone he could impress. He marched back and forth along the shelf, parading like a general. He rocked and swayed, puffed up his chest, bristled the thick black hair on his shoulders and back, all to make himself look strong and powerful.

The woman smiled and laughed. Clearly the big monkey liked her.

"Isn't he funny?" she said, and her child nodded.

They were so trusting, the moms with their golden bangs and their tanned shoulders, shining in the sun. They almost never caught on to what was really happening. But sometimes, if the women stood there long enough, watching Herman strut, a hint of recognition played across their faces. Possibly they had encountered other males who acted this way. In a bar, maybe, or in the last hazy hours of a party.

When the moms turned and left, taking their children with them— and all of them left soon enough, whether they'd figured it out or not— Herman cried out after them. He knew when he was being dismissed. After more than thirty years at Lowry Park, he had endured more than his share of rejection. For the record, he was not a monkey. Chimpanzees are apes. It was understandable if some of the moms were offended. No one goes to the zoo expecting to be propositioned by an ape. The women might not have taken his advances personally if they had understood that Herman's mixed-up libido was not his fault. If they had known his background, they might have understood how things had gotten so turned around inside him.

His early life had unfolded like something coauthored by Dickens and Darwin. Born in the wilds of west Africa, he was taken from his mother as an infant—he almost certainly saw her die, trying to protect him—and then sold in an orange crate for twenty-five dollars. He was raised as a pet for the first few years, then was eventually brought to Florida and donated to the zoo, where he was installed in a cage and taught to depend on the imperfect love of strangers. He charmed Jane Goodall, threw dirt at the mayor of Tampa, learned to clap and smoke cigarettes—whatever it took to entertain the masses. Whatever was required to survive.

Herman reigned through the death of the old Lowry Park and the birth of the new. He still executed handstands and blew kisses. Now, though, the flirtatious behavior had evolved into something beyond mere performance; underneath the playfulness ran a streak of possessiveness and frustrated desire. He thought of the female keepers as his, and if he spied a man standing next to one of them in front of the chimp exhibit, a clump of dirt was certain to fly in the interloper's direction.

"We better move out of sight," the keeper would say.

To anyone who lingered in front of the exhibit for more than a few minutes, it became obvious that Herman suffered from an identity crisis. For all his intelligence and personality, he did not appear to fully understand that he was a chimp. His early years, with a human family who had clothed him and diapered him and taught him to sit at the dinner table, had left him in profound confusion, and his years of isolation in the cage had increased this confusion and imbued him with an unceasing need for human attention. Though his alpha status conferred upon him sexual privileges, he never tried to breed with the three female chimps available to him. Instead he was attracted only to human females, preferably athletic blondes. Herman demonstrated this cross-species fixation every day. When female keepers greeted him in the mornings, he often became aroused, especially if he happened to glimpse the skin of their shoulders under their Lowry Park polo shirt. Herman had a thing for shoulders, which explained his fetish for tank tops.

The misdirected libido was disastrous for Herman, since it prevented him from ever mating or reproducing or joining fully with his own species. Surrounded by other chimps, he remained fundamentally disconnected. The female keepers understood this and felt for him. They found it a little odd to be regarded as a sex object by a chimp, but they didn't make a big deal of it. They respected Herman, quirks and all, because he had so many other admirable qualities that far outweighed his obsession. From watching him with the other chimps, the keepers knew he was a benevolent leader, ready to reach out to any chimp who was vulnerable. He was a good listener. He was loyal and forgiving and patient. Looking into his brown eyes, they had no doubt that he possessed a soul.

Being the alpha was not easy. "Drama queens," the keepers called the chimps, and for good reason. They were always cycling through another episode of their daily soap opera. They shrieked and screamed, raising such bedlam it seemed impossible there were only six of them. They chased one another in circles, arms flailing, and jumped into the dry moat that curved along the front of the exhibit. They climbed the high mesh wall at the back and cried out to anyone who would listen. The staff almost never knew what triggered these outbursts, but usually they could count on Herman to resolve them. He had a gift for keeping the peace and for observing the social formalities. He knew when to stomp after the others and intimidate them into submission, and when to stand back and let them release the tension on their own.

Eventually the chimps would calm down, grooming one another and climbing into the tree at the center of the exhibit to gaze toward the horizon. But even when they were quiet, the emotions percolated, elemental and palpable, sometimes even frightening. It was like a force that could barely be contained.

Herman's job was to monitor that force and channel it. He had done it for longer than almost anyone at the zoo could remember. As long as he kept doing it, everything would be fine.

The queen entered from the back, through a hidden corridor that led to the waiting eyes of her public. The Sumatran tiger had been lounging in her private quarters, in the suite of secret rooms where she was born, where she saw her mother for the last time, where she now passed her nights and the idle hours of her mornings, preening and flying into rages at her minders, where she toyed with any males misguided enough to believe that they could possess her. Now she was ready for a walk.

A door slid open, and Enshalla appeared, cloaked in a calm both hypnotic and terrifying. She moved through dappled shadows and into the sun, every step a promise, every breath a warning. She padded across ground littered with bones and stained with blood, past the large picture window where admirers stood with mouths agape, so close they could see the emerald of her eyes and watch the shoulder muscles shift beneath her stripes.

"Here kitty-kitty-kitty!" a man called out.

Enshalla ignored the taunt. She raised her great head and sniffed and tested the air to see if her attendants had left her a token of their devotion. They loved to please her. Knowing that tigers revel in different scents, the keepers would venture into the exhibit in the early morning, when Enshalla was still locked away in her den, and spray the area with dashes of cinnamon, peppermint, even perfume. She preferred the muskier brands. Her favorite was Obsession.

That August, the staff was introducing Enshalla to a male Sumatran named Eric. The zoo hoped that eventually the two tigers would breed, but the outlook was not promising. Eric was only four years old and sexually naïve. Enshalla, almost twelve, was more experienced and confident. Born at Lowry Park, she viewed the tiger exhibit as her territory and ruled it with the titanic force of her personality. She was perhaps the most beautiful creature at the zoo and certainly one of the most fierce. She was imperious, independent, hostile to the expectations of not just humans but other tigers.

By human standards, Enshalla's family history was like a Greek tragedy. Her mother and father had been brought from zoos on two continents and paired at Lowry Park. Her mother had accidentally killed one of her first cubs. Later, when Enshalla was still young, her father had slain her mother in front of a crowd of onlookers.

There was no way to know if Enshalla had any memory of her parents. She seemed to glide through her days in a state of perpetual now, unconcerned with the past and unburdened with any awareness of the future. Words have not been invented to adequately describe how she moved, though the poet Ted Hughes came close when he wrote about another big cat whose stride, he said, contained "wildernesses of freedom." Everything Enshalla did, even the way she curled on the ground for an afternoon nap, radiated both fluid grace and a sense of terrible power.

The staff was enthralled with her. They adored her haughtiness, the deep orange of her coat and the dark black of her stripes and the long white fur that ringed her neck like a mane, the daintiness with which she approached the water at the front of her exhibit, trying not to get too wet. Sumatrans have webbed toes and tend to be excellent swimmers, but Enshalla usually preferred to stay dry. Her delicacy fooled no one. She was remarkably aggressive, even for a tiger, and especially for one born into captivity. Her keepers noted her skill as a huntress, even within the confines of her enclosure. They held their breath every time a neighborhood bird was foolish enough to land in her exhibit and linger.

Over the years, various suitors had been brought to the zoo for Enshalla's approval. With each of them, there had been no doubt who was in charge. The male Sumatrans had the advantage of size and brute strength. But Enshalla, relatively petite at 180 pounds, dominated them all with the force of her will, making it clear that the exhibit was hers and that she would do as she pleased. If she was in estrus, she would warm to them, chuff at them, rub her cheeks against theirs, roll playfully at their feet—give all the signals that she was ready to mate. But when they responded, she ran away or even turned on them. Ignoring the fact that they could easily have killed her, she chased them and cornered them and stalked them as though they were her prey.

Now it was Eric's turn to test her defenses. The staff had not yet released the tigers together into the exhibit to mate. They were letting the couple get acquainted slowly, putting the two of them in separate but adjoining dens in the night house so they could eye and smell each other up close without either of them getting hurt. Lethal violence seemed unlikely from the new suitor. Eric had arrived on loan from the National Zoo in Washington, D.C., and was still getting acclimated to his new environment. He looked and sounded ferocious enough. When he growled, his lips pulled back to reveal canines longer than human fingers. But compared to other male tigers, Eric so far seemed relaxed. Too relaxed, perhaps, for the task before him. Enshalla bristled with a menace he could not muster. Against her cunning and experience, the young virgin hardly stood a chance.

The staff remained hopeful that Eric would find some way to assert himself and overcome Enshalla's resistance. Like so many species at the zoo, Sumatran tigers were rapidly dwindling toward extinction. With fewer than six hundred left in the wild, they were the single most endangered subspecies of tigers and one of the most critically endangered animals on the planet. If Sumatrans were to survive, they needed to reproduce, either in their native forests in Indonesia or in institutions such as Lowry Park. As an added bonus, it would also be a boon for the zoo's bottom line. Animal babies of many species tended to be a good draw at the box office. But tiger cubs, with their soft fur and tiny growls, were golden.

Nobody at Lowry Park was crass enough to talk about this out loud. Nobody had to.

The keepers pairing Enshalla and Eric weren't thinking about filling Lowry Park's coffers. What they wanted, more than anything, was to populate the planet with more tigers. It wasn't even up to the keepers, or the zoo, to decide whether Enshalla and Eric could breed. Before putting them together, Lowry Park had to seek permission from a program that oversees the welfare of endangered species in captivity. The program was called the Species Survival Plan, and it was run by the Association of Zoos and Aquariums. Under the AZA's direction, there were plans for dozens of different species in captivity—not just Sumatran tigers, but frogs, cranes, giant pandas, lowland gorillas—and the plans tracked thousands of animals' reproductive histories to make sure that no single individual's DNA was over-represented. Since neither Enshalla nor Eric had any offspring so far, there had been no problem getting permission to put them together. If the tigers produced a litter of cubs, it would be good for the genetic future of their species. And for Lowry Park's profits.

At the zoo, higher aspirations overlapped with economic motives. The desire to save the planet was woven with the necessity of economic survival. The zoo was a nonprofit organization, but it still had to earn its way. In that summer of 2003, the zoo had embarked on its expansion and was building the new exhibits for the elephants and the other African species. To make all these things happen, Lowry Park needed more money, more attractions, more paying customers pouring through the gate. A few baby tigers added to the mix wouldn't hurt.

Before that could happen, Enshalla would have to decide if she was willing to surrender. It would be her choice, not Eric's, and at the moment it seemed almost impossible.

Gazing down at Enshalla from the boardwalk, watching her stealthily crawl toward a sparrow, it was easy to understand the ambivalence so many people felt toward zoos. To know that she had spent her entire life in captivity, on the other side of the world from the peat swamp forests where she belonged, it was impossible not to feel a sense of loss. But watching Enshalla triggered wonder as well. Suddenly she was not just some vague notion of a tiger, a picture in a book. She was a Sumatran, one of the few remaining in the world, and the untamed reality of her—the specificity and physicality and undeniability of her—made onlookers catch their breath.

The same tangle of reactions twisted inside visitors as they stood in front of Herman's exhibit and watched him with the other chimps. The conflict nagged at them as they walked through the rest of the zoo and saw all the animals collected inside these walls. Joy vied with regret. Delight was weighted with guilt.

All zoos, even the most enlightened, are built upon an idea both beguiling and repellent—the notion that we can seek out the wildness of the world and behold its beauty, but that we must first contain that wildness. Zoos argue that they are fighting for the conservation of the Earth, that they educate the public and provide refuge and support for vanishing species. And they are right. Animal-rights groups argue that zoos traffic in living creatures, exploiting them for financial gain and amusement. And they are right.

Caught inside this contradiction are the animals themselves, and the humans charged with their well-being.

Keepers see the realities of zoo life up close, every day. More than anyone else, they know when animals are treated well at their zoo and when they are not.

"The keepers," a veterinarian at another institution once wrote, "are the core of the zoo's conscience."

At Lowry Park, most of the keepers would say, even in private, that they worked at a good zoo—not a perfect zoo, but one where the animals were generally well cared for and where the staff took pride in the difference it made in the survival of so many species. Yet these same keepers admitted that to work in any zoo was to live with ambivalence. They saw it when they went to the grocery store and glimpsed the delight on some shoppers' faces, and the distaste on others, when they spied Lowry Park's insignia on their shirt. They saw it at parties when they told someone where they worked and the other person grimaced.

The keepers wrestled with their own thicket of emotions. They loved animals and were deeply attached to the ones in their care. But their attachment did not blind them to the moral complexities of what they did for a living. Since it was announced that Lowry Park and San Diego were purchasing the eleven elephants from Swaziland, many keepers had reacted with quiet unease. The difficulties of caring for elephants were well known in zoo circles. The journey from Swaziland— all those animals crated in the hold of the plane for all those hours—was almost too much to contemplate. Making elephants fly across an ocean represented a fundamental inversion of the natural order. It required a confidence that bordered on hubris.

At Lowry Park, the staff had heard the official rationales and read the press releases describing the importation as a mercy mission to rescue the elephants from another cull. Yet for all the altruistic pronouncements, there was no question the zoo was gaining four coveted and valuable prizes in return. Once the elephants went on display, profits were certain to spike. Taking these creatures from the wilds of Africa was complicated enough, even if it did save their lives. But to build a new vision of the zoo on their backs? Some keepers worried about what this move would mean for the well-being of the elephants, what it might reveal about the future priorities of Lowry Park and the compromises it was willing to make. To them, the zoo's resources had already seemed stretched to the breaking point, even before the bulldozers had broken ground on the multimillion-dollar elephant facilities. What would happen to all the other species, with so much money being diverted to the new wing? In so many ways, the importation had become a battle over the zoo's very existence—a crucible that challenged its vision of itself as an ethical institution where animals were revered above all else.

PETA and its warriors may have been ideologues, uninterested in facts that clouded the purity of their dogma, but that didn't necessarily mean they were wrong. Did it make sense to bring these elephants to the United States? Even some members of Lowry Park's staff weren't sure. They wondered if their zoo, in its dreams of expansion, might have crossed a line from which there was no return.

3

Night Delivery

The Swazi Eleven arrived in America just before midnight, in the rain, in secret. When the 747 finally touched down at Tampa International Airport, an armada of police cruisers and unmarked FBI vehicles was waiting to escort them to the zoo. In the sky, a police helicopter searched for trouble.

"We had intelligence there would be an effort to sabotage the convoy," said a Tampa police captain.

The notion of trying to hide a jumbo jet as it ferried eleven elephants across an ocean was absurd. Lowry Park had cloaked the flight's itinerary in a deliberate fog. In the days before, as the appeals from the animal-rights coalition sputtered in federal court and it became clear the elephants would soon be in the air, the protests had grown increasingly desperate. In San Diego, a caller threatened to burn down the zoo and a woman was arrested after breaking into the director's office. In Tampa, three activists, including a PETA organizer who had traveled from the group's headquarters in Virginia, bought admission to Lowry Park and then stormed into the administrative suite, where they knocked items off desks and slammed phones and yelled "Free the Swazi elephants!" and "Born free! Live free!" The police had escorted the trio away in handcuffs and charged them with burglary, trespassing, and disorderly conduct. Rattled, Lowry Park's staff wondered how far the resistance could go. The answer came shortly before the flight was scheduled to take off from Africa, when the FBI's San Diego office passed along a lead indicating that activists might try to interfere somehow with the delivery of the animals after they were unloaded from the 747.

"Hopefully," an FBI agent wrote in an internal memo, "all of our efforts will prevent elephants on the tarmac."

When the 747 taxied toward the cargo area, a delegation from the zoo formed a receiving line. Lex Salisbury was there, along with David Murphy, the zoo's veterinarian, and Brian French,* a former circus star and longtime elephant trainer recently hired as the assistant curator in charge of the new Africa section. Also on hand was Lee Ann Rottman, Lowry Park's curator. Lee Ann was one of the zoo's true believers. As the woman in charge of the entire animal collection and all of their human keepers, her identity had meshed so thoroughly with the institution's that it was difficult to envision the place without her. She knew every creature at Lowry Park and often enumerated their individual qualities as though they were her own children. When the mandrills were going through a stressful time and needed reassurance, she had been known to climb into their exhibit and groom the hair on their backs, as though she were a baboon too. When a baby screech owl was orphaned, she would take the fuzzy white chick home and let him practice flying around her bedroom as she slept.

"If animals aren't in heaven," she liked to say, "I'm not going."

That night, as the 747 rolled forward on the runway, Lee Ann was worried about the condition of the elephants. She knew that Mick Reilly and Chris Kingsley, the South African vet, had been watching over them. Still, the risks of animal transports were well documented. Over the decades some had died from shock or stress while being moved to zoos or game parks over much shorter distances. Just the year before, three wallabies had died as Dr. Murphy drove them to Lowry Park in a rental truck from Ocala, a city only ninety miles north of Tampa. With their strength and ingenuity, elephants presented a special challenge; sometimes they reacted to transports in unpredictable ways. In one case, an Asian elephant at another zoo was loaded into the back of a trailer to be moved to another facility. A zoo employee following in a car spied the animal's trunk dangling underneath, perilously close to

---

* No relation to the author.

the road. When the truck was stopped, the workers discovered that the elephant had repeatedly dropped to her knees until she smashed a one-foot hole through the vehicle's thick oak floor. That incident had occurred only ten miles or so into the trip with a normally docile elephant already inured to captivity. The Swazi elephants were still wild, had just been forced through a voyage of eight thousand miles, and had been confined in their crates, under extremely disorienting conditions, for more than fifty hours. In her mind, Lee Ann had listed all the things that could have gone wrong and had braced herself for the possibility that one or more of the animals had died. When the plane finally shut down its engines, she hurried into the cargo hold. The moment she saw them, the heaviness inside her lifted. They were quiet and showed no signs of distress. In fact, they seemed remarkably calm. As Lee Ann peered into their crates, saying hello and softly sweet-talking them, they extended their trunks toward her and sniffed her. There wasn't much time to linger, though. While the plane refueled, preparing for the next leg of its flight to California, a heavy-duty forklift lowered the four crates with Lowry Park's elephants from the hold, while a crane waited to load them onto two flatbed trucks. Customs officials and wildlife officers checked the permits and paperwork, and finally the elephants were secured on the trucks and ready for the last few miles of their marathon journey. Shortly after midnight, the long line of ground vehicles—the trucks, the unmarked cars, plus dozens of cruisers with their flashing lights—left the airport. Lee Ann, riding in the cab of one of the trucks carrying the elephants, was stunned.

"It's like a presidential escort," she said.

The convoy turned east on Hillsborough Avenue, then headed north on Dale Mabry Highway toward Lowry Park. The cruisers moved in an ever-shifting tactical formation, some weaving forward out of the line to take the lead, others suddenly dropping back. The lanes had been cleared. Cross streets had been blocked off. Sharpshooters, the zoo had been told, were positioned in undisclosed locations. Hovering above them all, the police helicopter cast the bright beam of a spotlight back and forth in the darkness.

....

The neighborhood was still asleep when the two trucks rumbled through the zoo's back gate and made their way toward the newly completed elephant barn, a big moss-green building at the northern edge of the grounds. The crates were unloaded from the trucks, and the elephants were invited to walk out, when ready, into chutes that led inside the barn toward stalls supplied with water and hay and apples and carrots and bananas.

Brian French studied the four new arrivals taking their first steps on a new continent. The sedatives were wearing off, but still they moved cautiously, their ears pushed forward and their trunks sniffing in every direction as they absorbed a profusion of strange sounds and scents. Brian had first observed them earlier that year, during one of the zoo's scouting trips to the game parks in Swaziland. One had been selected from Mkhaya's herd. The others all came from Hlane and had grown up together and knew one another well. That shared history was likely to help the three of them through the transition to captivity.

As the elephants moved into neighboring stalls, Brian noted which of them extended their trunks through the thick bars in greeting and which held back. He watched their posture, the flapping of their ears, the swishing of their tails. He wanted to see if their movements were erratic or fluid, if they were easily startled, if they seemed rattled or anxious, how one of them reacted when one of the others moved. He paid special attention to their foreheads, because he knew that when elephants communicated through the infrasonic rumbles—the same low-frequency sounds that the scientists were scrutinizing in such detail—the effort sometimes caused the muscles in their foreheads to move. Even if his human ears could not detect the rumbles, he wanted to see who was talking and who was responding, who was connecting and who was keeping to themselves. He needed to learn their respective temperaments, their habits and quirks, the things that unnerved and calmed them. Any clue that might offer even the smallest glimpse into their inner worlds.

"Learning to read the animals," Brian called it, and he had plenty of practice. Although he was only twenty-nine, he had been around elephants since before he could walk. Born into a family of circus performers known as the Cristianis, he was the seventh generation to work with animals, the fourth to train and perform with elephants. By age three, he was being lifted onto their sloping backs; at six, he was riding them in the ring in Japan. Under the performing name of Brian Cristiani, he trained elephants at Ringling Bros. and other circuses around the world. Like many circus people, he starred in a variety of acts, working not just with elephants but with horses and tigers. He rode a motorcycle inside the Globe of Death and walked the high wire in a seven-man pyramid. When asked about it now, he shrugged. "It was normal life to me."

It was hard to picture Brian balancing on a wire forty feet in the air, because he suffered from a fear of heights—a liability he'd overcome with many hours of practice—and because he did not have an acrobat's typically waifish physique. Just as dog owners often resemble their pets, Brian was built uncannily like an elephant. He was big and powerful, with a hulking presence and a low center of gravity, but also surprisingly graceful and nimble on his feet. All his life he had felt a special connection to elephants. He admired their intelligence, the complexity of their character, the way each had a distinct personality waiting to be discovered underneath that thick gray skin. Working with them required empathy, the patience to form a rapport. Bigger and stronger than their human keepers, elephants always had the power to say no.

"Everybody thinks they have to respect you," Brian said. "Well, you have to respect them, and they know it. They actually learn to like you, and that's what binds everything."

He described the relationship in almost mystical terms. When the training went well, he grew to know certain elephants in such depth that it seemed as though he could sense what they were thinking and as though they could read his thoughts in return. In this blissful affinity, the divide between man and animal fell away. He called it "the flow." Achieving such intimacy with the Swazi elephants would not be easy, however. Brian had never worked with elephants freshly taken from the savanna. In his experience, African elephants, even those who had grown up in captivity, were often more challenging than the Asians. "It's like the difference between a mustang and a quarter horse," he explained. The African species tended to be more high-strung and fidgety, even stubborn. If they didn't get their way, they sometimes pouted like children.

Despite the emotional bonds that developed between elephants and their human keepers, both the African and Asian species remained extremely dangerous to work with. One study showed that over a fifteen-year period, one elephant handler was killed in the United States every year—a fatality rate three times that of coal miners, the most deadly occupation tracked by the federal labor department. The job was especially hazardous when their human keepers worked side by side with the elephants under a protocol known as free contact. To survive under free contact, which called for them to enter the same space as the elephants, many keepers believed they had to not only join the herd but maintain dominance. Essentially they had to become a human version of the matriarch. This was never easy, given the differential in size and strength, but it became particularly hazardous when the lead handler was off-duty and a subordinate had to take over. As elephants maneuvered for position in the hierarchy, they would push or bump their handlers to test them. If the person wasn't experienced enough or fell down in front of them or showed another sign of vulnerability, one of the elephants would sometimes see an opening and attack.

Lowry Park had been using free contact in 1993 when an Asian elephant killed Char-Lee Torre, a young keeper who had only recently begun working at the zoo. Char-Lee's death had been the most disturbing moment in Lowry Park's history. Lex Salisbury, the zoo's CEO, had been curator at the time and still remembered the awful chaos after the attack as other handlers tried to get the elephant under control and the paramedics fought to keep Char-Lee alive long enough for her to reach a hospital. A decade later, as Lex and the rest of the management prepared to exhibit elephants again, they were determined to prevent another tragedy. Even before the four newcomers arrived from Swaziland, the zoo had instituted an elephant management system called protected contact. Used increasingly in zoos around the country, protected contact required staff members to maintain a barrier between themselves and the animals, even when they had to get close enough to check the pads of their feet or exfoliate their skin or perform other tasks crucial to the everyday care of captive elephants. The alternative protocol was also considered more humane for the elephants, since it relied on positive reinforcement. The elephants were not dominated or prodded or punished, as they often were with free contact. Through a system of food rewards, they were encouraged to follow the trainers' commands, not intimidated into compliance. The new protocol did not allow for the same intimacy between the elephants and their handlers, but in zoos where it was used, keeper injuries and fatalities had virtually disappeared. San Diego Zoo's Wild Animal Park would also be relying on protected contact with their seven Swazi elephants arriving on the 747. Although protected contact had been in use for more than a decade, the approach had never been tested with wild elephants. Some critics were already predicting that it was doomed to fail. Elephants who had spent their lives in the bush and who had never been trained before, the skeptics said, would not be bribed by a few treats as if they were overgrown collies.

Lex was not swayed by the arguments. He believed that protected contact would work, even with what were commonly referred to as "naïve elephants," and he had gone to great lengths to make sure that the transition went as smoothly—and safely—as possible. Lowry Park had spent five million dollars constructing the elephant building with state-of-the-art equipment designed for protected contact, including hydraulic doors and gates that opened by remote control, chutes that helped the staff to move the elephants indoors and outdoors, and a giant metal box known as a Hugger that gently restrained an elephant whenever the staff needed to get close to perform an exam or work on the animal. Outside the building, the zoo had created several acres of exhibit space, including two yards to separate the bulls when their hormones were raging and a massive pool where the animals would eventually swim and spray themselves with their trunks.

To help the four newcomers adjust, the zoo had acquired a fifth elephant, an eighteen-year-old female named Ellie who was also born in Africa but who had been taken into captivity as a young calf and then spent almost her entire life in American zoos. Because she was older than the four young adults from Swaziland, the zoo hoped Ellie would assume the role of matriarch and teach the others how to live inside the confines and structure of a zoo. The new arrivals, it turned out, would almost certainly be teaching Ellie a few lessons of their own. In her early years, Ellie had lived at the Gulf Breeze Zoo in the Florida Panhandle. But as the only elephant in the small zoo's collection, she had never learned the social skills required to maneuver within a herd. Eventually she had joined a group of elephants at the Knoxville Zoo. But she was so awkward, the other elephants bullied her. Finally Ellie's keepers decided to separate her for her own protection, leaving her even more isolated. By now she was more comfortable with humans than her own species.

"She doesn't really know how to be an elephant," said one of her keepers at Lowry Park.

Now that Ellie was in Tampa, the zoo had done what it could to tilt the odds in favor of her dominance. Her transport from Knoxville had been arranged several months before, so that when the newcomers arrived she would have already established the elephant building and the adjoining yards as her territory. Ellie was at least two feet taller than the others and had the natural advantage of already being familiar with zoo routine. Still, elephants have a gift for defying human plans. There was no way to guarantee what would happen inside the hierarchy that would take shape in the months ahead. It was possible that Ellie might never summon the confidence to become the matriarch. After years of growing up in the bush, learning how to jockey for position and status among their native herds, the wild elephants might simply prove too strong.

That first night, Brian French stayed up to watch over the four new arrivals, who were clearly exhausted from their long journey. If anything went wrong—if they stopped eating or drinking, if they battered their bodies against the thick metal bars that enclosed their stalls—he wanted to know immediately. He had already set up a cot in the hall outside the barn. He planned to babysit them around the clock for the next couple weeks, or however long it took for him to be sure that they were settling in safely.

Night-vision cameras had been installed inside the barn, hooked up to monitors in the office, so Brian could see how the elephants were doing even when the lights were turned off. He wanted to know which of them was dozing and which stayed awake. Elephants can sleep either while standing or lying on their sides, but if they lie down, it usually means they've dropped their guard. In those first hours, Brian watched the grayish-green feeds from the cameras and was pleased to see that three of the four newcomers felt relaxed enough to lie down. They were on their feet soon enough, but it was a start. It was possible that they were suffering from an elephant version of jet lag and that their body clocks, set to the passage of the sun and moon over the savanna on the other side of the globe, would need a couple days to reset. Ravenous after their long journey, the four of them devoured their hay and slurped gallons of water—another good sign. As morning arrived, they were already comfortable enough with Brian and other staff members that they were slipping their trunks through the bars of their stalls, the moist ovals of their nostrils opening and closing at the tips of the trunks as they inhaled the signature scent of each human. Soon they were eating from the keepers' hands.

The first critical hours of the transition were unfolding about as well as the zoo could have hoped. Even so, it was impossible not to wonder what the elephants made of this strange new tableau.

To say they had never been in captivity before does not fully describe how alien these experiences must have been to them. Until now they had never set foot inside a building; there was no way for them to have any notion of what a building was. All they had known was the open vault of the African sky above them, the dirt and grass of the savanna beneath their feet, the wind from the Indian Ocean blowing through the knobthorn trees. They had never stood on cement floors, enclosed by walls and a roof, or been asked to walk through a doorway, or shivered in the artificial breeze of ventilation fans. For years they had drunk from streams and rivers and reservoirs. Now, for the first time, they were tasting water drawn from the Florida aquifer and poured for them into stainless-steel containers. From birth onward, the soundtrack of their lives had been the bellows of hippos, the cries of snake eagles, the snorting of wildebeests. At the zoo, all of that auditory context was gone, replaced instead by siamang duets and tiger roars and a host of other calls from species they had never heard or seen before. Although they had grown up in the presence of the rangers and the tourists in the Swazi game parks, their daily movements around the parks had been directed almost entirely by the matriarchs of their herds. Now they were stranded in an environment created and controlled by humans.

What exactly did this monumental shift in circumstance mean to them? What inner calibrations had they made to retain any sense of a life they recognized as their own? How much did they understand of what had happened to them and how they had been brought to this place? Contemplation of these questions required a leap of empathy into the elephants' inner world—a landscape many people believed was inaccessible. For centuries, ethicists and philosophers had debated whether humans could fathom the internal lives of animals.

"Even if a lion could speak," Wittgenstein wrote in *Philosophical Investigations*, "we could not understand him."

The line was clever, but ultimately self-defeatist, since it suggested there was no point in even attempting to interpret animal behavior. It was also demonstrably wrong. In the decades since the famous comment had first been published, researchers had begun to decode the communications—verbal, visual, chemical, facial, electrical, vibrational, behavioral—of myriad species, from dolphins to fireflies. At Lowry Park, the keepers recognized that they would never understand everything about the animals in their care. But that didn't stop them from trying. The primate staff knew that when Herman and the other chimpanzees grinned and showed their teeth, it meant not that they were laughing but that they were afraid. When Enshalla chuffed at her keepers, they recognized it as a greeting, not a threat. Wittgenstein might never have made his observation if he'd tried listening to elephants, whose communications have been extensively mapped. Field researchers among herds in Kenya and professors in a bioacoustics lab at Cornell University are working together to assemble a lexicon that catalogues the meanings of more than seventy distinct elephant calls. They can identify the rumble that matriarchs use to tell their herds to keep moving, the roar that warns intruders to keep their distance, the chorus of trumpetings that females sound to rejoice over the birth of another calf.

It's not farfetched, then, to try to reconstruct some semblance of what the long journey to captivity was like for the four elephants at Lowry Park. Although they arrived safely, some of the elephants' behavior on the plane—Mbali's apparent despondency, the bulls' trumpeting and restless attempts to push through the walls of their crates—hinted at how difficult the trip must have been for them, despite the efforts to calm them. Anyone who has ever been squeezed into the middle seat of a passenger jet on a transatlantic flight has some notion of what it must have been like inside those crates. But to be confined for two full days without understanding where they were going or what was happening—lacking even the most basic notion of a plane—must have been disorienting almost beyond description. Surely some of the elephants had glimpsed the exterior of the 747 when they were first loaded into the hold, back in Africa. What did they think it was? All that time they were traveling across the Atlantic, did they believe they were inside the belly of some great winged creature?

Imagine the landing in Tampa. Begin with what it must have been like to descend through the clouds—that curious sensation of slowly sinking, the leveling of the wings, the cascading change in altitude. What would that have felt like to an elephant? Did their ears pop? Then came the buzz of the landing gears lowering beneath their feet and the shaking from outside as the air resistance increased. Then the bump of the landing and the sense of rushing forward on solid ground and a roar from outside as the plane slowed and finally stopped. Something opened, and a series of unrecognizable faces and scents approached their crates. Then the whirring of the forklift and a groaning from the crane, accompanied by the sensation of being lifted and lowered. A rush of fresh air, the patter of rain. Night, unfurling outside the metal box that had become their world. A mechanical growling as they were propelled forward on the trucks. A forest of flashing lights. The *thunk-thunk* of helicopter blades, rotating somewhere above.

The Swazi elephants would have recognized that last sound. Elephants throughout southern Africa had been fleeing from it for decades. These four had heard it when they were young calves in Kruger National Park and the culling teams came gunning for their herds. The metallic chop, approaching from the distance, was usually the harbinger of what was about to happen. The helicopters appeared overhead, and shots rang out, and then the families of the calves—their mothers and aunts, their younger siblings, everyone in their herd—dropped and did not get up. The lingering trauma to the generation of orphans spared in the Kruger culls was well-documented. But there was no way to know what exactly the four Swazi elephants remembered from the specific culls they had survived, or what associations might have been triggered by the presence of the police helicopter as they traveled that night through Tampa. Could they still feel the waves of panic and confusion washing through their herds as they stampeded through the bush? Did they recall standing in the swirling dust beside the bodies of their mothers? Did they see the white-uniformed disposal teams moving around them, slitting the throats of the fallen corpses with their pangas?

The Swazi elephants had been visited by another helicopter only several months before their flight to the United States, when the game-park crew darted them from the air to knock them out before their transport to the boma. There was no way for the elephants to have known that this time the helicopter was on a different mission. For them, the darting would have almost certainly reverberated with echoes of the culls. Once again, a helicopter appeared, and elephants all around them collapsed to the ground. When the selected bulls and cows awoke in the boma, all they knew was that they had been taken away to some-place different, just as they were after the culls, and that the other members of their herd were gone.

To the Swazi elephants, the chop of a helicopter was linked to memories—both old and recent—of dislocation, death, the end of every-thing they knew. In the midnight convoy through Tampa, as that sound ushered them toward the zoo, what could have been going through their minds? Did they wonder if they were being led to another kill zone? Did they brace for the crack of a rifle?

Given everything else they had gone through since birth, perhaps it was not so surprising that they had shown such resilience during their journey from the Swazi bush to the concrete veldt of Tampa. In the months that had preceded their arrival in the United States, they had been cast as refugees, victims, tragic icons, political pawns, vessels of genetic hope. But the most reliable description was also the simplest: They were survivors. Somehow they had lived through not one but two death sentences, through a storm of legal wrangling and political grand-standing and through an epic voyage halfway across the globe. As night fell on the elephants' first day in their new home, the staff at Lowry Park was already memorizing their names.

Msholo.

Matjeka.

Sdudla.

Mbali.

They had been named by rangers inside Mkhaya and Hlane. Msholo, pronounced um-show-lo, roughly translated in siSwati as "the one who appears from nowhere"—an allusion to Ted Reilly and a lifetime of surprising poachers. Matjeka (muh-chay-guh) meant "skewed tusks." Sdudla (stood-luh) meant "stout or sturdy." Mbali (um-bahl-ee) translated to "pretty flower."

For now the four of them would remain out of sight, away from the public's gaze. They would need several months to learn how to live inside a zoo. But soon, if all went according to plan, they would venture out into their exhibit and walk and throw dust on their backs and trumpet in front of Lowry Park's visitors. Mothers and fathers with toddlers riding on their shoulders would draw near and point. Groups of schoolchildren would be told their names and, even though many would instantly forget those names, they would call out to the four of them, not knowing the wild place they came from, grasping nothing about the losses they carried, the memories swimming within them, everything they had endured to be standing here, on display in a zoo.

4

Siren Song

Inside the zoo, time was not human. More precisely, time moved outside human expectation. It did not settle into a single groove. Zoo time was fluid, changeable, unpredictable. It unfolded in different rhythms, at variable speeds, calibrated to the heartbeat and breathing patterns and behavior of each species.

The staff and visitors wore wristwatches and carried cell phones adorned with digital displays of the hour and minute as agreed upon by Homo sapiens. But all of this fell away once people stepped inside the mini-aviary that was home to dozens of lorikeets—rainbow-hued parrots from Indonesia and Australia. To enter the lorikeet domain was to be absorbed into a cloud of otherness. The birds murmured and chattered and swooped from every direction, their wings whirring like soft bursts from a velvet machine gun as they flew back and forth in a blur of blue and yellow and red. The lorikeets landed on visitors' arms and shoulders and hair, then darted away, then came back. The birds meant no harm; they were simply curious and hoped for a sip of nectar from cups sold in the gift shop. Even so, people found their pulse accelerating, their own hearts beating faster, their sense of themselves becoming fragmented. Some were so overwhelmed they would lie on the ground until the birds went away. Others turned around and around, wondering where the next machine-gun burst would come from, and what made the lorikeets' wings sound like that, and oh my God, how did nature turn up the dials enough to paint that shade of red in their chest feathers—a supercharged red constantly bursting like fireworks as the lorikeets careened above and around and back and forth in crisscrossing arcs.

"Whoa," the humans said, not even realizing that they had spoken.

Inside that nebula of color and sound, the world sped up and slowed down simultaneously. Visitors forgot how long they had been standing there, even if it was only for thirty seconds, because the idea of a second and the notion of the number thirty were both out of reach. They had no time for time. They were caught up in the choreography of the lorikeets.

Wherever people went at Lowry Park, whatever animal they watched, one construct of time was obliterated, and another construct replaced it. Once visitors emerged from the lorikeet aviary, they could walk over to the python exhibit, only a few steps away, and study the seventeen-foot reticulated python and the two carpet pythons and the three Burmese pythons, all curled like shiny still lifes on the other side of the glass, their heads turned toward the humans but not moving, their eyes open but unblinking, their coils betraying nothing. People wondered if the pythons would ever move. Time slowed to something close to a full stop—no longer a linear progression, but a breathless waiting. If it was feeding day, the keepers would deposit dead rabbits inside the exhibit, and then the pythons would uncoil toward their prey in a flash, almost too fast for the onlookers to follow. In that microsecond, as the rabbits' ears and heads disappeared down the pythons' throats, time became an explosion that blossomed instantaneously from inertia to lethal movement. Children, their faces pressed close to the glass, would gasp and cry out.

Life was less violent over in the manatee exhibit. Visitors could walk down the tunnel that led to the underground viewing area and gaze as long as they liked, and they wouldn't see the manatees eating anyone. The most aggressive behavior inside the pools came from the male turtles who swam beside the giant marine mammals and repeatedly tried to mount them through some insane overestimation of their sexual prowess. The manatees did tussle occasionally. Sometimes they bumped their heads into each other's torsos or nudged each other with their tails. But these conflicts were fleeting and never resulted in injury. Most of the time, the manatees at Lowry Park lived up to the peaceful reputation of their species, spending their days quietly drifting around the pools, their bodies twisting and turning and slowly spinning as they nibbled on hydrilla and carrots. Occasionally they paused in front of the picture windows, suspended, and gazed toward the humans on the other side of the glass. If visitors stood there long enough, they soon relaxed, especially on a weekday afternoon when the zoo was quiet. Time became something graceful and seamless.

If you happened to be on the other side of the pools, where the keepers worked from a deck along the water's edge away from the bustle of the crowds, the sense of calm was hypnotic. You followed the gray shapes moving beneath you, tracing parabolas in the depths, and you heard the occasional splash of their tails and the eruptions of air that burst forth every few minutes as they raised their whiskered nostrils above the surface, breathed deeply, then dropped back below. Soon you found yourself waiting for the next exhalation, and your own breathing would slow. In the distance another human's voice would break the silence, and suddenly you realized that you had lost track not only of the time but what day it was. Without even knowing it, you had slipped outside of yourself.

Epiphanies like these were one of the reasons Lowry Park and other zoos endured. Despite all their flaws, zoos wake us up. They invite us to step outside our most basic assumptions. Offered for our contemplation, the animals remind us of nature's impossibly varied schemes for survival, all the strategies that species rely upon for courtship and mating and protecting the young and establishing dominance and hunting for something to eat and avoiding being eaten. On a good day, zoos shake people into recognizing the manifold possibilities of existence, what it's like to walk across the Earth, or swim in its oceans, or fly above its forests—even though most of the animals on display will never have the chance to do any of those things again, at least not in the wild.

The staff at Lowry Park confronted this paradox every day. Only for them, it cut deeper because it was not an abstraction but a living, breathing reality that stared them in the eye. They understood, better than anyone else, the inherent difficulties of holding living creatures captive. But they also recognized that the public tends to romanticize nature. They knew that the notion of freedom is a human invention and that creatures in the wild are rarely free and are in fact confined by territory, hunger, and the constant threat of predators.

Against all this logic, some staff members still wished sometimes there was some way they could let the animals go.

"Any good keeper absolutely feels a guilty conscience," a veteran on the staff confided one evening after Lowry Park was closed. "There are definitely days when you walk in and you look at the animals, and you say, 'I wish they didn't have to be here.'"

The only part of the zoo where the paradox got turned inside out—where animals were routinely returned to their native habitat—was the manatee section, which featured not only the viewing pools but a small hospital built around medical tanks. The sirens, as some called them, came in torn up by boat propellers or tangled in fishing line or suffering from cold stress, the marine version of frostbite. Sometimes they were on the edge of death from toxins they'd ingested during another outbreak of red tide. Lowry Park would slowly nurse them back to health, pumping them full of antibiotics to fight infections, feeding them vitamins to help them build back their strength, even performing surgery when necessary. Once the patients recovered, they were eventually set free again. Over the past decade the zoo had released sixty-four manatees back into the wild.

"We take 'em in, patch 'em up, and send 'em out," said Dr. Murphy. It was a beautiful promise that reminded the staff why they worked at Lowry Park. Delivering on that promise was one of the more difficult logistical challenges at the zoo. Working with wild creatures that often weighed close to a ton required patience and brute strength. If Murphy needed to draw blood or gather a fecal sample—relatively routine procedures with most of the other species—the staff would isolate the manatee in a medical tank, then drain the water so that several people could climb in with the vet and hold the patient down. The keepers would drape themselves over the manatee's body. They tried to be gentle; they would stroke the manatee's thick skin and coo and tell it to relax. But they had to hold the animal as still as possible. If it decided to roll or lash out with its tail, one of the keepers could easily wind up with a broken leg.

"Watch it," Murphy would tell the team when a manatee began to thrash. "Let him calm down a minute."

Manatees did not appreciate being handled. Often, they would expel prodigious amounts of droppings as the humans worked on them. Murphy, accustomed to such indignities, seemed not to notice when the dung oozed between his toes.

As exhausting and hazardous as these procedures were, keepers from all over the zoo happily volunteered to help, especially when it came time to assist in a release. Nothing was more satisfying to the staff than seeing a manatee healed and returned to open water. A team would maneuver a giant sling under the animal, and a crane could lift it onto a bed of mats inside a truck. Keepers would sit in back with the manatee, dousing it with water and monitoring its breathing while Murphy drove to the release point. Usually they tried to release the manatees fairly close to wherever they'd initially been found—a river, a freshwater spring, an inlet off the Gulf of Mexico. The team would attach a satellite transmitter to a belt around the manatee's tail, so researchers could follow its progress in the months ahead, and then hoist it down to the water and watch it swim away. Cheering was common. So were tears.

Not all of the manatees made it back to the wild. Often they arrived at Lowry Park in such forlorn condition that they didn't survive. The odds were particularly daunting with newborn calves whose mothers had abandoned them or been killed. Many of these orphans died shortly after they were found, before a rescue team could rush them to the rehab center. The calves that did reach the zoo still faced an uphill struggle. They'd lost their mothers. They couldn't nurse. They had trouble adapting.

"They don't know the ways of the world," said Virginia Edmonds, the assistant curator of Florida mammals, who oversaw the manatee section along with Dr. Murphy.

One day in May of 2003, not long before the elephants arrived from Swaziland, two fishermen in a boat in the waters of Buttonwood Bay, near Naples, spied a small gray leathery object on a beach and realized

it was a newborn calf, maybe a day old, stranded and apparently abandoned by its mother. The calf was brought to Lowry Park, where the
staff dubbed him Buttonwood. Usually they named the manatees after
the body of water where they had been found; it was a way of remem-
bering where the animals came from, and where the keepers hoped they
would eventually return. For Buttonwood, as with all abandoned calves,
the first forty-eight hours were crucial. If they could make it through
two days, their chances improved dramatically.

From the start, it was a challenge getting enough food into Buttonwood for him to gain weight. The keepers tried bottle feeding him different combinations of formula and Pedialyte, but it didn't work. His
weight, already low when he arrived, remained unstable.

"It's like finding a baby in a Dumpster," said Murphy. "He's in a
very guarded condition. Cross your fingers."

Buttonwood's plight catapulted him into a media sensation. Soon
his whiskered, rumpled face appeared in newspapers and on TV across
the state. Elementary schoolchildren were phoning the zoo to check on
his progress. Lowry Park decided to place Buttonwood on display—a
risky move with a young animal whose survival was still far from
certain. To accommodate the demand, the staff moved him from one
of the medical tanks in the back into a brightly colored kiddie pool
where the keepers could work with him in public view. Children were
so mesmerized, they swarmed in front of a fence low enough for them
to see the famous calf but high enough to keep them from trying to pet
him.

The keepers were trying to feed Buttonwood around the clock.
Sometimes, as they held him, he would fall asleep in their arms. But
with his weight still rising and falling, they moved him back into one of
the medical tanks and placed him with a lactating adult female manatee
named Sani, hoping she would let him nurse. It worked for a couple of
days, but then Sani rejected him. Finally the staff switched to a feeding
tube, trying to pump vegetarian formula directly into his stomach. It
appeared to be working. At last Buttonwood was gaining weight. But in
mid-July, a couple of weeks after he started to improve, one of the keepers went to check on the calf and found his small gray body floating
in the shallow water. When people from other departments heard the

news, they didn't want to believe it. Wasn't Buttonwood growing stronger? The manatee keepers were too devastated to answer.

That fall, a second abandoned manatee calf arrived at the zoo. Another male, only several days old. This one was named Loo, because he was found in the Caloosahatchee River, a couple of hours south of the zoo. Now Virginia and the other manatee keepers were working around the clock to save Loo, just as they'd done with Buttonwood. After the emotional ups and downs of that experience, they knew the odds. The zoo's public relations department understood as well. This time there were no press releases alerting the public to the drama quietly unfolding in the manatee section. Whatever was going to happen, it would be between Loo and his keepers. They placed him in one of the medical tanks, and every two or three hours they would climb in to feed him with a bottle. At night, when the rest of the zoo was closed and dark, one of the keepers stayed late to watch over him. The keeper would put on her wetsuit—at this point, almost all of the Florida mammal staff was female—and reach through the black water until she found the calf. Loo weighed barely sixty pounds and was relatively light, so the keeper pulled him onto her lap, cradled him in her arms, and tried to get him to take the bottle. If even a few ounces of the formula reached the calf's stomach, it would increase the odds.

The feedings continued night and day for weeks. Virginia and the rest of her staff would not give up. Though it was not their habit to say such things out loud, they knew all too well that they were Loo's only hope. At daybreak, as they held the calf in the water and tried again, they could hear the rest of the zoo rousing to life around them. If it was quiet enough, they could even make out the faint calls of the adult manatees in the nearby pools when they walked down into the underground viewing area. The vocalizations were like the chirping squeak of a dolphin, only more quiet; manatees are sometimes described as "soft-spoken." Scientists believed that the species used the sounds to express fear or anger, to stay in contact with one another, to keep their calves from straying.

The high-pitched calls were both beautiful and enigmatic. It was easy to wonder what the sirens were communicating at that moment, what the calls sounded like to them rippling through the water. Whatever the message, perhaps Loo was listening too.

Summer was over, allegedly. According to the calendar, it was now October. But a stroll through Lowry Park still felt like a tour through the inner chambers of a giant kiln. By midmorning, an invisible shroud of heat settled over the grounds. It reflected off the walkways that curved past babirusa digging with their tusks and muntjacs darting in the shadows, and shimmered over the placid green water of the moats surrounding the ring-tailed lemurs and the Colobus monkeys, and burned in the scrub pines where the zoo's lone red wolf patrolled the fence at the edge of his exhibit, avoiding eye contact.

The inferno did not slow the stream of cars and minivans pouring into the front parking lots. Observing each new wave of visitors was like standing before an exhibit that endlessly renewed itself. The species on display, however, was hardly soft-spoken. Elementary schoolchildren tumbled out of buses, fidgeting and scratching without shame, the girls quickly bunching into whispered huddles as they reinforced old alliances or established new ones, the boys elbowing and pushing as they maneuvered for position in their secret hierarchies. Adult couples smooched and locked hands and giggled loudly at coded allusions, public proof of their private pair-bond and a warning against interference from any potential reproductive competitors. In biological terms, the signals they were sending could not have been more clear. Walking toward the ticket windows, they rubbed each other's shoulders and brushed dirt and picked lint off each other's shirts and ran their fingers through each other's hair—all classic precoital grooming behavior. (Possibly postcoital.) Mothers and fathers lingered at the rear of their Expeditions and Escalades—glittering emblems not just of status but of their determination to protect the future of their genetic line—and unloaded strollers built like tanks, designer diaper bags overflowing with juice packets and sanitary wipes, and enough sunblock to slather an army. In their car seats, their toddlers waited to be waited upon, spoiled like so many young primates, whining and kicking their legs like tiny despots impatient for their retinue to convey them forward.

If the visitors were listening, they could already detect the roar of Eric, the male Sumatran tiger. Possibly he was restless, eager for his turn in the exhibit. Definitely he was sexually frustrated, since his attempts to court Enshalla had so far been met only with scorn. If the humans heard the roar, it was doubtful that they would have guessed what animal was making it, or why. The deep bass note repeated over and over, punctuating the morning. It didn't sound like tigers in the movies. More like a bellow than a roar, it declared the presence of something vaguely big and clearly ferocious and maybe hungry. Perfect. Much more enticing than the jungle drums, still pounding from the loudspeakers.

As visitors paid their money and pushed through the turnstiles, the predictable soundtrack reassured them that what awaited inside was not true wildness but a carefully staged illusion of wildness. At an almost subliminal level, the true message of the drums was that the zoo's staff would control the experience ahead and that all the leopards and bears and panthers—not to mention any tigers—were safely behind lock and key and would not be allowed, no matter how peckish they might feel, to snack on any children.

Lowry Park prided itself as an institution custom-made for families with young kids. Even though the zoo was growing, it remained compact enough that it was possible to take in the highlights in a couple of hours or less. This was no accident; the new zoo had been designed not to overwhelm. The size of the place was ideal for a four-year-old's attention span. Moving at a reasonable clip and fortified with enough liquids to stave off heat stroke, parents could whisk their brood from one end to the other and be gunning for the exit just as the little one crashed into a blissful stupor. From start to finish, the experience was tailored for the delight of impressionable children. The front courtyard was graced with a fountain where manatee statues swam in the air and toddlers squealed with joy as they jumped through jets of burbling water. Wallaroo Station, featuring species from Australia, offered a rock-climbing wall for older kids. At Stingray Bay, over in the Aquatic Center, children reached inside a shallow tank and ran their fingers along the sleek backs of Southern stingrays whose tail barbs had been removed. Every day, families crowded into an outdoor theater for *Spirits of the Sky*, a birds-of-prey show where the handlers invited the guests to admire Smedley the vulture and cued Ivan the Eurasian eagle owl to fly directly over the audience, his massive wings flapping so close that the churning air ruffled their hair. Inside the Discovery Center, kids studied toxic toads up close and were allowed to fondle a replica of a raccoon dropping. For their birthdays, children were encouraged to celebrate at the zoo with their friends, pet a skink or snake, and play Pin the Tentacle on the Octopus. On special evenings, the zoo sponsored slumber parties where third-graders climbed into sleeping bags next to the underwater viewing windows, drifting off to the sight of the manatees swimming. At Halloween, preschoolers were invited to a camp with bats and tarantulas. At Christmas, they met real reindeer and a not-so-real Santa.

One of the most popular attractions, all year round, was the petting zoo, a dusty corral where children waded happily among bleating sheep and fed them grain pellets and ignored the teeth and gums pulling at their clothes. Unbeknownst to parents, the herd included a billy goat named Cody who had somehow mastered the art of contorting himself so he could urinate on his own head. To impress the nanny goats, of course.

"We call him Pee Goat," a keeper said under her breath one day, maintaining a safe distance. "He's disgusting."

Many of the kids, no doubt, would have been ecstatic to learn of Cody's special talent. They howled at the raccoon poop. Why not a malodorous goat? From a child's perspective, nothing could have been more enchanting.

Perched on a branch, two golden lion tamarins peered out with their tiny old-men faces, chirping as though they were birds, not tiny monkeys.

With silky, reddish gold manes that swept backward toward their shoulders, the tamarins were among the most striking creatures at Lowry Park. Weighing less than two pounds each, Kevin and Candy did in fact look like miniature lions. If they could have growled, they would have been doing so right now, because they were in the middle of a heated argument with Lee Ann Rottman. The best they could do was glare at her.

"You see 'em?" said Lee Ann, shaking her head as she pointed them out.

The curator and the defiant monkeys were facing off inside the zoo's free flight aviary. Knowing how much the public loves tamarins, Lowry Park had long kept a pair of them inside the giant screened enclosure along with the emerald starlings and the masked lapwings and all the other birds. In their native forests of Brazil, tamarins lived in the canopy and nested inside holes in the tree trunks; at Lowry Park they roamed through the oaks of the aviary and slept in a camouflaged Igloo cooler that hung high among the branches. For years, another pair of tamarins had lived in peaceful coexistence with the birds and the human visitors, but recently they had grown too old and the staff had replaced them with Kevin and Candy. The two newcomers had become a headache, because they had chosen to spend their days on a branch that hung too close to the sidewalk that led guests through the trees. Much smaller than the average housecat, the tamarins were relatively harmless. But their teeth were sharp and they had been known to bite when their keepers approached to feed them crickets or fruit. The zoo had posted a sign warning not to touch the monkeys, but they were too cute to resist and too feisty to be trusted. Sooner or later, somebody was likely to get a hand chomped.

The keepers had tried everything they could think of to make Kevin and Candy abandon the low-hanging branch and choose another perch farther from the sidewalk. They had even collected some of Eric the tiger's urine from his den and used it to spray the area, hoping the pungent menace of his scent would intimidate the monkeys. No luck. Nothing seemed to scare them, even the two boat-billed herons who grew agitated one day when Kevin and Candy wandered too close to the large birds' nest.

"They were clacking at them," said Lee Ann. "The tamarins didn't care."

Candy, the female, was especially territorial. She didn't like taking orders from other species, no matter how much they dwarfed her.

Whenever the keepers drew near, she retaliated with angry chatter. She was doing it now to the acting curator.

"She's a little bitchy," said Lee Ann.

Obviously Kevin and Candy were not destined to be permanent residents of the aviary. The staff would have to move them back to their previous home, a smaller enclosure with other tamarins and marmosets in Primate World. It was just one more task for Lee Ann's never-ending to-do list. She was the ultimate troubleshooter, constantly dealing with the neuroses and complaints and quirks and insecurities and problems of multiple species. If a baby chimp was forsaken by its birth mother, Lee Ann found it a surrogate. If one of the Sarus cranes lost its appetite or a kangaroo suffered a miscarriage, she needed to know why. If an orangutan hurled her droppings at a bank president or the Bactrian camels humped again in front of the second-grade field trip, she heard about it. If one of her keepers was going through a divorce or couldn't take another day of beak-pecking from the emus, typically they ended up crying in her office. Sometimes the humans acted like animals—not necessarily a bad thing in her view—and sometimes the animals behaved like complicated humans. All of it was her problem.

In a zoo, where dominance is often maintained through physical size and brute force, Lee Ann was a remarkably small and delicate alpha. Five feet tall, with a slight build and a natural shyness, she appeared almost frail. In reality, she possessed reserves of strength and resilience that had sustained her through emergencies most people could not imagine. Over the years, she had periodically taken leaves from the zoo to study and work with wild chimps in Uganda and Cameroon, and during her travels she had contracted typhoid, amoebic dysentery, and cerebral malaria. One day, as she and a group of other people were floating on a river in inner tubes, a hippo surfaced directly beneath her boyfriend and dragged him in its jaws toward the river bottom. Hippos are much more dangerous than their ungainly appearance would suggest—in Africa, they kill more humans than lions and elephants combined—and as she watched her boyfriend going under, Lee Ann was screaming. She doesn't know how long he was down there, but suddenly he broke free and reappeared above the surface, bleeding from huge bites to his torso. At the hospital, doctors determined that the hippo's teeth had barely missed his spinal cord and femoral artery. During his recovery, Lee Ann slept on the floor beside his bed and held his hand as he hallucinated.

The boyfriend survived, but the relationship did not. Eventually Lee Ann returned to Lowry Park with a vivid new appreciation for just how dangerous animals could be. The zoo was a more controlled environment than the wilds of Africa, but the hazards and difficulties of the job could not be discounted, as had been demonstrated by the fatal elephant attack on Char-Lee Torre. Caring for the animals at Lowry Park was so demanding, both physically and emotionally, that many keepers only lasted a few years before moving on. Lee Ann had stayed for more than a decade, starting in the primate department and then working her way up through the ranks. Being curator was easily the hardest position she'd ever had. Whatever situation she was dealing with, a dozen others awaited her immediate attention. Her face was often streaked with sweat. Her boot soles were caked with the droppings of who knew how many species. It was an exhilarating, appalling, glorious mess of a job that devoured almost every moment of every day, from before dawn until after dark. It required her to be a general, a therapist, a mind-reader, a diplomat, and a den mother to almost seventeen hundred individuals, some of whom walked on four legs and could kill her without even trying.

One of Lee Ann's favorites was Rango, the zoo's only adult male orangutan. Stopping in front of Rango's exhibit, she waxed on about what a good father he was to his young son and daughter, who at that moment were climbing in some netting nearby.

"He's very handsome, I think," she said. "He has the most sensitive eyes."

Lately, though, Rango had been snubbing Lee Ann, avoiding eye contact with her. He was mad because she was so busy that she hadn't come to see him lately. She felt guilty, but what could she do? With the opening of Safari Africa on the horizon, she was more swamped than ever, coordinating the arrival of giraffes and zebras and monitoring the progress of the four Swazi elephants and Ellie. Lowry Park had great hopes that these five would form the nucleus of a breeding herd. In the coming spring, before the new wing opened, the zoo planned to attempt an artificial insemination with Ellie. The two females from Swaziland were not yet old enough to safely get pregnant, and the two males were not yet tall enough to mount Ellie. Considering Ellie's skittishness with her own species, no one could predict how she would react if one of the bulls tried to breed with her. The fact that she'd never mated or been pregnant before complicated her chances of being able to conceive in the future. Just as with humans, elephant females can develop endometriosis as they get older, leaving cysts and scar tissue that render them infertile; such health issues are especially prevalent in elephants who have never been pregnant. If the zoo wanted Ellie to have a baby, then she needed to do it soon. Already the staff was tracking her menstrual cycle to determine the optimal time for the AI and was consulting with two specialists from Berlin—Drs. Thomas Hildebrandt and Frank Göritz, the same two who had carried out the field sonograms in Swaziland. These two specialists had distinguished reputations, but at zoos around the world, they were known as "the Berlin boys." Soon the zoo would fly them to Florida.

Although the fears of sabotage from animal-rights activists at the airport had never materialized, Lee Ann and the rest of the staff were on alert for the possibility of further protests. Work crews had already raised the height of Lowry Park's perimeter fence to make sure no one entered at night to interfere with the elephants. Lee Ann did not harbor antagonism toward PETA or the other groups that had fought the elephants' importation. Speaking to the docents one evening, she acknowledged that the coalition's campaign had ultimately been useful because it focused everyone's attention on the elephants' well-being.

Even so, Lee Ann knew how far such activism could go. Fifteen years before, in the wake of highly publicized criticisms over the treatment of an Asian elephant at the San Diego Wild Animal Park, a shadowy group called the Animal Liberation Front had vandalized the homes of three of the park's elephant keepers, splashing red paint and paint thinner on the keepers' cars and houses. The letters "ALF" were etched into a window with acid.

Lee Ann steered clear of such extremes. She was aware of her institution's appalling history. She knew the sad stories of how so many animals had ended up in captivity over the centuries, the terrible losses different species suffered as various zoos dispatched animal traders into jungles and forests around the world to seize new wonders. But she was also aware of the role that Lowry Park and other zoos were now taking to defend many species against obliteration.

The golden lion tamarins were a compelling example. Kevin and Candy had been born in captivity. But in decades past, the tamarins had been so coveted for their beauty—and so prized by zoos and private collectors—that they had nearly been hunted to extinction before a coalition of scientists and zoo officials led a battle to protect them in their native swamp forests of Brazil. Thirty years ago, fewer than a hundred were left in the wild, but since then their numbers had surged, thanks partly to the introduction of breeding males and females born at the National Zoo and other institutions and then released into the forest populations. Zoos, in other words, had been agents of both the golden lion tamarins' annihilation and their resurrection. The rampant desire to display them as gorgeous trophies had pushed them to the brink. The recognition that such practices were not only repugnant but harmful to the future of the planet had then led to a coordinated campaign for their conservation. Despite these efforts, the tamarins' future is considered bleak. Logging and farming have destroyed more than 90 percent of their habitat in Brazil. Unless something changes, the only golden lion tamarins found on the planet by the end of this century are likely to live in zoos.

Lowry Park had been involved in the campaign to increase the tamarins' numbers in the wild. Over the years, the zoo had placed other tamarins in an oak on the grounds to acclimate them to living in the trees in preparation for a return to the Brazilian forest. But none had ever been selected by the program. Still, in the years since, the institution had tried to do its part for conservation, especially with its work in rehabilitating manatees and releasing them back into their native waters. Lee Ann was proud of these efforts and wanted the zoo to do more. Like many keepers on her staff, she would have preferred to see Lowry Park's animals returned to the wild.

"In a perfect world," she said, "we wouldn't have animals in captivity."

With most of the animals at Lowry Park, though, freedom was impossible. Take Rango, for instance. It would be wonderful, Lee Ann said, if someone could spring the male orangutan out of Lowry Park and transport him around the world to the forests of Borneo, where remnants of his species still live high in the trees, eating figs and mangos and lychees. But after a lifetime in zoos, Rango would have no idea how to fend for himself. Some captive-born animals can learn those skills, but it's almost always a complicated transition. Over the decades, hundreds of orangutans have been rescued from the illegal pet trade and returned to the forest canopies. But many of these captive-born animals were released without any training to teach them how to search for food and fend off predators, and researchers believe that most did not survive. When they were taken into the wild, some of the orangs would not even attempt to climb into the trees. For Rango, it was far too late. Besides, there wasn't much wild left for him or any other orangutans. Most of their habitat had already been cleared away for gold mining and logging and palm oil plantations. Bornean orangutans were so endangered that some experts predicted they could vanish from the wild in the next few years.

The same dilemma repeated itself over and over. For many of the species at Lowry Park, very little of the wild remained. Outside the zoo, there was no place else for them to go.

Lee Ann wasn't convinced that most of the zoo's animals would have been happier in the wild, even if they'd had the choice. After her stints in Africa, studying chimps in the forest, she could testify that nature played nothing like a Disney movie. During her travels she had seen animals dying of hunger, dying in droughts, in the teeth of predators, in the gun sights of humans who hunted them for bushmeat.

"The wild," she said, "is not all it's cracked up to be."

For most of the animals she worked with, maybe the zoo was the best option left.

5

Royalty

The king and queen of Lowry Park ruled over twin kingdoms, enclosed by high walls and electrified wire and deep moats, erected to ensure that the king and queen never set foot in the outside world and that the outside world never reached them.

Though their domains stood less than a hundred yards apart, they had never met or even laid eyes on each other. Their species, in fact, hailed from tropical forests on opposite sides of the world and were never intended to cross paths. Still, the queen had grown up hearing the king's hoots and cries, and like nearly everyone else at the zoo, he undoubtedly had spent years listening to her roars and moans. Their individual histories could not have been more different. He had been born in the trees of Africa but had long since lost almost every trace of wildness. She had been born and raised in the care of humans but had never been tamed. He had forgotten who he was and would one day pay for that omission. She had always remembered, and would pay for that, too.

In ways neither could begin to understand, their lives would be intertwined forever.

Liberia, December 1966. An American named Ed Schultz, working for an iron ore mining company in the west African port of Buchanan, got word that someone at the mess hall was selling baby chimps.

Schultz knew all about the bushmeat trade. Hunters killed adult chimpanzees, knocking them from the trees, then sold their flesh for food and their young as pets. The mothers made for an easier target, because as they held on to their young they could not flee as quickly through the trees. The hunting had been going on for decades, with chimps and other species, and would continue for decades more. The losses were devastating. For every chimp sold as a pet, many others— sometimes ten or more—would be slaughtered.

When he heard about the man in the mess hall, Schultz saw it as a chance to save one of those babies. Four decades later, he would still remember that day. He went to the mess hall and found a man waiting with an open orange crate. Inside were two chimps, each only a few weeks old. One looked up at Schultz and reached up with both arms.

"You're my Herman," said Schultz, scooping up the chimp. He didn't know where the name came from. It just seemed right.

Schultz paid $25 in cash, got a receipt marked with a thumbprint—the seller didn't know how to write—then took Herman home to meet his wife, Elizabeth, and two young children, Roger and Sandy. At first, the family put Herman in diapers and fed him from the bottle Sandy used when she pretended to feed her doll. A few months later, they started caring for another young chimp, a female named Gitta. Before she came to the Schultz household, Gitta had been confined almost exclusively to a small cage and was extremely shy and unsure of herself around humans. When she saw Herman, she clung to him and rocked nervously back and forth. Herman tolerated her neediness; even then, he seemed more patient than other chimps. Though Herman and Gitta slept in a crate on the front porch, the Schultzes often treated them more like members of the family than pets. Herman, naturally affectionate and overflowing with personality, featured more prominently in the family's daily life. The Schultzes taught him to sit at a table and drink from a cup and eat fruit without making too much of a mess. They dressed him in children's clothes and tickled his feet and toted him on their shoulders and took him swimming at the quarry. They let him play out in the yard and climb high into the trees. As the years passed and the Schultz children grew, their parents penciled their changing heights on the wall. As Herman and Gitta grew, height marks were made for them, too.

"Herman was probably as close to a human as a chimp could be," said Roger Schultz, recalling those days. "I don't think he really believed he was a chimp."

LAMCO, the multinational company where Ed worked in Liberia, employed people from around the world, including an abundance from Sweden. At company parties and picnics, Herman—young, impressionable, and decidedly male—was constantly being swept up in the arms of Swedish women. It was during this time period when he apparently developed his weakness for blondes. Most of the Swedish women at the gatherings were blond. Mrs. Schultz was blond, too, and so were the Dutch girls who came to the house. If Herman had not been ripped away from the forest, he would have spent his infancy in the arms of his mother. Instead he was surrounded by fair-haired human women who showered him with attention. He never recovered from their kindness. The Schultzes hoped that he would eventually mate with Gitta, but as he grew older, it became apparent that he had no interest. Though he was friendly to Gitta and other female chimps, his libido had already turned away from his own kind. The Schultz family did not foresee any of this. Believing they had saved Herman, they embraced him into their lives without realizing exactly what that embrace would mean.

A year or so later, when Schultz found a new job back in the United States and moved the family to Ohio, he arranged for both Herman and Gitta to join them. Their first Christmas back home, they bundled Herman into winter baby gear and carried him outside to play in the snow drifting across their front lawn. When he tried to walk, he tumbled into a snow bank and cried for someone to pick him up and dust him off. In a photo from that day, Ed Schultz is shown balancing the chimp on his knee. In front of them stretches some kind of animal, possibly a lion, that the family had made in place of a snowman. Herman, his small head tucked inside a bonnet knitted with a pompom, stares out at the frozen landscape, bewildered.

Soon Schultz took another job in Tampa, working as a manager for a phosphate company, and moved the family with him. Herman and Gitta, almost five years old and on the cusp of chimp adolescence, spent increasing amounts of their time in a large cage the family constructed in the backyard. The chimps were growing stronger and more difficult to control, and Elizabeth Schultz and her daughter were no longer comfortable taking them into the house on their own. It became clear that Herman and Gitta were reaching an age when they could no longer safely stay with the family. Unlike the precocious young chimps seen grinning on old TV sitcoms, adult chimps can be extremely dangerous. They're bigger than most people realize and much stronger than humans. Even in the presence of people they know and trust, chimps are volatile. When they get upset or angry, they simply react. Over the years, adult chimps have repeatedly mauled humans with startling brutality, sometimes biting off their fingers or even plucking out their eyes. In a 2009 incident in Stamford, Connecticut, a pet chimp who had been raised like a human—taught to drink from long-stemmed glasses, to dress and bathe himself, even to use a computer—took his owner's keys from the kitchen table and slipped outside. When the owner asked a friend to help retrieve him, the two-hundred-pound chimp attacked the friend in the driveway and refused to be pried off her even when the owner stabbed the animal with a butcher knife. "He's ripping her apart!" the owner told a 911 dispatcher. By the time police arrived and shot him, the chimp had blinded his victim, severely maimed her hands, and torn off her nose and much of her face. She survived but remained hospitalized for months.

Ed Schultz did not believe that his beloved Herman or Gitta would attack his family. But he wasn't willing to take the chance. So in 1971, he donated the chimps to Lowry Park. In exchange, the family made two requests. The first was that Herman and Gitta be allowed to live out their lives at the zoo, without being sold or transferred to another facility and possibly ending up in some research lab.

"We weren't going to let anybody put an electrode in Herman's head," recalls Schultz's son, Roger.

The second request was that on the off-chance Herman and Gitta ever mated, the family wanted custody of their offspring, at least for a few years. If Herman and Gitta had a baby, the Schultzes wanted to ensure that it was well cared for, and they had little confidence that the zoo was up to the task. At that time, Lowry Park was still more than a decade away from its remodeling. Herman and Gitta were headed for the shabby old zoo, which was small and claustrophobic and had no facilities for raising an infant chimp. Ed Schultz knew Lowry Park was far from ideal. Even so, he believed it was the only realistic choice available. Besides, the zoo had promised to give Herman and Gitta a cage of their own—one larger than the one that housed them now in the family's backyard—that would keep them safely away from another chimp known for his aggressiveness. The staff had also agreed to allow Schultz to visit Herman and Gitta whenever he wanted and even hold them, provided he still felt safe getting that close.

On the morning of the big move, the Schultz family drove the chimps to downtown Tampa for a ceremonial visit at City Hall. A *Tampa Tribune* photographer snapped pictures of Mayor Dick Greco hamming it up with Herman and Gitta. One shot showed the chimps seated beside Greco, pondering the city budget. The staged frivolity did not take away the bittersweet emotions of the day, but the Schultzes were pleased to see Herman reveling in the spotlight. From the moment he'd entered their lives, his hunger for human attention had always made him quick to please. That day, as he posed for the news crew, he was being trained to perform for a larger audience. For better or worse, he was about to become a star.

Once they finished at the mayor's office, the family escorted the chimps to Lowry Park. On their way inside, Herman scaled a light pole. After a childhood in the trees, he would never again have a chance to climb anything that tall. When the zoo staff led them to Herman and Gitta's cage, the Schultzes climbed inside with the chimps. Roger and his little sister, Sandy, understood the reasons for the move. But as they said good-bye to their friends, the children could not help crying.

It's almost impossible to envision what a shock the farewell must have been for Herman. Already confused about so many things, he would have had no way to understand why he and Gitta were being abandoned. When the cage door locked shut and the Schultzes walked away, he called out after them, as he often did when they placed him inside his cage at home. When they didn't return to retrieve him the next day, or the day after that, did he still harbor some hope that they would eventually return to retrieve him? How long must it have taken before the truth sank in?

That was the start of Herman's third life. First he had clung to his mother in the forest, only to be ripped away from her and everything else he'd known. Then he had been adopted into his human family and had learned to act as though he were one of them. Now that family was

with the chimps that one day he actually fell asleep in the cage. When he awoke, Herman and Gitta were napping beside him.

"Whoa. What time is it?" he said, checking his watch. "Fellas, I gotta go."

The adventures inside the cage didn't last. A keeper told Schultz it was too much of a risk to allow him direct contact with the chimps, especially as they grew older. Schultz reluctantly agreed but continued to visit, spending so much time there that he soon signed up as a volunteer.

As the years stretched on, Herman's charm gained him legions of admirers. When Jane Goodall visited Lowry Park in 1987, the renowned chimpanzee researcher instantly fell for him, praising his glossy coat, pleasant personality, and the "lovely, open expression on his face." "Wonderful," she called him. "Magnificent." Along the way, she also offered some insight into Herman's ostentatious display behavior in front of human alpha males.

"He wants to be the boss," Goodall explained. "He doesn't want you to be the boss."

By then, the city of Tampa had closed the old zoo and was handing over the facility to the Lowry Park Zoological Society, a newly created nonprofit organization that would be running the zoo from that point on. Goodall was an ardent supporter of the new zoo and its expanded focus on endangered primates and other threatened species. She returned repeatedly to tour the remodeled grounds and to enthrall the public with heart-rending stories from her generational studies of chimps in Tanzania's Gombe National Park. Speaking one afternoon at a Girl Scout luncheon, she greeted her audience with a rousing imitation of a wild chimpanzee call.

Goodall, famed around the world, gave the remodeled zoo a fresh stamp of legitimacy. Even before the grand opening, she spoke glowingly of the more naturalistic setting where Herman and the zoo's other chimps would soon be moved. The open exhibit, much bigger than his cage, was flanked by the canyon walls and featured a termite mound in which they could poke sticks in search of food, just as Gombe's chimps did in the wild. Goodall was pleased that Herman would be able to walk in the elephant grass and feel the sun above his head.

In truth, the "naturalism" of the zoo's new exhibits was a conceit. Like the rocks and the waterfall, the termite mound was not real. It didn't even contain termites; instead it tempted the chimps with hidden caches of honey and jelly. As with so many other exhibits at zoos around the world, many of these design elements were carefully constructed props installed as much for the entertainment of the humans gazing into the exhibits as for the animals themselves. The public has long had a distaste for seeing animals in cages or enclosures with bars or other boundaries that symbolize captivity. Man-made waterfalls and other special effects, such as fake rocks made to appear weathered with air-brushed mineral stains and simulated bird droppings, encourage zoo visitors to feel as though they are witnessing wild creatures in their natural habitat and that in fact those creatures are roaming at will, perfectly happy to be there. The principle guiding such aesthetic touches has been called "imitation freedom." Animals of any intelligence, presumably, are well aware of the difference. Certainly they are not fooled by the fake bird droppings. Some zoos are so determined to make their exhibits appear "natural" that they hide electrified wires around the trees and plants to prevent the animals from touching them.

The creators of Lowry Park's new chimp exhibit had not taken their naturalistic designs that far. Electrified wires had been installed along the perimeter to discourage the chimps from climbing out, but no shocks awaited them in the tall grass of the moat. Though the exhibit was hardly a substitute for the verdant complexity of the African forest where Herman had been born, it was unquestionably a great improvement over the claustrophobic box in which he'd been trapped for the past decade and a half. The new exhibit was so radically different that it promised yet another life for Herman. Gitta, it turned out, would not get the chance to come with him. After so many years together, first with the Schultz family and then inside the cage, the female chimp fell ill with a viral infection and died shortly before the two of them were to be moved together.

Herman would not be alone for long. Other chimps were added to Lowry Park's collection. For the first time since he was a baby, Herman became part of a chimpanzee social group, learning their habits and rhythms and negotiating his way atop the group's hierarchy. On his first day in the new exhibit, as he stepped into the open air and walked onto the grass and the ground for the first time in years, Herman appeared tentative. Soon, though, he was climbing the exhibit's tree and had claimed his perch on the rock shelf beside the waterfall, using the higher ground to survey both the crowds of human onlookers as well as the other chimps. In those first years, it was just him and a female named Rukiya and two sisters, Jamie and Twiggy, and a young male named Chester. As the elder male, Herman initially assumed control as the group's alpha. But when Chester grew older and stronger, he challenged Herman and ousted him in a sudden coup. It didn't take much, because Herman was not a typical alpha. Chester only had to attack Herman once, pummeling and biting him, and Herman immediately surrendered.

A counter coup was out of the question. Having been raised among humans, Herman was far too nice. He had no combat experience to guide him, no idea how to hold his own amid the violent upheavals at the heart of chimpanzee politics. In both the wild and captivity, male chimps vying for power will battle aggressively. Usually these conflicts do not result in serious injury, but on occasion rivals will resort to brutality. In one gruesome case at the Arnhem zoo in the Netherlands, two males apparently conspired to kill their group's alpha one night when their keepers were gone. The next morning, the alpha was found in his cage with his toes and testicles bitten off, bleeding to death from numerous wounds. One primatologist, recounting the incident, called it "an assassination." In Gombe, the forest where Jane Goodall conducts her research, males from one chimpanzee group have been repeatedly observed waging war on other chimp groups, hunting down and exterminating their weaker rivals. Males will kill females and their infants, eating their flesh. Sometimes, in the midst of these war raids, several male chimps will hold down an enemy while others dismember him.

"Their culture is just so aggressive—so naturally aggressive," said Andrea Schuch, another primate keeper at Lowry Park. "It always surprises people."

Even after seizing power, Chester continued to chase and slap Herman and the other chimps as a matter of routine, just to maintain his dominance. The primate staff didn't want to interfere; they thought it best to let the chimps work out the power shift in their own way, provided the situation didn't reach a point where the animals were getting hurt. Sometimes, when tensions between Herman and Chester grew high, the keepers would separate the two males, hoping to calm them. But the physical domination continued.

Lee Ann Rottman, still a young primate keeper at the time, remembers how upsetting those days were for Herman. It wasn't just that he'd been overthrown; it was that he could not defend himself or the other chimps. Powerless to stop Chester from picking on the females, Herman showed signs of confusion. He would pace the exhibit, grinning with his mouth open, the chimp signal for fear.

"He didn't know what to do," Lee Ann said. "He would be very scared."

Sometimes, when Chester was coming after him or one of the other chimps, Herman would turn to any keepers who happened to be nearby and reach his hand toward them. For a chimp who identified so closely with humans, the woeful gesture must have made sense. He had no way of comprehending the keepers' reluctance to intervene. All he knew, from his decades at the zoo, was that people were his friends. Surely they would save him. Surely they would help him protect the others.

Chester's behavior was to be expected of an alpha chimp. In many ways, his reign brought new life to the group. He was full of energy and verve, and unlike Herman, he was keenly interested in breeding with the chimp females. Still, he was a problem for the staff. He had a habit of cupping fresh droppings in his hand and hurling them at visitors. Even more disturbing, he displayed a talent for climbing up the rock wall beside the waterfall and eluding the electrical wire that ran across the top. He never wandered far. He seemed content to stand on the roof of the chimps' night house, and when he saw the keepers coming, he simply climbed back down into the exhibit. Still, these excursions did not bode well. What if Chester really got out and hurt someone? A year or so later, he was shipped to another zoo, and Herman reclaimed his position at the top of the hierarchy.

The possibility of an escaped animal was something Lowry Park took seriously. The keepers communicated all day on walkie-talkies and had different codes for different emergencies. Code One signified that one of the animals had gotten out of its enclosure. Code Two meant a visitor had fallen or climbed into an exhibit. Code Three meant a venomous snake had bitten a keeper. The staff prepared for these emergencies, especially Code Ones. They had protocols for species on the loose—what to do if it was a wolf or a clouded leopard—and drills to practice carrying out those protocols. The zoo even had a weapons team, made up of keepers who were trained by law enforcement to use firearms, if other measures failed.

Lee Ann often considered what it would be like to hear the crackle of the radio and then the words, "Code One, chimp." Inside her head, she would play through the scenarios. If Herman got out, what would she do? What if it was Rukiya or Twiggy? Lee Ann knew each of the chimps' personalities better than some parents know their own children. She was fairly sure that she would feel safe approaching Rukiya if she were loose. Among the staff, the joke was that if Herman ever escaped, he'd just find a blond visitor and strip off her clothes. Still, the keepers knew they had to be careful, and never entered the exhibit with the chimps except in emergencies. Lee Ann did not believe she had anything to fear from Herman, either. But there was no telling what another chimp might do.

In the primate department, some preferred the orangs. Some had a thing for the lemurs. Lee Ann's heart, always, was with Herman and his group. Showing the chimps to a newcomer inside the zoo, she would rhapsodize about how handsome Herman was, how smart and thoughtful and considerate of the other chimps, how he managed to be both strong and gentle.

"If I could meet a man like Herman," she said, "I would marry him."

For his part, Herman was deeply attached to Lee Ann, whose hair fell somewhere along the border between light brown and blond. He thought of her and the other female primate keepers as his. Once, when Lee Ann's father visited the zoo, he placed a hand on his daughter's shoulder, and Herman exploded, screaming and pounding his body against the walls of the exhibit. Lee Ann wasn't offended. She understood that chimps were extremely emotional and that whatever they felt usually flashed straight to the surface. She identified with this trait, because sometimes she felt overwhelmed by her emotions too.

In the years since Chester had been sent away, Herman had ruled unchallenged over Lowry Park's other chimps with a soft touch unusual for alphas of his species. If he needed to keep the others in line, he would shriek at them and sometimes even chase them. Afterward, the keepers noticed, he would always reconcile. He was their protector and leader. When a baby chimp named Alex was introduced into the group in 1998, Rukiya became his surrogate mother. But it was Herman who refused to leave Alex's side when the baby got his head stuck in some netting.

Not long after Alex joined the group, another chimp—a male, a few years older than Herman—was brought to the zoo from another facility. Bamboo was a pathetic sight. He had almost no teeth and was therefore vulnerable, and when he arrived at Lowry Park, he was obviously shaken and unsure of himself. Another dominant male might have ignored him or beaten him to put him in his place. Herman welcomed Bamboo and accepted him before any of the others did.

Always, Herman was different. When new keepers were hired, he welcomed them by extending his fingers through openings in the mesh, offering to put the fingers in their mouth. In chimp language, this was an expression of faith, demonstrating that he believed the keepers would not bite off the digits. He wanted them to understand that he trusted them, and that therefore they could trust him.

At times, Herman seemed uncannily human, understanding things that eluded the other chimps. His unusual relationship with Dr. Murphy was a good example. Like many of the animals at Lowry Park, most of the chimps disliked the veterinarian because they associated him with the sting of a tranquilizer dart and other indignities required for their medical care. One day, Murphy appeared in the chimp night house with a tranquilizer gun so he could attend to Herman. Murphy was a good shot and almost never missed. But this time, his aim was off. The other chimps would have run and hid. Herman just picked up the dart, walked over to the mesh, and handed it back to Murphy so he could try again.

Enshalla's life was so much simpler. Everything about her was clean and clear and imbued with ruthless purity. Unlike Herman, she never betrayed the slightest confusion about what she was. She didn't perform. She didn't accommodate or negotiate. She was a tiger through and through, with almost no interest in humans, except when they brought her another slab of horse ribs. When her keepers worked in her night house, she would wait until their backs were turned, then leap toward them against the mesh, growling and hissing.

Tigers have distinctive personalities, both in zoos and in the wild. Some have been characterized as daring and rash, others are relatively mild-mannered. Even though she had been born and raised in captivity, Enshalla's personality was irredeemably, wondrously savage. She was such an intimidating animal, some keepers from other departments were reluctant to walk down the narrow, dimly lit corridor that led past her den, only a couple of feet past the piercing stare of her emerald eyes. Even though these keepers knew they were safe, it unnerved them every time she jumped at them, so close they could see her fangs gleaming in the semidarkness.

To those who worked with her every day, Enshalla's unwielding ferocity only deepened her beauty.

"What I loved about her the most was that she was nasty," said Pam Noel, who had worked with her for years. "She was true to her species."

The public found Enshalla mesmerizing. On the boardwalk that overlooked her exhibit, people would throng at the railing to stare and point and yell. They loved to watch her circle the perimeter, lick her paws, jump onto her elevated platform. They were especially fascinated when the staff tossed her another serving of meat. Once, a man had asked one of the keepers why they insisted on serving meat to the zoo's tigers. Wouldn't a vegetarian diet be better? The keeper explained that tigers are carnivores with deeply bred instincts for hunting prey. The man was not satisfied.

"Couldn't you give them tofu shaped to look like their prey?"

Enshalla ignored the crowd's provocations. She didn't bother growling at the gawkers who called out to her from above, and she didn't pounce against the viewing window even when they pointed at her from the other side, only a few inches away. The visitors would pound the glass, trying to prod a reaction. Enshalla would gaze in the opposite direction with regal indifference, refusing to acknowledge the humans' vulgarity with so much as a twitch of her ear.

She was an independent female, born from an independent mother. Her parents, Sumatran tigers named Dutch and Tuka, came to Lowry Park from zoos in Rotterdam and San Diego. Their early courtship bore a strong resemblance to the dynamic that would later unfold between Enshalla and Eric. Just like her daughter, Tuka was older and more experienced and confident than the male suitor brought before her. Just as with Enshalla, she lived at Lowry Park first and considered the tiger exhibit her kingdom. When Dutch arrived, she treated him as an intruder. Even though he outweighed her, Tuka dominated him at first, snarling and hissing until he hid from her wrath.

Finally Tuka relented and allowed Dutch to get close enough to mate. Even then, though, the danger was not over. Fatal violence between tigers is common. In the wild, they tend to be solitary animals, highly protective of their territories, and when two males cross paths, their conflicts sometimes end in death. Males and females typically don't meet unless the female is in estrus; even then, the male may kill the female. And once a female gives birth, it's not uncommon for her to kill a cub, either accidentally or to protect it from another threat. Dutch and Tuka lost their first cub, Shere-Khan, in the spring of 1990 to just such an accident. Witnesses reported that Shere-Khan was sitting near the pond that lined the front of the exhibit when he called out to his mother in a low growl, sounding like a whiny child demanding attention. Tuka went over to the cub and picked him up by his throat instead of the scruff at the back of his neck. As she held him, seemingly unaware of his distress, Shere-Khan struggled and suffocated. Once he went still, Tuka carried his body to the water at the front of the exhibit. As sobbing visitors watched, she pulled the limp cub through the water, as though she were trying to revive him. When keepers coaxed Tuka back into her den inside the night house, she dropped Shere-Khan and left his body in the exhibit. A vet tech ran out to retrieve the cub, and several staff members performed CPR and mouth-to-mouth resuscitation for an hour, to no avail.

Six months later, Dutch and Tuka had another cub, a female named Kecil. Then, on August 24, 1991, Tuka gave birth to a litter of three more cubs—Raja, Sacha, and Enshalla. For the first few months, the cubs stayed inside Tuka's den, nursing and walking on wobbly legs. For their protection, they were kept separate from their father. When the cubs were about eight weeks old, Tuka's keepers decided to briefly take Enshalla from her mother, too. Enshalla had a sore behind her ear and the keepers had noticed that Tuka was overcompensating, licking the sore incessantly. To give Enshalla a chance to heal, the staff hand-raised the cub for a couple of weeks, taking turns bringing her to their homes at night.

Ged Caddick, then the assistant general curator, remembers the young Enshalla padding across the wood floors of his south Tampa home. She slept in a pet carrier in the kitchen and accepted feedings of a gruel made of formula and meat powder, squirted into her mouth with a syringe. Before he fed her, Caddick would put on gloves so as not to leave his scent in her fur. He would pick her up by the scruff of her neck, just as a mother tiger would, and feel her body go limp. Even then, she was far from docile. She wasn't eager to be held and had no desire to cuddle.

"She wasn't aggressive, but she wasn't seeking human companionship," said Caddick. Still, "she was cute as the dickens. Cute as can be."

Taking the cub home was a rare treat for her keepers. Once Enshalla grew, it would be far too dangerous for them to venture into the same room with her. In the zoo world, big felines are notoriously unforgiving of humans who get too close. A senior keeper at the Miami Metrozoo was slain one day when he walked into the Bengal tiger exhibit without realizing that one of the tigers was still inside the paddock. The tiger heard the keeper approaching through the night house and was waiting for him the moment he opened the service door. In another incident, a keeper at Busch Gardens was giving a behind-the-scenes tour for her parents and boyfriend when she briefly steadied herself against the bars of a lion's cage. The lion bit down on her hand and severed her arm near the elbow. She survived, but doctors were unable to reattach her arm.

Cradling young Enshalla late at night, feeling her squirm in their laps as she gulped down the gruel, allowed Caddick and the other keepers to appreciate her with a vivid intimacy that would never again be possible. Even wearing the gloves, they could stroke her paws, which seemed far too big for the rest of her body and held the promise of how much she would grow. They could touch the smooth brown pads under those paws, and feel the rhythmic rise and fall of her lungs. When she was full and yowled to get down, they could sense the vibration rising from her throat. Holding a baby tiger is nothing like holding a housecat. The body of a fully grown cat is not nearly as thick or muscular as that of a tiger cub, and cats tend to turn in your arms with a lightness that's completely missing from a cub. Even when it's being playful, a baby tiger moves with a heaviness that has nothing to do with how much it weighs and everything to do with what it's becoming. When you hold a tiger cub, it's impossible to forget even for a second that very soon this stunning creature now nuzzling your arm will be capable of hunting and killing you. The tension between those opposites—the adorability of the fluffy cub, the menace of the apex predator waiting to emerge—is electric.

Enshalla was soon returned to Tuka. That November, she and her siblings were introduced to the public. In preparation, the staff baby-proofed the exhibit, lowering the water in the moat to eighteen inches, and allowed Tuka to take the three-month-old cubs out on a trial run, early one morning before the zoo opened, so that they could explore the exhibit quietly. By then the staff had also built a platform, raised five feet off the ground, where Tuka could retreat when she needed a moment of peace from the clamoring litter. The next day, the cubs made their debut. Tuka stepped out first while her cubs remained inside. She studied the gawkers on the boardwalk above, then decided it was safe enough to bring out the babies. She went to the doorway where the cubs were waiting and chuffed at them, making a sound, similar to a cough, that tigers use for greetings or friendly encouragement. To the crowd, it sounded like she said "poof." At once the cubs bounded forward into the light. For the next hour or so, they followed their mother, jumping on her and splashing through the pond and shredding the exhibit's plants and batting one another with their paws.

The cubs were an instant hit, but their time together would be brief. As they turned one, they were all shipped to other zoos. Kecil had been sent away too. Lowry Park's tiger exhibit and night house was not spacious enough to hold them all as they grew. Enshalla and Rajah were sent on loan to Zoo World in the Florida Panhandle. By the time she arrived at the Panama City zoo, Enshalla was no longer a fuzzy cub. She had grown into a juvenile tiger, still maturing but already showing her fiery temperament. Don Woodman, now a veterinarian in Clearwater, Florida, worked at Zoo World at the time and was one of Enshalla's keepers. He remembers her as extraordinarily beautiful, even for a tiger, and extremely aggressive. Her moods were mercurial. She seemed torn between a desire for affection and a determination to attack anyone who tried to give it to her. When Woodman approached her den, she acted friendly and rubbed the white fur of her cheeks against the bars of her cage. But when he turned, she threw herself at him against the bars. Even though he always knew what was coming, the explosions startled him every time.

"She was a mean little cuss," Woodman said. "If you moved, she would hiss like she was going to rip you apart."

Enshalla's brother, Rajah, lasted less than a day at Zoo World. The night he and Enshalla arrived, the two young tigers were still recovering from the sedatives they'd been given for the journey from Tampa. Both of them were out of it when the keepers placed them in their dens. The next morning, when the staff returned to check on them, they found Rajah dead with an injury to the back of his neck.

At first, the cub's death was a mystery, since he had been in his den alone. But during the necropsy, it became clear that his injury was a fatal bite from a fully grown male lion in the adjoining den. During the night, the lion had managed to raise the drop gate that separated them—a guillotine gate, it's called—and attacked Rajah while he was still half-asleep. Enshalla, housed in a different den, was not harmed. Although she had only been a few feet away, it was unclear if she would have been sufficiently awake from her drug-induced sleep to see or hear her brother being dragged into the lion's jaws. Already separated from her mother and other siblings, she was on her own.

Sudden death hovered over Enshalla's family, striking again and again across the generations. First Shere-Khan, then Rajah. Then one spring day in 1994, Enshalla's father killed her mother. Dutch and Tuka were still at Lowry Park, on their own after the cubs were sent away. Although their earlier courtship had been tumultuous, the two tigers had been together for five years and seemed to be getting along well enough that the keepers were routinely pairing them. They were outside in the exhibit around noon one day when something set them off. Whatever it was, the fight did not last long. When it was over, Dutch had crushed Tuka's windpipe. Dr. Murphy, who performed the necropsy, said afterward that the zoo did not know what had led to the death.

"Whatever produced the exchange between the two, I know that instincts took over with the male, and he reacted," said Murphy.

In the days after, the keepers saw Dutch skulking through the dens in the night house, obviously looking for Tuka. "Certainly he knows she's missing," said Murphy.

Eventually, Dutch was sent to the Louisville Zoo. His departure, and Tuka's death, left Lowry Park with openings in its tiger exhibit, and Enshalla was brought back from Panama City later that year. By then she was turning three, a fully grown young adult, much stronger and more indomitable than when she'd been sent away. Returning to the place where she had been born, she was ready to claim it as her own.

In the nine years since, male Sumatrans had been rotated into the exhibit for Enshalla's approval. With each of them, there had been no doubt who was in charge. The keepers admired her refusal to submit, either to other tigers or to humans. Even when the keepers fed her, leaving her meat inside her den, Enshalla would growl at them to get out and let her eat in peace. They were trained to check and recheck every lock in her night house and to maintain a safe distance. They never entered the same enclosure with her or the other tigers. These precautions did not lessen the heart-quickening awe Enshalla inspired. In the early mornings, when she was still inside her den and the keepers went into her empty exhibit to clean and rake, they saw horse ribs scattered on the ground and smelled the tang of the scent she sprayed to mark her territory. Standing in that place, they knew they were no longer at the top of the food chain. Still, they did their best to let Enshalla know they loved her. At Halloween, they gave her pumpkins to tear open. For Cinco de Mayo, they gave her a pinata stuffed with horsemeat. They even learned to chuff for her. Sometimes, she chuffed back.

One of her keepers, Carie Peterson, showered her with sweet-talk.

"Hi, baby girl," Carie called out to her one morning. "Hey, princess."

Enshalla answered with a half-roar, half-snort.

"She's mad at me," Carie said, laughing.

She didn't mind the tiger's moods. Enshalla was her favorite, and she made no attempt to hide it. She insisted that Enshalla was hers and hers alone.

"She's my cat," Carie would say. "If she ever leaves, I'm leaving with her."

Like the rest of the staff, she was closely following Enshalla's and Eric's courtship dance. She prayed that eventually Enshalla would warm to the young virgin and that together they would conceive a litter, thereby adding to the world's dwindling number of Sumatran tigers. Even so, as a modern woman with modern notions, Carie took great satisfaction in Enshalla's refusal to automatically concede to the male imperative. It made the keeper happy that many of the female animals she worked with dominated the males in their exhibits.

"All our girls are like that here," said Carie, beaming.

Enshalla's invincibility posed a threat to the future of her species. Feminism was a human invention, just like morality and ethics and the vegan principles espoused by the man who wanted to feed the tigers tofu. Nature was indifferent to the hopes embedded in these ideas. It unfolded outside our notions of progress, justice, right and wrong. If Enshalla was going to ever have a litter, it had to be soon. She had just turned thirteen and was approaching the end of her reproductive window. If she rejected Eric, how many more suitors could be brought before her? How many more chances did she realistically have? Like her species, she was running out of time.

Patrolling her territory, the queen circled quietly. She slinked past the rock walls that held her in and traced a path along the edge of the moat. In the water, her reflection moved with her—a shimmer of orange and black, disappearing.

Across the way, the king was chasing his minders. It was a game they had played for years, and one of his favorites. The keepers would dash along the exterior of the high mesh wall at the back of the chimp exhibit, and from the other side, Herman would tear after them, laughing and nodding ecstatically.

The keepers loved it too. It made them happy to lure Herman away from another nap on his rock shelf and to see him so engaged and excited, running hard, showing a glimpse of youthful energy. To many staff members, Herman *was* Lowry Park. Waves of primate keepers had worked with him, and as they all came and went, he had always been there. Zoo-keeping tends to be a young person's profession, and many of his current keepers had not been born when he first arrived. They could not picture Lowry Park without him. Still, they wondered how much longer he could hold on. Sooner or later, his heart had to give out, or another chimp would topple him from the throne.

At the moment, Herman had no rivals. There were still only two other males in the group. Bamboo was even older and slower than him and was relegated to such a lowly status in the hierarchy that the females sometimes felt at liberty to bully him. Alex, the adolescent male, looked up to Herman so much that he often imitated him, puffing himself up and rocking back and forth and acting as though he were in charge. But inside any chimp group, even a small and stable one like Herman's, power is always fluid. Alliances shift. Secret deals are made. A new male, stronger and more ambitious, could be transferred from another zoo and take over, just as Chester had done before. Alex, growing fast, might look at Herman one day and gauge the slowness of his gait and decide it was time for a change.

It was hard to imagine what Herman would do then, what he would have left. If he were no longer the king, who would he be?

No need to worry about that right now. There were no threats on the horizon, no challengers looming. For the moment, Herman could while away whatever days he had left, indulging in the privileges of his position—flirting with pretty women, rolling in the dirt with Bamboo, sticking his long black leathery feet through the mesh of his den so his keepers could give him another pedicure. Sometimes, when the afternoon light turned amber and they summoned Herman inside for the night, the chimp ignored them. If he was especially stubborn, they asked one of his favorite blondes on staff—he was particularly enamored of a woman in the Asia department—to stand near the door and call his name. Ever hopeful, Herman would race toward her, running on all fours.

After so many years in this place, he had become a gray eminence. An old man at dusk, hanging on.

6

Cold-Blooded

The burning heart of the day was always the most quiet. Hours passed when nothing happened, when a hush fell over the grounds and the sunbaked toddlers passed out in their strollers and all the other species seemed to have retreated into the shade to doze and dream. Then without warning, the spell would break and the zoo would explode back to life. In a flash, the animals were licking newborn babies clean or plotting a rival's downfall or courting another sexual conquest—giving themselves over to lust, greed, rage, vanity, ambition, even something that might be called love. For a moment, the world would open and offer a glimpse into its logic and design, its random joys and casual cruelties.

That October, Virginia Edmonds and the other manatee keepers were still working around the clock to save Loo, the abandoned calf found in the Caloosahatchee River. He'd been having trouble adjusting to the formula. One Friday evening, Virginia was in the medical tank with Loo, feeding him with the bottle again, when the calf began to shake. He seemed to be seizing. Murphy was summoned, and a small oxygen mask was placed on Loo's small gray face. But it was no good. A few minutes later, he died in Virginia's arms.

After losing Buttonwood only a couple of months before, the other keepers were better prepared for Loo's death. It hurt, seeing another calf slip away. But after eleven years at Lowry Park, they had learned to accept that some animals would die, no matter how much care they gave them.

"We have a lot of death, no matter what we do."

A necropsy would be conducted to determine how Loo had died. Maybe the zoo would discover something that could help. Some kernel of insight that could improve the odds, ever so slightly, the next time an abandoned calf was brought to them and they held him in the cold water through the night.

Death was part of the daily fabric. Mice disappeared down the digestive tracts of eagles. Bears got old and passed away. Squirrels made the fatal error of venturing into the chimp exhibit on a day when Rukiya and Twiggy felt like hunting.

Immersed in the everyday drama of so many species, the staff saw the cycles of life and death endlessly repeating. Sometimes the wheel turned so fast, it made them dizzy.

The keepers in the herps and aquatics department were grinning. One of their male sea horses had just given birth to a new brood.

A male, yes. The way it works with sea horses, the female deposits the eggs into a pouch on the male's stomach. He fertilizes the eggs, then carries them in the pouch for two weeks. "Pregnant males," they're called. When the babies are big enough to swim, the male pushes them into the water.

"They're good at birthing," said Dan Costell, one of the herps keepers, pointing toward the tank where the sea horses were swimming.

Floating near their parents, the babies looked like specks of dirt. Viewed through a magnifying glass, though, they were revealed as tiny dragons, with blinking eyes and shivering dorsal fins and S-shaped bodies plated in crenellated armor from their coronets to the ends of their curving tails. More than a hundred of them had been born into this brood—not unusual for sea horses. They were wondrous creations, somehow both majestic and otherworldly, and in all likelihood, most of them would soon be dead. Sea horse babies have high mortality rates, sometimes 90 percent or more.

The prospect of their deaths did not weigh heavily on Dan or the rest of the herps staff. They accepted that this was the way of things for sea horses, and they knew that soon enough another pregnant male would hatch another huge brood. When biologists talk about reproductive strategies in the animal kingdom, they break it down into two categories of species. Some, known as K-selected species—usually larger mammals such as manatees or tigers or humans—produce only one or a few offspring at a time and then concentrate on rearing and protecting those handful of their young. If one dies, the loss can cut deep, both emotionally and genetically.

In the herps department, the calculus of life and death was figured differently. Most of the time, the staff worked with what are called r-selected species—fish, turtles, frogs, spiders, and other creatures that typically reproduce in greater number, with a much higher mortality rate and the parents devoting virtually no energy to the rearing of those young. Emotion is largely removed from the equation. Inequity abounds, at least by human standards. Some species of frogs, Dan explained one day, typically produce multiple clutches of eggs. The female lays the first clutch, then the male fertilizes them and carries them on his back toward a suitable hatching ground—someplace moist and warm and dark, such as a nutshell or a bromeliad leaf filled with rainwater. When the first clutch hatches into tadpoles, the female lays another clutch and delivers them, unfertilized, to the tadpoles to eat. The second clutch's entire function, then, is to provide a meal for the first clutch. Those eggs are devoured before they ever get a chance to wiggle in the water.

"Whoever hatches first, wins," said Dan.

In the herps department, where the animals were cold-blooded and the staff preferred them that way, sentimentality died quickly. It wasn't that the herps keepers didn't care about their animals. They were as devoted to the well-being of their geckos and marine toads as Lee Ann Rottman was to the chimps or as Carie Peterson was to the tigers. They just didn't see the point in projecting human values onto life forms so utterly different.

The keepers had a running catalogue of stereotypes they deployed to mess with one another, depending on the kind of animals to which they were each assigned. Staffers who worked outside of the aviary joked about asocial misfits fixated on any species with wings and a beak: "those bird nerds." Primate keepers were portrayed as hypersocial: nonstop talkers, slightly crazed, desperate for attention, and prone to extended outbursts of weeping—much like the chimps. The primate staff did not necessarily disagree with this assessment. In fact, a couple of them prided themselves on their talent for dramatic displays and epic banter.

The most withering jokes were reserved for the herps keepers, typically characterized as testosterone-laden freaks obsessed with species the rest of humanity despised. This was not entirely fair, since a couple of the herps keepers were women, seemingly well-adjusted, with nothing freakish about them. But when it came to Dan and his boss, Dustin Smith, the assistant curator in charge of the department, the stereotype was pretty much dead-on. Dustin and Dan—as they were invariably called, and always in the same breath—took boyish pleasure in the outlandish qualities of the species housed in their department, which included not just herps and aquatics but also large spiders and a lonely colony of naked mole rats, exiled in a back room while the zoo figured out where to display them.

Dustin gave lengthy discourses on inspecting the anal notches of turtles to determine their sex and on the virulence and variety of bacteria lurking inside the saliva of Komodo dragons. He talked about how male snakes have two penises, called hemipenes, and how the females have a cloaca, and how they mated side by side. When he gave behind-the-scenes tours of the herps building, he would escort visitors to the edge of the big tub that contained the naked mole rats and explain that although they were mammals, they lived in an underground hive like insects and were ruled by a queen.

"The wildest thing about them?" Dustin said. "When one member of the colony has a baby, every adult lactates, both male and female."

He was fanatical about turtles and tortoises—if it had a shell on its back and lumbered, he was happy—and was always conniving to sneak more of both into exhibits. At the moment he was campaigning for the addition of some Aldabra giant tortoises, a massive species from the Seychelles, off the east coast of Africa. Amazing creatures, Aldabras have one of the longest life spans on the planet; reportedly, they can live for more than a century. Dustin was convinced that Safari Africa, the zoo's soon-to-be-completed new wing, cried out for Aldabras. He had once worked with several of them. They had personalities; he swore it.

They were always following him around, he said, waiting for him to hand over a banana.

"Like puppy dogs!"

Dustin was so persuasive he could almost convince you that a tortoise was the most fiendishly entertaining animal on Earth. Dan tended to be more quiet and was not as prone to the hard sell. He wondered aloud at the ability of snakes to move across deserts, over mountains, and across the seas, all without the aid of limbs. He marveled at the brutal efficiency of male tarantulas, who kill each other on sight to eliminate any potential rival. The herps department kept several tarantulas in one of the back rooms, including a goliath bird-eater, the biggest spider in the world, with legs that can span a dinner plate. As Dan spoke, he was feeding it a breakfast of crickets.

"They won't eat their prey," he explained, "unless it's alive."

His favorites were the poison-dart frogs peeping in the small room modeled after the rain forest. Dan was the minor god who held sway over the air and the earth of this miniature ecosystem, calibrating the misters and the thermostat and the lights to re-create the conditions the frogs would have been experiencing if they lived in the wild and not a closet in a zoo. He made sure their water was clean, that none of them showed signs of spindly leg, and that the room temperature never went below seventy-five degrees or above eighty-five. He was watching over several species of the dart frogs, including the powder blues. They were almost gone from their native Suriname, but for now their numbers in captivity were stable. He thought the world needed more and was encouraging the powder blues to breed. He had fashioned breeding huts for them—coconut shells where they could hide from the light. Usually he put two males in a tank with one female, so that the males would feel competitive and wrestle.

"They've got to do a little sparring to be in the mood," Dan said.

When he found eggs in the breeding huts, he carefully gathered each clutch and tended to it inside a deli cup from Publix. He dreaded going on vacation because he worried some tadpoles would die while he was away.

Dan's precision was a perfect match for his boss's exuberance. He and Dustin were a team, united in their fascination with all that slithered and slunk. Once, when a Burmese python sank its jaws into Dan's hand during a feeding and would not let go, it was Dustin who finally pried the snake off by wedging his Lowry Park ID badge into its mouth.

One of the things that made them such a memorable pair was their physical dissimilarity. Dan was a walking fortress, with a flat-top mohawk and bulging muscles and a Harley parked outside. A tattoo of a dart frog was emblazoned on his right arm, and a Komodo dragon coiled itself around his left, lashing its tongue. The tattoo artist who endowed him with the dragon had free-handed it during a marathon session. Under the needle for more than three hours, Dan had not even winced. He had once been a counselor for juvenile delinquents and also an amateur boxer; recently he had climbed into the ring in a Toughman Contest.

Dustin was short and slightly scrawny and looked as though he'd just escaped from the eighth grade. Although he was actually twenty-five, with a wife and a mortgage and a title, he had no trouble calling forth his inner adolescent. All day long, he messed with the other keepers. His standard greeting, when he passed them on the zoo's back road, was to flash an "L" sign.

"Loser," he would say, smirking.

Usually, they rolled their eyes. "Dustin—"

"Whatever," he'd say, cutting them off.

Like the boy who waves snakes and spiders in front of girls to make them scream, he was not above placing an occasional centipede on someone's arm. Not surprisingly, half of the women on staff had dedicated their lives to devising a suitable revenge. None had succeeded as consistently as his nemesis, who happened to be a female orangutan.

Dee Dee was known around the zoo for her general dislike of men and particular dislike of Dustin. He could not fathom why she hated him so much. As far as he could remember, Dee Dee was one of the few females whom he had never slighted. Perhaps, like Herman, she had a gift for reading people. For years now, whenever Dustin's duties took him past the orang exhibit, Dee Dee had hurled her droppings at him. She had a good arm. One day, when he was zipping by in a golf cart, she calculated the velocity and movement and led her throw just enough for the bull's-eye.

"Women," he said afterward, shaking his head.

For all the abuse Dustin invited, he retained a scruffy appeal. Watching him counting the scutes on a turtle's shell, it was easy to see the child who had preceded the adolescent, the waif who wandered the fields for hours, peering under every piece of rotted wood to see if he could catch another water moccasin, and who was allowed by his mother to bring home countless orphaned creatures, as long as they didn't devour the family cat. The women at the zoo empathized with his wife. They assumed her patience was heroic.

Word had spread that she was pregnant with their first child. The idea gave pause even to his friends.

Dustin was spawning.

In spite of himself, he was held in great regard by the staff. It helped that he was brilliant and knew more about herps than seemed humanly possible. Also that he was possessed with that strangely winning passion for species almost nobody else wanted to touch. He recognized the depth of the bias his department was up against. Humankind had held a grudge against reptiles ever since the Garden of Eden. Even the chairman of Lowry Park's board, Fassil Gabremariam, detested snakes. Once, when he stepped onto an elevator with one of the zoo's keepers who happened to be carrying a ball python inside a small crate, Gabremariam had visibly shuddered and backed against the elevator wall, putting as much distance as possible between himself and the serpent.

Dustin could quote the studies that showed how little time most zoo visitors spent in front of every reptile exhibit. He knew that endangered mammals were much more likely to get attention and funding and protection than any toad on the edge of extinction. None of this lessened his fervor as a defender of downtrodden amphibians, maligned arachnids, anything that oozed or puffed a dewlap. To follow him through the zoo was to be regaled with a rapid-fire rant on the discrimination that plagued cold-blooded creatures.

"I don't know why we call them cold-blooded anyway," he'd say, headed toward the herps building. "Most of the time, their blood's about eighty-eight degrees. Do you think that's cold? I don't think that's cold."

The preceding is only an approximate rendering of what he said. He was talking fast and walking even faster, making it impossible to catch every word. Wait. He wasn't done yet.

"I think we should call them ectotherms."

He explained that the term referred to any animal whose body temperature matched the temperature of its surroundings.

This was Dustin's crusade. He wanted the warm-blooded world to embrace ectotherms. He understood it wouldn't be easy, but he was in no hurry. He and Dan and the rest of their staff were biding their time, working under the radar on behalf of all reviled species: feeding bunnies to the pythons, urging the frogs and spiders to increase their numbers, slipping another turtle into public view.

The sun was barely in the sky when the keepers ducked into the night houses to start the daily routine.

In the primate department, a cluster of howler monkeys eager to be let out whooped in rhythmic, escalating waves that echoed off the cement block walls. A few feet away, in their den, the Colobus monkeys stayed silent, unable to compete with the howlers' volume. But the alpha, Grimaldi, declared his presence with an emphatic stream from his bladder.

"Lovely, Grim," said a keeper named Kevin McKay, mixing a breakfast of mashed bananas and ground-up vitamins.

In the Asia department, Carie Peterson sweet-talked Enshalla and Eric, as always, and said hello to Naboo, the male Indian rhino, and teased Madison, one of the clouded leopards, for being so shy.

"You're such a crazy girl," Carie said.

A pair of bar-headed geese honked and complained when she went into their exhibit to rake. Their names were Ken and Barbie, and Carie insisted that they were the meanest animals in the zoo. In the wild, their species soared above Mount Everest. At Lowry Park, where their wings are pinioned, they could only nip at their keepers' ankles.

"Stop," Carie told them, gently nudging them away with the rake. "You're brats."

Inside the venomous snake room, above the copperhead and the rattlers and the young crocodiles, Led Zeppelin wailed on. There was something perfect about the union of the thunderous music and the deadly species. Also something slightly supernatural, since Led Zeppelin always seemed to be blaring from the radio on the shelf.

A few feet away, in the dart-frog closet, Dan Costell shuffled between the terrariums to check on the powder blues. Looking under the breeding huts, he stopped and smiled.

"Eggs," he said.

Carefully, he transferred the clutch to one of the deli cups. As his hands reached into the terrarium, the nearby frogs looked extra tiny. He didn't have to worry about them touching him. In the wild, poison-dart frogs carry paralytic alkaloids on their skin that can indeed be deadly; one species, the golden poison-dart frog, is said to be so toxic that a single frog can poison fifty men. In captivity, Dan explained, poison-dart frogs did not secrete the toxins, because they were no longer eating ants in the rain forest that had consumed the plants from which the toxins are synthesized.

When Dan talked about the frogs, he usually referred to them by their scientific names. The bumblebees, bright yellow and black, were *Dendrobates leucomelas*. The powder blues were *Dendrobates azureus*. He distinguished the individuals by their size and markings; if necessary, he could refer to the numbers under which they'd been registered at the zoo. What he pointedly did not do was name them.

"Forget it," he said. "I'm no bunnyhugger."

Aside from their respective departments, many of Lowry Park's keepers unofficially divided themselves into two groups. There were bunnyhuggers, and there were non-bunnyhuggers. Bunnyhuggers spoke in baby talk to the animals, remembered their birthdays and baked them cakes, gave them wrapped presents at Christmas. More than anything else, perhaps, bunnyhuggers relished thinking up new names. They named the animals after candy bars, famous gangsters, characters on *Seinfeld* and *Will & Grace*, even one another. Naboo the rhino? Anakin the howler monkey? Bunnyhugger names, given in tribute to a much-admired veteran keeper who worshipped all things *Star Wars*.

Sometimes bunnyhuggers grew giddy with naming. In the Asia

department, Carie christened every creature that wandered into view. She had even become attached to an anole—a small brown lizard commonly seen in Florida, often sunning themselves on sidewalks—that had recently staked a claim to a log inside the tiger dens. Carie named him Timmy.

"Everybody's named," she said. "Every single plant. Every emu."

In the herps department, almost everyone was a certified non-bunnyhugger who scoffed at the notion of naming frogs or snakes.

"I just can't see a reason," said Dan.

Beneath the surface of this seemingly frivolous debate, an important question simmered. Namely, how should we relate to nature? The bunnyhuggers were drawn to whatever aspects of their animals reminded them of something in themselves. They watched Enshalla dominating male tigers, and they identified with her. They saw the siamangs bonding for life—even holding hands when they went to the clinic together—and it reassured them that enduring love was possible. The non-bunnyhuggers reveled in the otherness of their creatures. The very qualities in the animals that terrified and disgusted other people, the non-bunnyhuggers loved.

The bunnyhuggers and the non-bunnyhuggers didn't sit around the break room and preside over philosophical discussions on Man and Nature. Instead they waged guerrilla warfare. The herps keepers resorted to shock and awe. They dropped spiders on unsuspecting shoulders; they slipped the molt of an emperor scorpion inside a bunnyhugger's work boot. The bunnyhuggers retaliated by sneaking into the herps office and plastering Dustin's and Dan's lockers with flower power signs and Barbie stickers. They coddled the feeder mice that the herps keepers saved for the snakes, brightening the bare tanks of the doomed rodents with wheels and tunnels and little mouse houses, anything to make their short lives more interesting.

Back and forth the battle raged. One day, Dan abducted Carie's lizard, Timmy. "She cried so much," Dan said, "that we gave it back." Carie denied that she had cried. She also insisted she did not yelp when she found one of the emperor scorpion molts in her boot.

Seeking vengeance, Carie told anyone who would listen that Dan was a closet bunnyhugger. Her evidence? The tenderness he bestowed on his poison-dart frogs.

"He makes houses for them out of coconut. He talks about them like they're his little kids."

Dan threatened to remove arms from the sockets of anyone who suggested Carie was right. Still, he acknowledged that he was not immune to the charms of warm-blooded creatures with names and personalities. He was especially fond of Bamboo, the oldest member of the chimp group. Even though Herman looked out for him, Bamboo remained the lowest-ranking adult. The three females still chased him and vented their frustrations at him.

When he wasn't busy in the herps building, Dan liked to stop behind the chimp exhibit and visit with Bamboo. When Bamboo saw him, the chimp ran up to the fence, head bobbing in excitement. Knowing that Bamboo needed a friend, Dan told him to hang in there.

"You'll be all right," said Dan. "Don't let the girls push you around."

7

Frontier

A Code One drill, again. This time for a black bear.

The Florida mammals department only had one at the moment, a female named Ladybug, but a new male was due to arrive in a few days, and Virginia Edmonds thought it would be a good idea to do a run-through, especially since there were several new keepers who didn't know what to do if one of the bears got out and ambled in their direction. Virginia didn't worry too much about Ladybug, because she was a low-key bear who had never shown the slightest sign of wanting to leave her exhibit, a placid swath of woods and thick grass, with a big dead log where she rooted for grubs and napped for hours.

The only way Ladybug was likely to escape was if someone accidentally left a gate open. Even if that did happen, she was likely to walk right back into her exhibit without a fuss if her keepers approached her slowly and waved an orange within range of her nostrils.

"Ladybug likes oranges and peanut butter," Virginia explained to a handful of keepers, all of them standing in a circle beside the black bear exhibit. "She's really easygoing."

As any keeper quickly learned, animals responded to different types of bribes. Some, such as Herman, were tempted by the promise of human attention. Others, such as Ladybug, followed their stomachs; keepers referred to such animals as "food-motivated." Since the other bear had not yet arrived at the zoo, Virginia knew nothing about his temperament. All she knew about Sam, the new male, was that he had been captured in the wild as an orphaned cub. If food failed to compel him, Virginia told the keepers, they might have to resort to pepper spray or air horns to frighten him into retreating back toward his exhibit.

"Would a hose turn him around?" asked one keeper.

Virginia nodded. Sometimes, when animals attacked one another in their displays, the staff separated them with a high-pressure hose. "It's usually a pretty good deterrent," she said, "except for when you have otters in a pair fighting. They don't care."

If either Sam or Ladybug slipped out, it would be imperative to get them back quickly, one way or the other, before they had any chance of barreling through the perimeter fence. This was more for their well-being than the public's. Black bears tend to be solitary and rather shy. But any large animal that stumbles into a city neighborhood runs a high risk of getting hit by a car or dying in a hail of police bullets, even if the animal hasn't so much as growled. Lowry Park's Code One protocols instructed the zoo's own weapons team—including not just Virginia, but Lee Ann Rottman and Dan Costell—to kill any potentially danger-ous animal before it managed to leave the grounds and enter the sur-rounding neighborhood.

The idea of shooting down Ladybug, or any other animal in the zoo's collection, was almost too upsetting for Virginia or the rest of the weap-ons team to contemplate. The assistant curators scheduled the Code One drills regularly, rotating between species, so that their staffs were well versed in all the ways to safely return an animal to its exhibit without resorting to lethal force. Zoos around the world have similar protocols, each adapted to the specific animals in their collections and other variables dictated by their layout and location.

At the Ueno Zoo in Tokyo, the staff prepares for a breakout by one of their polar bears, the species known among zookeepers as among the most likely to kill humans when confronted face-to-face. The keepers stage drills twice a year to simulate a polar bear escaping through a damaged exhibit during an earthquake.

Natural disasters, the ultimate rebuke to human assumptions of control, have a way of obliterating a zoo's defenses. In the predawn hours of July 17, 1969, a torrential rainstorm flooded the polar bear moat at the Brookfield Zoo outside Chicago and enabled seven of the hulking predators to swim to solid ground. At that hour, the zoo was still virtually empty of humans, but the other exhibits teemed with living snacks the bears could have easily devoured. "However," writes Vicki Croke, who chronicled the escape in *The Modern Ark*, "these were the days when zoogoers fed the animals, and the bears headed directly for the snack stand. They ripped open the ice-cream chest and cash register. And after gorging on chips, marshmallows, and ice cream, they were herded back into their enclosure by a Volvo, a pickup truck, and a few blasts from a shotgun."

When Hurricane Andrew roared through south Florida in 1992, much of the Miami Metrozoo was smashed to rubble, even though its building had been designed to withstand winds of up to 120 miles an hour. The free-flight aviary had literally been blown away and with it several hundred rare birds, including hornbills and fairy bluebirds. The majority of the zoo's most dangerous animals were secure, having been locked up before the Category 5 storm made landfall, but the crocodile pool was jammed with so much debris that the keepers literally couldn't see if the man-eating reptiles were still in the water. Later, one croc was discovered strolling in a service hallway. Other animals roamed aimlessly among the ruins. An antelope was seen walking through what was left of the administration building. A 450-pound Galápagos tortoise was recovered from a nearby street. A state trooper sighted an argus pheasant on the Florida Turnpike and returned it to the zoo in the backseat of his cruiser. A group of monkeys was caught while running down Coral Reef Drive, but it was later discovered that the storm had liberated them not from the zoo but from a nearby primate research center.

Lowry Park, located a short distance from the warm waters of the Gulf of Mexico, had been buffeted by tropical storms in the past, but had never taken a direct hit from a monster like Andrew. The zoo's hurricane plan called for most of the animals, including the birds, to be evacuated into the zoo's night houses and into the underground chambers of the manatee viewing center. Even so, there was no guarantee that the manatees would be spared from whatever was cast into their pools or that the buildings could withstand a sustained assault by Category 5 winds. The possibilities of such a catastrophe were sobering.

But if an animal were going to be freed from an exhibit at Lowry Park, it was likely to be due not to nature's fury but to human error. The majority of zoo escapes, all around the world, result from mistakes made by keepers or by the architects who design the barriers. In recent decades, as cages have been replaced by open exhibits bounded by moats and walls instead of metal bars, the challenge of containing the inhabitants has become more complex. Sometimes zoo designers underestimate how high a certain species can leap or how well it can swim. No matter how carefully the humans draw their blueprints, they cannot predict every variable that might motivate an animal to act in unexpected ways that propel it into the world waiting on the other side of the moat.

In one of the more disturbing animal escapes of recent years, a Siberian tiger named Tatiana scaled the wall of its grotto at the San Francisco Zoo just as the zoo was closing on Christmas Day. She attacked three young men, killing one and severely injuring another. Calling 911 from his cell phone, one of the men frantically pleaded with a dispatcher to send the paramedics to help his brother, who was bleeding from bite wounds. Both of them were outside one of the zoo's snack bars, but the manager would not let them inside because he believed they were drunk and had been fighting. The dispatcher explained that the paramedics could not enter the zoo grounds until police went in first and located the tiger.

"What do you mean?" said the caller. "My brother's going to die out here!"

"OK, calm down, all right? . . . I'll stay on the line with you. If the paramedics get hurt, they cannot help your brother, so you need to calm down and—"

"Send more paramedics, then! . . . Can you fly a helicopter right here? Because I don't see no ambulance here."

As officers made their way to the scene, they found the dead man on the ground outside Tatiana's exhibit, his throat gashed, and a trail of blood that led to the snack bar, where the seriously wounded man and his brother had fled as the brother called for help. By now the tiger had stalked the two survivors to the outside of the snack bar and was standing over the wounded man. As the officers approached, she pounced on him again and continued biting him until the officers distracted her and got her to move away before they opened fire and killed her.

The San Francisco Zoo and police investigators scrambled to piece together some explanation of how Tatiana had managed to climb over a wall that had held her inside for years. Reports quickly surfaced that the three young men might have antagonized the tiger. Shortly before the attack, two of them had been seen taunting lions in a nearby exhibit. An attorney for the men denied they had done anything wrong, but later, one of the men acknowledged to his father that he and the others had stood on a railing in front of the tiger's wall, yelling and waving at Tatiana. In the blizzard of news articles that followed, zoo officials theorized that perhaps the men had dangled a branch or even their legs over the wall, giving Tatiana something to grab. Chunks of concrete had been found in her hind claws, suggesting the intensity of her determination to climb the wall. It became clear that the zoo bore some responsibility, however, when investigators announced that the wall was only twelve and a half feet high—barely half the height the zoo had previously claimed and several feet shorter than the AZA recommended for tiger enclosures.

The zoo drew more criticism that March when a team of AZA inspectors completed a report showing that the zoo was seriously understaffed and generally unprepared for a serious Code One. Although the inspectors praised the zoo's response once it became clear that a tiger was on the loose, the report laid out the failings that had combined to turn the incident into such a nightmarish muddle: the refusal of the snack bar manager to give the two injured men safe haven inside the restaurant; confusion over how many tigers had escaped, or whether it was a tiger or a lion; rusted and broken cages in the night houses that had almost resulted in the escape of a snow leopard earlier that year; employees who either didn't know or didn't follow the Code One protocols; others who had left their walkie-talkies back in their offices and therefore had not heard the warning. Because it was Christmas, almost all of the staff had been sent home early. Only two keepers and one vet tech remained on the grounds, and one of those keepers—a member of the weapons team—did not have keys to the room where a shotgun was stored. Once he got the shotgun, he could not find the keys for a zoo vehicle to drive to the site of the attack. The inspectors saved their most damning criticism for the final paragraph:

> It appeared to the inspection team that the zoo lacks enough supervisory personnel in the animal care department to effectively train, oversee, and enforce existing policies and procedures. The zoo is too often chasing problems rather than proactively addressing known concerns. This will require a shift in culture and the supervisory and maintenance to make it happen.

The message was clear: An understaffed zoo with untrained employees, attempting to watch over dangerous animals, was a tragedy waiting to happen. If more keepers had been on duty late that day, one might have seen the young men teasing the lions and kicked them out of the zoo before they moved on to the tiger grotto. Nobody would have died. Tatiana would have been called back into her night house to sleep through what remained of Christmas.

On the night of the tiger escape, the AZA's top public relations official received an emergency call from the San Francisco Zoo's P.R. man, alerting him to the bad news. The AZA spokesman, an expert in crisis management, was just leaving a holiday celebration at his in-laws' house, but he and the San Francisco spokesman immediately began coordinating a response to the coming deluge of media phone calls. For the AZA, and for all zoos, a high-profile escape resulting in the death of a human being was a catastrophe that struck at the core of their mission. For years, the AZA had been working to counter the critiques of PETA and other animal-rights groups who dismissed zoos as wretched prisons and publicized lists of all the occasions when animals had broken free and attacked. From the organization's viewpoint, almost nothing could be more horrendous than an escaped Siberian tiger slashing one man's throat and then stalking another in front of a snack bar.

A high-profile escape was much more damaging than a barrage of scare headlines. Such incidents undermined the promise on which all zoos are built and the assumptions that all visitors embrace as they enter the front gates. Whenever an animal unlatched a gate or leaped a fence, it breached the allegedly impenetrable divide between the spectators and the spectacle, proving that the humans were not in control and that the animals retained a will and a determination that could not always be thwarted. Every animal escape, even with a species that was relatively harmless, was a slap at our claim of dominion.

The truth was, animals broke out of their enclosures more often than zoos were eager to admit. Gorillas burst through doors of their night houses. Elephant calves squeezed through the bars of their stalls. In the majority of cases, the animals were returned safely without injury to them or anyone else. The San Francisco tiger case was the first time a zoo escape had resulted in the death of a visitor at any AZA institution since the group had been founded in 1974. One of the most unsettling things about the case was that the young men had stepped to the edge of the barrier between themselves and the tiger and essentially dared her to cross it. Convinced of their own inviolability, they seemed unaware that they were at the precipice, taunting death.

Humans are drawn to danger every day in zoos around the world. Like the young men in San Francisco, many feel at liberty to lean over the railings and yell. Sometimes they throw things, just to provoke a response. Other visitors stand in silence, mesmerized by the awareness that they are staring across a frontier between life and death, the past and future, the noise of their own interior monologues and the unmapped worlds inside the animals. At that frontier, primal energy surges. A few people, overtaken with mania, climb across the rail and into the exhibits, compelled to either embrace nature or conquer it. In *The Looming Tower*, Lawrence Wright tells how Taliban fighters became possessed with such a sense of omnipotence after the fall of Kabul that one jumped into a bear's cage at the city zoo and cut off the bear's nose, "reputedly because the animal's 'beard' was not long enough. Another fighter, intoxicated by events and his own power, leaped into the lion's den and cried out, 'I am the lion now!' The lion killed him. Another Taliban soldier threw a grenade into the den, blinding the animal. These two, the noseless bear and the blind lion, together with two wolves, were the only animals that survived the Taliban rule."

In Berlin, where the crowds swooned over the hand-raising of a polar bear cub named Knut, a man climbed into the shallow pool of the polar bear exhibit in 2008 and tried to approach Knut, who by then was two years old and weighed 440 pounds. Keepers managed to lure the young bear away with a leg of beef before he reached the intruder. As the man was led away, soaked and cold, he explained that he had felt lonely and believed Knut was lonely too. A few months later, a teacher despairing over her inability to find a job climbed into the same exhibit and sloshed through the water toward several bears sunning themselves nearby. One, not Knut, promptly swam out and bit her arms and legs. She survived, but only after the staff pushed the bear away with poles and lowered a rope and harness to rescue her. Afterward, a spokesman noted that the woman had endangered not only herself but the staff and the bears. If necessary, he said, the zoo's weapons team had been prepared to shoot the bear if that had proved the only way to save the woman.

A number of people have entered zoo enclosures to commit suicide. At the Lisbon Zoo, a man mourning the death of his son jumped into a pit with a pride of ten lions and was quickly dispatched by a lioness who broke his neck. In Washington, D.C., a drifter distraught over a custody battle for her children climbed down a nine-foot wall in 1995 and swam across a moat at the National Zoo to sacrifice herself in the jaws of two lions. A paranoid schizophrenic with a history of violent episodes, the woman told people she was the sister of Jesus Christ and that she and Jesus had grown up together in a house with President Clinton. She had once told a police officer to shoot her. The morning after she crossed the moat, a keeper discovered her body, face-up and mauled beyond recognition. Her arms and hands had been chewed off. On the blood-covered ground investigators found a barrette dislodged from her hair and a Sony Walkman containing a cassette of Christian singer Amy Grant's *House of Love*.

At Lowry Park, no one had ever heard a Code Two come across the walkie-talkies. As far as the staff could recall, a visitor had never fallen or climbed into any exhibit with a dangerous animal. A number of Code Ones had been declared over the years, but none where an animal or person was hurt. The primate department held the record for escapes. Chester was still infamous for his repeated ascents to the roof of the night house. From there it would have been no trouble for him to make a break into the rest of the zoo, but he never showed an interest. Perhaps he just coveted the glory of being able to gaze upon his fellow chimps from such a height. On another occasion, one of the Colobus monkeys had climbed onto a branch that reached too far across a moat and used it as a bridge to the public sidewalk. Covered in long black hair fringed with white, Colobus monkeys are striking, and this one gave visitors a jolt as it tore through the grounds, clearly distressed and lost. The monkey was soon retrieved, and the tree branch was trimmed.

The zoo's most serious Code One had occurred in 1991 when the radios crackled with a report that one of the orangutans was out. Lex Salisbury, then the curator, worried for a moment that it might be Rango, the big male. But it turned out to be Rudy, a young female who inched her way up a rock façade and then scaled the roof of the orang building. Visitors who had watched her stage the breakout alerted the staff and then were evacuated. Once he arrived, Lex took over, as usual. He was confident that Rudy didn't intend to attack anyone. She was new and was having trouble fitting in with the other orangutans and had only climbed out of the exhibit to escape another confrontation. Lex called to Rudy, holding out his hand, and she made her way down to him, ready to surrender. Obviously frightened, the orang needed comfort and climbed eagerly into his arms. She would not let go until he carried her back to the safety of her bedroom in the night house.

"As soon as I saw it wasn't Rango," Lex said afterward, "I knew it wasn't going to be a problem, because the females we can walk right up to."

In the zoo world, orangutans are known as escape artists. Typically much calmer and quieter than chimps, they are inquisitive and love to spend hours figuring out how to put things together or take them apart. Their species practices these engineering skills high in the jungle canopies of Indonesia, where they have been observed tying branches and vines together and manipulating the tension of saplings to move more easily through the trees. In zoos, they are famed for their ability to devise ingenious ways of slipping from their enclosures. According to Eugene Linden, author of *The Octopus and the Orangutan*, they sometimes make handcrafted tools to escape captivity. One orang used a wire to pick a lock, and another used a piece of cardboard to dislodge a security pin that held the doors of his cage closed. Others have proven their skill at unscrewing bolts. "Orangutans," Linden writes, "have made insulating gloves out of straw in order to climb over electrified fences."

In the twelve years since Rudy's field trip on top of the orang building, there had been no particularly memorable escapes. A turkey got out one day, and guinea fowl were known to sneak from their pens and strut with impunity through the grounds, prompting the staff to send out an alert on their walkie-talkies.

"Code One, rooster," they'd say, stifling giggles.

No one joked about the possibility of an elephant Code One, especially since the arrival of the four wild juveniles from Swaziland. Elephants were extremely unpredictable, especially ones who were unaccustomed to captivity, and their size and strength made them difficult to stop or bring down. When they broke free of their handlers at circuses or in parades, they sometimes went berserk, bulldozing through fences and into traffic, killing anyone in their path, even after they had been shot multiple times. To make sure that everyone on the staff knew what to do in case one of the elephants escaped, Brian French had posted a set of Code One recommendations on bulletin boards.

Do not approach animal, hide behind something,
i.e. tree, vehicle, building, etc.

Do not fall down when getting away. This is what they look
for when attacking.

Do not try to scare animal to direct it, it will take this as a
challenge and likely charge. (Females will be more likely to
complete the charge and males will likely stop about 10 feet

short, but do not hold your ground, get out of sight, they
can run 32 mph for about 10 minutes.)

If elephant is out of sight of its building, it will likely have to
be shot, so all gun-trained staff (ACs, curators, vet) should be
equipped with appropriate weapons. (We do have tranquilizers
strong enough for elephants but can only be used in certain
situations.)

Clearly the possibilities were awful. The perimeter fence, which ran
only a few yards from the elephant building, would not present a serious obstacle. If an elephant went on a rampage, it would not take more
than thirty seconds for the animal to break through and charge into
neighboring backyards. By the time the weapons team was summoned,
the elephant could easily be deep into the neighborhood.

In case anyone at Lowry Park needed reminding as to how dangerous elephants could be, a wall of the keepers' break room was adorned
with a memorial to Char-Lee Torre, the handler killed by an elephant.
Char-Lee had worked at Lowry Park in the early 1990s, not long after
the new zoo opened. Like so many keepers, she grew up with animals
and was constantly rescuing cormorants and turtles and iguanas. When
one of her animals died, she would preside over a funeral in the backyard. When she was hired, she had just received a degree in education
from the University of South Florida. She was interested in conservation.

"The night before she died," remembered her mother, Cheryl Pejack, "we were talking about her getting a bachelor's degree in zoology."

Char-Lee wanted to be the curator of a zoo. But at twenty-four, she
knew she had to prove herself. Not long after she arrived at Lowry
Park, she had been offered a chance to become an elephant trainer and
work with Tillie, an Asian elephant who had spent most of her life in
captivity. Around Tampa, Tillie was a minor celebrity. Aside from performing in shows every day at the zoo, she starred in television com-
mercials for Bob's Carpet Mart, where she was shown walking across
carpet to prove the fabric's toughness. At the time, Lowry Park's elephant handlers worked side by side with the elephants, escorting them

to and from the elephant building and guiding them through their daily performances, signaling them to raise their trunks and stand on their hind legs and turn in circles. For all her obedient displays, however, Tillie had begun acting erratically, repeatedly nudging and pushing Char-Lee.

The incidents followed a pattern frequently observed with Asian elephants contemplating a fatal attack on a keeper. According to a survey of elephant care managers from around the country, African elephants tend to lash out suddenly, while Asian elephants typically show more patience, waiting for the right moment to strike. Often they give warnings, shoving their keepers against a wall or flicking them with their tails. Sometimes the elephants are testing their keepers, assessing whether they're weak enough to be nudged aside in the hierarchy; sometimes they simply don't like the human assigned to care for them. New trainers, still learning the moods and personalities of their elephants, are particularly vulnerable. It would not have been surprising, then, if Tillie was contemplating a move against her new trainer. Char-Lee was not just the most inexperienced member of the elephant-care staff but also the youngest and smallest. And although she tried to be as commanding a presence as possible, Char-Lee exuded a gentleness that would have made it difficult for her to assert dominance over a thirty-three-year-old elephant. By the time she was introduced to Char-Lee, Tillie had spent three decades in captivity and was infinitely more experienced at judging the power dynamics between her species and humans. Tillie had been at Lowry Park, watching keepers come and go, for more than five years. Moved between institutions and owners most of her life, she had been studying a long line of handlers and had been assessing their strengths and weaknesses literally since Char-Lee was in kindergarten. How long would it have taken Tillie to size up her new trainer? A week? A day?

That spring, as Char-Lee struggled to assert her authority over Tillie, elephant-care managers across the country were sounding warnings at the alarming rate of deaths among keepers working free contact. The movement was already under way to abolish free contact and replace it with protected contact. Originally developed by animal behavioral specialists at the San Diego Wild Animal Park, the new protocol radically challenged the methods humans had used to train elephants for thousands of years.

San Diego had decided to try the new safety protocol after the death of one of their own elephant keepers and after a particularly ugly scandal over the park's treatment of its elephants. In 1988, the city erupted over the revelation that some of San Diego's handlers had beaten a disobedient elephant for days with ax handles while she was chained and screaming. Backed up by their superiors, the handlers defended the beating by arguing that it had been necessary to bring a dangerous elephant to heel. Without physical discipline, they said, more keepers would die.

Protected contact, modeled after training methods used with killer whales, showed another way. Keepers would not step into an enclosure with the elephants. A barrier would always stand between them, allowing a handler to back safely away if an elephant became aggressive. Positive reinforcement and operant conditioning would guide every action. If an elephant followed a command, he would be rewarded with an apple. No more beatings. No more screaming. The worst thing that would happen to an uncooperative elephant would be for the keeper to withhold attention. Essentially, physical discipline would be replaced by a time-out. The elephant would always have a choice, and the keeper would no longer have to become the matriarch. The system was more humane for the elephants and much safer for the humans.

Skeptics scoffed, saying that elephants were not cocker spaniels who could be bribed with a biscuit. But a test run, conducted over months with some of San Diego's most intractable elephants, proved otherwise. One subject, a twelve-thousand-pound African bull named Chico, was considered the park's most dangerous elephant. He was so aggressive, his keepers risked their lives every time they went near him. He had been chained for years. Inside a zoo, caring for an elephant's feet is essential. Their toenails and the thick skin on the soles of their feet require regular pedicures, because elephants tend to walk much shorter distances than they would in the wild, and their foot pads grow faster than they wear down. If the pads aren't trimmed, the skin can crack and develop an infection that sweeps through the rest of the body—the leading cause of mortality in captive elephants. The San Diego staff was so terrified of Chico, no one had dared give him a pedicure in years.

When the team of behavioral specialists decided to try protected contact with Chico, they cut some openings, fitted with doors that locked, in the high gate of the African bull yard. A bar was welded over the top of the gate so Chico couldn't get to them with his trunk. Then, using sliced apples and carrots and praise, they trained Chico to raise his feet, one at a time, into a cradle fashioned beside one of the openings in the gate, so the staff could reach his toenails and footpads. Sometimes the bull reverted to his old aggression and charged. When he was truly angry, he would lunge up onto the wall, roaring and rearing up like Godzilla. It didn't matter. The keepers would back away and let him have his tantrum. When he calmed down, they'd lure him back with another treat and return to their work. By the time they were done, Chico had a pedicure on all four feet, and San Diego was ready to switch to protected contact for good. The behavioral specialists wrote papers detailing their methods and results—pamphlets for the revolution—and the word spread.

Resistance was apocalyptic. Veteran keepers insisted that the new protocol would not work, that it was unacceptable to erect a permanent barrier between them and the animals. They understood that free contact was dangerous, and believed it was their right to take that risk. Elephant handling was one of the few departments of the zoo where male keepers outnumbered the women, and the men responded the way male primates often do when confronted with a challenge. At San Diego, the elephants adapted quickly to the new system, but the humans did not. At first the old guard tried to ignore the specialist heading the conversion. Then they debated him. Then they vandalized his car. In the end, they lost anyway. Every keeper who had worked in free contact quit or was transferred. Soon the revolution reached other zoos, and protected contact gradually began to supplant the old system.

In the midst of these upheavals, Char-Lee stood next to Tillie every day and looked up into the eyes of an animal already plotting her death.

Both the young handler and the elephant were trapped in a system of dominance that was already outdated. Tillie had certainly suffered under free contact. Like so many other elephants, she too had been punished over the years and was still chained every night in the elephant house. None of this was her fault, or Char-Lee's. Lowry Park's management was aware of the changes sweeping through elephant care at other zoos. For the moment, though, Lowry Park was sticking with the old system. In 1993, the new zoo was busy celebrating its five-year anniversary. The focus, in those early years, was the conservation of threatened Florida species such as the manatee, a cause whose importance was undeniable. Lowry Park was already receiving the highest praise.

"I consider it to be one of the very best zoological parks of its size anywhere in the country," said the chief administrative officer of the AZA.

The zoo's budget, even smaller in those days, was already stretched by the massive expenses involved in the manatee care. There was little chance of scraping together the millions of dollars required to build the new facilities necessary to carry out protected contact. Besides, Lex Salisbury and others believed that with two cows and no bulls, the risk was minimal and manageable. Tillie and the other female, Minyak, had been working side by side with their keepers for years without serious incident.

Maybe Char-Lee wondered why protected contact hadn't yet been adopted at Lowry Park. Maybe not. But she knew something was wrong. Tillie's warnings began almost immediately after Char-Lee started working with her. One day in April, the elephant tried to edge her off a platform. That June, during one of the daily shows in front of the public, Tillie ignored Char-Lee's commands and shoved the young trainer into the hip-deep water of the moat that bordered the performance area, and kept the elephants back from the crowds.

"No," Char-Lee told Tillie, managing to keep her balance.

The aggression worried her enough that she talked about it with her supervisors. One of them later wrote her a note referencing "your incident with Tillie." The supervisors were concerned too—so much that they took the unusual step of flying in a nationally recognized elephant handler from a Chicago zoo to review the procedures and talk with Char-Lee and the other elephant keepers. At home, Char-Lee put on a brave face. Her mother sensed that she was scared and was not telling her everything. Char-Lee didn't want to worry her mother and felt she could not afford to look timid in front of her fellow keepers. It made no sense to Cheryl Pejack. Why was a novice being allowed to continue working with an elephant who was clearly testing her? Char-Lee weighed 105 pounds. Tillie weighed close to four tons. One night late that July, Char-Lee's mother asked her daughter what she would do if one of the elephants attacked. "Are there guns there?" Pejack remembered asking. "Is there a place you can hide yourself?"

Char-Lee told her mother she would do what she could. When her little brother asked about her safety, Char-Lee reminded him that she carried a buck knife on her belt. Her mother couldn't believe it. A knife?

"What's that going to do?" Pejack said.

Char-Lee said she'd be fine. She felt privileged to work with such magnificent creatures.

The next morning, July 30, Tillie decided the moment was right. Char-Lee had just unchained her and was preparing to lead her out of the barn when Tillie knocked her to the ground and began to kick her. Char-Lee tried to crawl to safety, but the elephant repeatedly dragged her back with her trunk. A nearby keeper fought to pull the elephant away. By the time Tillie stopped, Char-Lee's torso and lungs had been severely injured and much of her hair and scalp had been peeled from her head. As she waited for a medical helicopter to land on the grounds and fly her to nearby St. Joseph's Hospital, she was still conscious. She said she couldn't breathe. She asked about Tillie.

"Don't hurt the elephant," she said.

By the time her family reached the hospital, Char-Lee was dead. That day, she had been carrying the knife she'd talked about with her little brother. In her wallet, her family found a folded piece of paper with several lines of verse copied in Char-Lee's cursive. The paper was yellowed. She had been keeping it for some time.

Mourn not for us, for we have seen the light . . .
Grieve but for those who go alone, unwise, to die in darkness . . .

Ten years after her death, photos of Char-Lee Torre still hung in the break room. One showed her with the two elephants she trained, including the one that would eventually kill her. In the photo, Char-Lee is beaming. Tillie towers beside her.

8

Berlin Boys

Outside one day, watching the elephants giving themselves another dust bath, Brian French saw something that made his heart lurch.

Msholo, the bigger of the two bulls, was testing the hot wires that created an electrified barrier around the elephant yards. The wires were so thin, they were almost invisible. But the elephants were aware of their presence and had even approached to touch them a few times, giving themselves a jolt. Now, as Brian watched, he saw Msholo weave his trunk through the space between the hot wires and reach toward a small live oak tree, planted at what everyone had thought to be a safe distance.

Brian immediately radioed the horticulture department to have the tree removed. If Msholo uprooted the oak, he could have pulled it through the hot wires, shorting them out and even possibly opening a hole. This hole would have only led the bull to another barrier—a thick cable fence, known to zoo designers as a ha-ha—that ran through the bottom of a deep trench. At Lowry Park, as at other zoos, the ha-ha served another function aside from containing the elephants. Because the fence stood lower than the rest of the grounds, it was easier to conceal it with bushes and other vegetation, reinforcing the illusion that almost nothing stood between the public and the animals.

Msholo's reach for the tree reminded Brian just how closely the staff had to watch the elephants. His fears were far from imaginary. Elephants are skilled tool-users who pick up grass and branches to scratch their backs, clean their ears, wipe cuts, and even to cover the bodies of their dead. Sometimes, they stuff grass or leaves into the mouths of a fallen member of their herd, apparently trying to revive her. Holding a stone or a stick in their trunks, they have been known to draw in the dirt. In zoos, they can paint when given a brush and paper, and some of their abstract works have been auctioned at Christie's and displayed in galleries. Whatever their artistic merits, elephants also have been known to wield tools as weapons, hitting people with sticks and throwing things at their cars. When park rangers in Africa opened a new road and used it for culls, elephants snapped branches and piled them into a makeshift roadblock. When the cull teams cleared away the branches, the elephants put them back, not just once but three more times.

Captive elephants have repeatedly demonstrated their ingenuity at overcoming human constraints on their freedom. They have dropped large rocks on electric fences to short them out. They've piled branches on similar barriers, knocked large trees onto them, even picked up smaller elephants and thrown them, just as they used Mbali as a battering ram in the boma. One morning in January 2004, not long before Brian caught Msholo reaching for the oak, an elephant named Burma hoisted a log from her paddock at the Auckland Zoo in New Zealand and dropped it onto an electric fence, shorting it out, and then broke through a gate. A married couple walking in a nearby park saw the elephant amble by and tried to talk to her, but she ignored them, possibly because they were speaking English and she only responded to commands in German, Maori, and Sri Lankan. Burma munched on leaves for about fifteen minutes before her keepers returned her unharmed, but not before she had proven once again that elephants had mastered at least the fundamentals of electricity.

"They're so smart," said Brian, gazing with admiration at Msholo and the others. He understood Lee Ann's allegiance to the chimps, but he had trained primates, too, and had no doubt that elephants surpassed them. It was awe-inspiring to watch their minds process information, work out problems, experiment with solutions. The four orphans from Africa weren't just probing the zoo's security measures. They were testing every aspect of their new lives—the routines, the equipment, their keepers, even one another. By now, several months had passed since the four of them had been loaded off the 747 and stepped out of their crates into their stalls. For weeks, Brian had stayed with the elephants around the clock. In the other departments, his superhuman vigilance immediately entered him into the urban lore of the zoo. Noting how rarely he was seen in the rest of the zoo, people began to talk about him as though he were some phantom hybrid of the Elephant Man and Mary Poppins.

If PETA's propaganda was right and the elephants were Brian's prisoners, then he was their prisoner too. When he couldn't keep his eyes open any longer, he would turn off every light and crash on the cot in the hall, plummeting into unconsciousness even as he listened for movement from the stalls on the other side of the double doors. Some nights his sleep was interrupted by trumpet blasts; other times he woke to rumbles that he felt as much as heard. Whatever roused him, he would force himself out of the cot and shuffle into his office, no matter the hour, to stare bleary-eyed at the feeds from the night-vision cameras. In front of him, in the dark, a new herd was forming.

In those first days, wildness radiated off the new arrivals. Msholo and the others didn't act like circus elephants or zoo elephants such as Ellie. Though they allowed their keepers to draw near, they were restless and uncertain. Brian kept them in separate stalls so they wouldn't take out their anxieties on one another. Three of them—Msholo, Sdudla, and Mbali—had grown up together in Hlane. Matjeka came from Mkhaya and was relatively new to the others, though they had spent months together in the boma. Ellie didn't know what to make of any of them and kept her distance. When they drew close to the thick bars that divided their stalls and extended their trunks to smell her, she'd cry out and back away. Who could blame her? Though they were from the same species, Ellie and the Swazi elephants spoke entirely different languages. She was attuned to humans and to their commands, while they communicated as though they were still on the savanna. After a few days, though, they all began to relax. Soon Brian was putting the two bulls together at night, giving them a chance to bond like other young males in a bachelor herd back in the bush, and pairing Matjeka and Mbali in a single stall too. He tried different configurations, looking to see which was the most harmonious. As Ellie calmed down and got to know the others, Brian tried putting her with Mbali, and then with Matjeka. Brian was already memorizing everything about the elephants—the way each of them moved, the way they thought, the sounds they made when they were hungry or irritated. He didn't need to peer up at their faces to know who was who. By now he recognized them from the curve and color and length of their tusks, from their posture and attitude and the notches and veins on their ears and the way they held their trunks.

"I can tell 'em apart," he said, "even by looking at their legs."

When Brian wanted to read their mood, he didn't look to their faces first. The anatomy of an elephant's face renders it much less expressive than, say, the face of a human or a chimp or even a dog. Their eyes are small and not particularly revealing, although an experienced handler or trainer can judge the level of alertness by how wide the eyes are open. Because elephants have no tear ducts, excess secretions flow down their cheeks, often giving the mistaken impression that they are crying. Any facial expression is typically overshadowed by the movement of the elephant's ears and trunk. Elephants that are excited or angry tend to flap their ears with more vigor. When they relax, their ears relax as well. They signal wariness by raising their heads, spreading their ears and holding them open, and extending their trunks in a "J" shape, with the tip pushed forward to gather olfactory information about whatever or whomever has raised their guard. When they want to show slight irritation, they tap their trunks on a smooth flat surface, similar to how humans drum their fingers when they're bored.

Day after day, Brian pieced together the clues, gaining traction on the personality and character of each elephant. Msholo, the big bull, was strong and already showed interest in breeding. Whenever possible, he gravitated toward the females and sniffed their urine to see if they were in estrus. Early on, though, Brian noticed that Msholo deferred to the other bull. Sdudla was extremely smart and a fast learner. Already he was finding his way through the routines of the zoo and the expectations of his keepers. As the dominant bull, Sdudla was more aggressive and did not let Msholo or any of the elephants boss him. Everywhere he went, his presence carried an extra charge.

"There's a little more pressure around," said Brian. "He pushes back."

Msholo and Sdudla had been competing almost since the day they arrived. In elephant herds, only the dominant male has breeding privileges. Out in the yards, the two bulls would butt heads to impress the females.

The contest swung back and forth. Sdudla ruled at first, but then one day he pushed his rival too far. They got into a brawl, and Msholo stood up for himself, and suddenly the balance of power tipped in his direction.

Mbali provided comic relief to the male posturing. At first she acted shy, almost demure. In the mornings, when the staff opened the gates to the yards and the other elephants hurried forward, Mbali hung back. She'd take a step or two out into the sunlight, then change her mind and turn around. For hours, she would stand at the doorway, reluctant to either venture out or return to her stall. She soon got past her timidity and assumed the role of the group's spoiled and slightly mischievous teenager. She liked to snatch things out of the keepers' hands and sometimes out of the other elephants' trunks. When the bigger animals were browsing on a tree branch that had been cut for them, she would sneak up and grab the branch and run away.

As the only elephant from Mkhaya, Matjeka was having trouble fitting in. When she stood near the others, she almost always positioned herself with her tail facing them, a sign of submission. Even though she was bigger and older than Mbali and should have outranked her, Matjeka had been relegated—or had relegated herself—to the bottom of the hierarchy.

"An outcast," Brian called her.

Ellie, so accustomed to humans, was the easiest to read. Brian kept a mental inventory of her likes and dislikes. Ellie didn't like female keepers. She quavered if a grasshopper landed near her feet. If she heard a truck driving by, she was fine. But the sound of a tractor set her on edge. As the months passed, Brian had also noted an empathy in Ellie not unlike what the primate keepers had observed so often with Herman. Perhaps this was not surprising, given that both the elephant and the chimp had been raised by humans and had imprinted on them instead of their own species. Herman's empathy had led him to reach out to the lowly Bamboo. Now Ellie's declared itself in the kindness she offered to the most woeful member of her group. The keepers saw Ellie browsing beside Matjeka, standing close to her, even looking out for her. When little Mbali grew feisty and tried to take advantage of Matjeka, Ellie would step in to defend her companion.

Although Ellie still had a great deal to learn about being an elephant, the keepers could see her confidence surging, especially with Matjeka.

Though they had come from opposite corners of the world and had known each other only a short time, the two females were rapidly growing into sisters. Every day they walked out together into the sun-drenched yards. At night, they were content when the keepers placed them in adjoining stalls and allowed them to sleep side by side. One had been in exile all her life. The other was an outsider. It was possible that they recognized something in each other—a social awkwardness, a sense of not belonging. Lifelong friendships had been built on less.

Ellie was guiding Matjeka and the others through the basics of zoo life, showing them how to stay calm when the humans touched their trunks or exfoliated their skin with brushes. For captive elephants to remain healthy, skin care was almost as important as their foot care. One of the most crucial things Ellie demonstrated was how to relax inside the ominously named Elephant Restraint Device, better known as an ERD. Located in the back of the elephant building, behind the stalls, the ERD was an updated version of the handmade equipment the behavioral specialists in San Diego had used to work safely with Chico. A giant metal box with thick bars and moveable walls, the ERD looked a bit like a big cage, except that nobody at the zoo uttered that word out loud anymore. The staff preferred to call the ERD by its more common nickname, the Hugger. To help the elephants grow accustomed to the Hugger, Brian and the other keepers made it an inescapable part of their daily routine. The elephants ate some of their food while standing in it. They walked through it to reach the yards and back through it again to return to their stalls. Every time an elephant entered the Hugger, a keeper pushed a green button, and the side walls closed in so that the elephant couldn't make any big movements. Keeping the animal relatively still was essential if the staff was to safely work up close, reaching through openings in the bars to bathe it, to train it with conditioning, to draw blood and urine and work on its feet and skin, to teach it how to inhale water into its trunks and then exhale it back again so that the fluids from inside could be tested for tuberculosis. Elephants are at special risk for TB. Over the years, several have died from it in captivity.

In a few weeks the zoo would use the Hugger to hold Ellie in place while the German specialists performed her artificial insemination. To some, it might have seemed odd to go to such lengths to produce another elephant calf in the United States when southern Africa overflowed with elephants. But Lowry Park's recent experience, importing the four juveniles from Swaziland, had shown just how complicated and contro-versial, not to mention expensive, that process could be. For months, the zoo had been monitoring the level of luteinizing hormone (LH) in El-lie's blood. Many female mammals experience an increase in LH just before they ovulate. Female elephants are unusual because their men-strual cycle, which lasts from fourteen to sixteen weeks, is keyed to a double LH surge. When the first surge hits, the second wave typically follows twenty-one days later, triggering ovulation and preparing the uterus for implantation of a fertilized egg. Researchers do not yet fully understand the function of the first LH surge; possibly it alters the cow's scent to alert bull elephants that she will soon be ready to con-ceive. Whatever function nature intended, the first surge was tremen-dously useful to any zoo hoping to schedule an artificial insemination. Once the initial surge showed up in the blood tests, it was almost cer-tain that the cow would ovulate exactly three weeks later.

Ellie's first LH surge had declared itself that January. The Berlin boys had been notified and had already booked their flights for mid-February. Soon they would bring their scopes and their ultrasound equipment and arrange to gather DNA from a bull at Animal Kingdom outside Orlando. They didn't want to collect the sample too far from Lowry Park, if pos-sible; it was extremely difficult to freeze elephant semen without damag-ing it. Once they had the DNA, they would bring it directly to Ellie.

In the meantime, Brian and his staff prepared Ellie for her appoint-ment with the Germans. Every day, they called her into the Hugger and rehearsed, so she wouldn't be startled or scared during the actual proce-dure. Ellie seemed fine. In fact, she seemed to like standing in the Hug-ger, because her keepers always gave her more hay to distract her. As Ellie waited patiently, wrapping her trunk around another mouthful of feed, Brian French would stand in front of her, stroking her leg and praising her. It was one of the few times he got to be so close to the ele-phants, and it felt good.

Brian had grown up with free contact, first training with elephants as a child and then later at Ringling Bros. Like so many other veteran keepers, he missed the intimacy of those days. When Brian had been hired at the zoo, Lex had already decided that the handlers would only work with the elephants in protected contact. Brian had agreed. He knew that for Lex it was personal, because on the day Char-Lee Torre had died, Lex had stood with the paramedics, waiting for the helicopter to take her to the hospital. Though Brian had only worked at the zoo for a year, he knew that once Lex made up his mind about something, almost nothing would change it. Accepting these things did not mean that Brian had to love protected contact.

One way or another, he was happy to be working with elephants again. He had known so many over the years that the stories flowed out of him. He still talked about a circus elephant he'd known who recognized commands in four languages: English, German, French, and Hindi. Sitting in his office, he recalled the time when he was six, performing in Japan, and he and his family rode out a typhoon in a railway car with their elephants.

As a boy, Brian's best friend was an elephant, owned by his family, named Shirley. "She was my elephant." When he was only three or four, Shirley would raise him up with her trunk, and he would climb onto her head and then wrap himself around her neck. Against his face, she felt warm. His body moved up and down with the rise and fall of her breathing. Often, he would nod off.

"Some kids ride in cars and they fall asleep right away. For me it was elephants."

So many years later, Brian would return to Shirley and the other elephants in his dreams. In these visions, he was small again, so light on their sloping backs. Sitting on high with a child's hands, touching their thick skin as the great beasts carried him forward.

All that power, fluid and effortless, rippling underneath.

In the elephant barn, the sacred and the scientific were being united. The two specialists from Berlin had arrived and were now trying to spark a new life inside Ellie.

She stood inside the Hugger, munching hay. By now she was accustomed to humans sticking her with needles and probing her body. Brian and another keeper, Steve Lefave, stood close by and reassured her.

"Steady," they told her. "It's all right."

Brian and Steve were up front, near Ellie's trunk. The two specialists, Drs. Hildebrandt and Göritz, were behind her, wearing helmets outfitted with ultrasonic goggles and plastic protective gear that covered their entire bodies. They looked like astronauts embarked on a perilous journey. Which was about right.

They had already inserted a catheter and an endoscope equipped with a light and a miniature video camera deep inside the opening of Ellie's ten-foot-long reproductive tract; in female elephants, this is called a vestibule. They had also inserted an ultrasound probe into Ellie's rectum, to follow the catheter's path toward Ellie's cervix on monitors positioned nearby. Early that morning, they had collected the DNA from the bull at Animal Kingdom. Other vets sometimes advocated gathering elephant semen by means of an electric shock to the rectum—a technique originally developed to allow paraplegic men to father children. Dr. Hildebrandt preferred not to rely on this technique, because he had learned from experience that the bulls sometimes were injured, either by the procedure or by the accompanying anesthesia. He found it more humane, and more effective, to reach a gloved arm inside the bull and manually stimulate the elephant until he ejaculated into a plastic sleeve.

Some would no doubt have snickered to even imagine such a thing. But for Dr. Hildebrandt, a boyish-looking thirty-nine-year-old with tousled brown hair, it was just another day in a remarkable career. Working with Göritz and other colleagues at the Institute for Zoo Biology, Hildebrandt specialized in reproductive medicine not just for elephants but hundreds of other species around the world. Known for his pioneering work in the use of ultrasound, he had probed the ovaries of Komodo dragons, tested the morphology and motility of rhino sperm, and evaluated the chemical signals transmitted in the urine of giant pandas. On the night the Berlin Wall fell and the streets of his city filled with ecstatic celebration, Hildebrandt was at the East Berlin Zoo, injecting a fertility drug into a rare yak.

"He'll ultrasound just about anything that lives or crawls," another zoologist once said.

Hildebrandt and his colleagues were best known for their unprecedented success at helping captive elephants deliver calves through AI.

For years, no one else had managed to pull it off. Captive elephant populations in the United States were slowly dying off. Using ultrasound equipment and probes they designed themselves, the Berlin boys had radically advanced the scientific understanding of elephant reproductive anatomy and developed new procedures that highly increased the chances of a pregnancy.

Obtaining the DNA from the male elephant, it turned out, is the easy part. Delivering the semen to its destination is much more tricky. The opening to an elephant's vagina is smaller than a dime—the mechanics of elephant reproduction do not require vaginal penetration by the male—and that opening is flanked by two false holes. "Blind pouches," Hildebrandt called them. The opening to the female's bladder is also nearby, complicating things even further. If the catheter doesn't reach the right hole, neither will the semen. Sometimes the procedure took hours. But Ellie was fairly calm. The two vets from Berlin worked quickly, adjusting their instruments, reaching deep inside Ellie to accomplish what no bull had ever attempted. The lights in the elephant barn were turned low to make it easier for the team to study the ultrasound and video feeds. Everyone who was gathered around Ellie worked quietly so as not to startle the patient. If Ellie suddenly shifted or took a wrong step, the humans behind and underneath her could easily have been injured.

As Hildebrandt and Göritz maneuvered with their probes, they spoke softly to each other in German. When they needed help positioning their patient, they spoke in English to Steve, who repeated the request to Brian, who was standing directly in front of Ellie with one hand on her chest.

"I need her to back up a little," said one of the vets, and then Steve told Brian, and then Brian told Ellie, and Ellie backed up.

"Good girl," said Brian.

To the zoo, the procedure was a triumph. Ellie did not appear traumatized. The vet specialists had lived up to their reputation for scientific prowess. Outside Lowry Park, though, some would have characterized the achievement in different terms. Here was Ellie, an African-born elephant so accustomed to captivity that when she arrived at Lowry Park she had forgotten much of how to be an elephant. Here were the specialists, inserting an array of machines. What were the implications of this enterprise? Just because humans had the mastery to accomplish such a feat, did that make it right, or even advisable? If Ellie became pregnant, any calf she bore would grow up either at Lowry Park or inside another carefully controlled environment. If that calf went on to have offspring of its own, those descendants were likely to live in captivity as well. And then their descendants, and theirs, on and on. The same future awaited Enshalla and Eric and other captive species at Lowry Park and other zoos. One did not have to be a critic of zoos to wonder what would become of these animals if they were permanently removed from the natural world.

Dr. Hildebrandt, asked about these issues later, said the key was the level of care and the quality of their habitat. Was the elephant kept alone or allowed to form relationships with other elephants, as would happen in the wild? Were they in cramped quarters, or did they have room to move during the day?

"We should try to make the life of an elephant as optimal as possible," said Hildebrandt. Lowry Park, he believed, had done an excellent job providing for its herd. He was impressed with the size of the yards and the expertise of Brian and Steve and the rest of the staff. Ellie and the other elephants appeared to be thriving. He also pointed out that the artificial insemination had not been performed simply in hopes of producing a calf. The procedure, he said, was crucial for Ellie's own health. If female elephants don't reproduce, they develop uterine cysts and tumors that can lead to cancer.

"It's for the best for Ellie," said Hildebrandt.

The respected doctor's conclusions were logical, thorough, calm. Even so, the question remained of what captivity meant in the long run for all the species at Lowry Park. If a bird couldn't fly, did it remain a bird? If a tiger could not hunt, did it slowly evolve into something more tame? As new generations of elephant calves were born at the zoo, would the herd gradually change in ways that could not be foreseen? Detached from the wild forever, would they cease to be elephants?

9

Mating

In the darkness beyond the edge of the sky, the satellite listened for manatee No. 9.

Five hundred miles above the planet's surface, the satellite was halfway through another orbit. From this vantage point, Earth almost overwhelmed the field of vision. A curving expanse of blue and green and brown, it appeared vast enough for an endless multitude of life. And yet even from space it was easy to make out the devastation pushing so many species toward extinction. The melting of the polar ice caps. The fires consuming the Amazon rain forest. The toxic blossom of another Red Tide outbreak spreading off the west coast of Florida.

Year after year, a network of satellites operated by the National Oceanic and Atmospheric Administration (NOAA) records the evidence of these and other catastrophes. The network gathers data on dozens of other missions for other researchers—taking infrared images of global cloud patterns, following the formation of thunderstorms and the path of hurricanes—and tracking manatees.

On March 16, 2004, as it crossed northward over the Caribbean and headed toward the middle of the United States, one of those NOAA satellites—known simply as M—was among several receiving signals sent by transmitters fastened to the tails of dozens of manatees in the waters around Florida. At 9:58 a.m., one of those signals reached M from the St. Johns River, from the transmitter attached to manatee No. 9, better known to hundreds of thousands of Floridians who grew up watching him, as Stormy. Born and raised in captivity and recently released into the wild, he was now trying, on a rain-soaked Tuesday morning, to elude the net of some humans who were attempting to capture him one last time.

"Beep . . . beep . . . beep . . ."

On the tracking boat, they heard the signal first, growing louder as the transmitter rose toward the surface. Then they saw the transmitter, bobbing. Then, finally, Stormy appeared.

"Over there! Three o'clock!"

The transmitter—the team called it a tag—was on a short tether attached to a belt around the base of Stormy's tail. Monica Ross, a biologist who has spent most of her life researching manatees, had fastened the tag and belt onto Stormy so they could track him by satellite and boat. Now Monica stood at the wheel of the tracking boat, her right hand steering, her left holding the antenna that picked up Stormy's signal.

"Beep . . . beep . . . beep . . ."

He was surfacing again.

"Tag up!" someone shouted. "He's there!"

Three boats were moving along the river that morning, all filled with manatee researchers and with staff from SeaWorld and Lowry Park. Virginia Edmonds was on board, along with Dr. Murphy. Both had known Stormy for years and were pleased to see him thriving. The manatee was navigating the river so skillfully, he was frustrating the team's efforts to catch him in their net.

"Our little Stormy isn't stupid," said one researcher. "Oh, no."

Few on the boats had believed this day would ever come. Stormy had been born at the Miami Seaquarium in 1985 and was later moved to Homosassa Springs Wildlife Park. In 1990 he was sent to Lowry Park, where he became the first manatee to live at the zoo. He stayed there for the next twelve years until the team decided to give him a chance in the wild and released him in the relatively warm waters of Blue Spring State Park, on the St. Johns River. His first time out, in early 2002, Stormy struggled. He lost weight and seemed reluctant to venture away from the spring. So the team recaptured him and brought him back to

Lowry Park. Once he recovered, the manatee had been released again into the same area with the transmitter attached to his tail. Now, a year later, Stormy was making the most of this second chance. He was holding his weight, had learned how to migrate to and from the spring, and had been seen socializing with other manatees. The team wanted to assess Stormy one more time, and if he looked healthy, they would remove the belt and transmitter for good. It was like a scene from *Born Free*, except it was set on a Florida river and Stormy had, in fact, not been born free at all.

"Beep . . . beep . . . beep . . ."

On the boats, more joyous yelping.

"Tag up!"

"There he is!"

"See the bubbles?"

Stormy disappeared again. The researchers wiped the rain from their faces and smiled.

A speedboat roared by, rushing through a part of the river where people were supposed to slow down. Monica hissed.

Finally the research team got a net around Stormy and took him toward the shallows, where they wrapped him in a sling and carried him onto the banks.

Stormy looked good—so big and so well-fed he almost seemed like a different manatee.

"Did we catch the right animal?"

They were definitely going to remove the belt and the transmitter and let him go. But first, Dr. Murphy wanted to do one more health assessment.

"Let's see if this old boy will hold still," said Murphy. The vet made sure the team collected samples of Stormy's blood and urine and skin and also took new measurements of his length and girth and weight. He was up to 1,090 pounds.

"Does anybody need a fecal?"

Amid all the prodding, Stormy decided he'd had enough and began to flex and roll.

"Get out of the way!" Murphy warned the others. He turned to Virginia Edmonds. "Virginia, talk to him."

"Easy, Storm," she said, leaning in. "Come on."

Soon the manatee calmed down. They removed his transmitter and lifted him in the sling to carry him back into the river, detached from the technology of his rescuers. No more satellites would listen to him from above. No more boats would pursue him with nets. As he swam away, Stormy was finally on his own.

Applause from the team. A few tight faces, fighting back tears. They were sad because they wouldn't be a part of Stormy's life anymore, and happy because they knew they shouldn't be.

Virginia let out a big sigh. "Oh, boy," she said.

The team climbed back into their boats and headed toward home, wind in their faces, rain still rippling on the water.

"How happy are you?" someone asked Monica.

The biologist grinned. "Very happy," she said. "Warm and mooshy happy."

That spring taught them all a new definition of hectic. The construction crews hurried to finish Safari Africa before the grand opening, and giraffes and zebras and warthogs were being unloaded from trucks, and Virginia and the crews seemed to be driving off every morning at dawn to release yet another manatee, and the primate department was admiring a new baby Colobus monkey—a surprise. The staff had not even been aware that one of the females was pregnant.

Kevin McKay walked by the Colobus enclosure one morning, and everything was normal. A few minutes later he passed by again and was startled to see a newborn male, still connected by the umbilical cord. Within a day or so, all of the females were competing to take care of the new baby. One would hold him, then another would snatch him away. Kevin suggested, to anyone who'd listen, that the little monkey should be named after him.

"I don't think so," said Lee Ann. She smiled and shook her head, knowing that Kevin was just practicing the art of being Kevin. He aspired, more than anything, to become an alpha and thought it would increase his chances if he could only get every male animal in the place christened in his honor. Kevin was a bunnyhugger, but not a baby-talking bunnyhugger. In his own way, he was classically male, trying to mark the entire zoo as his territory. When other departments weren't looking, he would sneak into their offices and scribble his name on calendars, on bulletin boards, on any blank space available.

In the Asia department, Carie Peterson had declared a temporary truce in the war between her and the herps department. Carie had been hatching a plan to stock Dustin's office with some Madagascar hissing cockroaches because she knew that Dustin, though he worked with spiders and millipedes, was terrified of roaches. She had wondered whether he would actually scream. But now she had no time for idle vendettas, because Enshalla finally appeared to be warming to the newly seductive powers of Eric. Most of the time she still growled. But on some mornings, she seemed smitten and rubbed against the mesh between their dens. Carie knew Enshalla was going into estrus because her urine was milky. Obviously, the time had arrived to chance putting the two tigers together.

The first meeting did not go well. Enshalla lowered herself close to the ground and began hunting Eric. He seemed oblivious to what was happening until she sprang at him and sent him running. Finally she cornered him and jumped onto his back. Watching on with a fire hose, the keepers sprayed water in the tigers' direction until Enshalla retreated. Eric did not seem to realize that he was strong enough to defeat her in a second, which was probably for the best. Eric licked his paws, looking frightened and confused. Enshalla sprayed her scent, then climbed to the top of the tiger platform to declare her supremacy.

Still the queen.

The Asia staff would not accept defeat. Knowing that Enshalla would remain in estrus for several days, they were determined to pair the tigers again. Only this time, they had resolved to be less quick with the hose. It was better, they thought, to step back and let the tigers handle it on their own. Maybe they would figure it out. Love was never easy.

One morning, in the middle of the mating season, Carie and Kevin and others joined forces to clean the moat around the lemur exhibit. The night before, the water had been drained. Now, in their boots, the keepers raked and shoveled and hosed the wet green muck, from which they extracted orange peels and corn cobs and a blue racquetball and a

Twix wrapper and a party horn, apparently left over from New Year's. Oh, and coins.

"We're doing pretty good," said Andrea Schuch, the primate keeper. "I think we have seventy-six cents."

They were sweating. They were trying not to touch their faces with their encrusted hands and trying not to inhale any whiffs of the ooze that surrounded them. Lemurs, they all knew, were dirty. The males staged stink wars, rubbing their tails onto scent glands on their arms, then waving the foul-smelling tails at one another. Cleaning the moat was a thankless task. And yet the keepers were laughing and singing and sporting shiny Mardi Gras beads around their necks. One of the women, covered in slime, sang a snippet from *West Side Story*.

"I feel pretty, oh so pretty! I feel pretty and witty and bright!"

Kevin, his face stained brown and green, began a dramatic recitation of every line from his favorite scene in *Monty Python and the Holy Grail*. The one where a peasant deconstructs King Arthur's explanation of how the Lady of the Lake granted him the monarchy when she handed him Excalibur.

"Listen," said Kevin, channeling the accent of the peasant, "strange women lying in ponds distributing swords is no basis for a system of government."

Andrea rolled her eyes, but he was only getting started.

"I mean, if I went around sayin' I was an emperor just because some moistened bint had lobbed a scimitar at me . . ."

Another keeper chimed in. "I didn't know we had a king," she said. "I thought we were an autonomous collective."

Through the divide that separated the lemurs from the orangutans, Rango watched the keepers bantering. Over in the chimp enclosure, Rukiya peered from the top branch of the exhibit's solitary tree. A moment later, she disappeared, and a pandemonium of screams and hoots erupted. Whatever had caused the disturbance, the keepers knew it was escalating; even from the depths of the lemur moat, they recognized the familiar thumping sound that meant Herman was hurling himself against the fake rock wall. It was probably nothing. Just to be sure, though, one of the keepers climbed from the lemur moat to go check. When it grew quiet again, everyone returned to the muck.

Kevin grabbed a stick and walked to the wall of the moat and scratched two words in the slime just below the waterline: KEVIN RULES.

With a stick of her own, Andrea added another word: NOTHING.

They had to make it fun. How else could they have kept going? They worked from dawn to dusk for a pittance. At that time, a starting keeper at Lowry Park made $7.50 an hour. They would have done almost as well pushing Big Macs at the McDonald's near the front gate. It was true, they got to work with animals—a passion for virtually all of them since childhood. But the job ground people up. Most keepers arrived at Lowry Park in their twenties, then moved on before their credit-card balances spiraled out of control. The zoo had no trouble hiring replacements. Other animal lovers were always clamoring for a position.

All day long, the keepers shoveled and raked and pushed wheelbarrows of dirt and hay and excrement. Sometimes the animals spit and threw things at them. The human visitors mocked them. When the keepers hauled another load of droppings, people would point and use them as an object lesson for their children.

"This," the parents would say, as though the keepers could not hear them, "is why you need to go to college."

On top of everything else, the work was dangerous. In case anyone at Lowry Park ever forgot, all he or she had to do was gaze into Char-Lee's face in the photos on the wall of the break room. For most of them, the job was worth it, at least for a while. They lived on Mountain Dew, lame jokes, the camaraderie of those who know they are expendable. They made friends on the staff they would never forget; some got married. Every day, they were immersed in the endlessly diverting and surprising lives of species from around the world. Holding a baby chimp, releasing a manatee into freedom—these were thrills they knew they could find nowhere else. And sometimes, the heavens parted and showered them with moments of savage joy.

On the last Thursday in March, the keepers in the Asia department bustled through their morning workload so they could get to the tiger sex. In the glow before sunrise, the keepers fed the tapirs and the muntjacs and the babirusa. They slipped a carrot to Naboo, then collected his droppings and saved them for Jamie, the young female rhino, so she could inhale Naboo's scent and consider the possibility that someday they might be paired too, when she was old enough and big enough that he wouldn't kill her.

In the rush of the morning, the keepers also collected and saved Enshalla's and Eric's droppings on behalf of a guy in the horticulture department.

"Bob wants more tiger feces," Carie said to another keeper.

"Bob does?"

"He claims that it chases the possums away."

Before they shifted Enshalla and Eric from their dens into the exhibit, the keepers fed them so they wouldn't be hungry and distracted when they were supposed to be mating. While both tigers ate breakfast inside their dens, Carie slipped into the exhibit and spritzed the rocks with tiny puffs of white gardenia body spray.

For Enshalla.

"Hey princess," Carie called, making kissy sounds.

Once the keeper was safely away, she let Enshalla into the exhibit. Behind her, from his den, Eric roared.

Carie smiled.

"He wants her so bad, and she's so mean."

The dance began at precisely 9:54 a.m. On cue, the door from the night house opened again, and Eric stepped into the bright light of the new day. Enshalla, walking by the edge of the pool, went to him immediately and rubbed her body against his, almost purring. Then she walked away.

"Wow," Carie said.

"Oh, God," said another keeper.

The two of them were watching from the dusty crawl space beneath the boardwalk that wound above the exhibit. They were roughly twenty feet from the tigers, protected by the moat and a wall of thick netting. Inches above their hair, cobwebs dangled. In the dirt beside them, the fire hose gurgled. They didn't want to use it, but they remembered all too well that Enshalla's father had slain her mother in this same exhibit.

Across the moat, a pattern was forming. Enshalla rubbed against Eric again, then ran away again. Eric, looking confused, slumped to the ground.

"He's still such a baby," said Carie. "A more mature tiger, an experienced tiger, would already be trying to get her."

Enshalla attempted to reclaim his attention, rolling on her back and raising her paws into the air. She crouched and crawled toward him. Somehow, she looked coquettish. Eric sniffed the nape of Enshalla's neck. Enshalla lowered herself and raised her hindquarters.

The two keepers held their breath. This might be it. When tigers mate, the female typically raises her backside—she "presents," is how the keepers put it—and then the male bites the back of the female's neck and holds her down. Before Eric could even consider such a thing, Enshalla slipped away. Soon she was running around the exhibit, Eric following.

"Shalla, you're such a brat," said Carie. "Just let him get on top of you, do the thing, and then you'll be done."

A small bird, maybe a grackle, landed nearby. Normally the tigers would make a quick meal out of birds that entered their exhibit. But now the tigers were distracted. Still, Eric stopped his pursuit to consider whether he should pounce. Carie couldn't believe it.

"You've got an inexperienced male and a bitchy woman who doesn't know what she wants—and then there's this bird!"

Carie blew her bangs out of her face with a tiny exhalation that sounded almost like a tiger's chuff. She could hear the chattering of the lorikeets. From the next section of the zoo came the unmistakable sound of Cyrus and Nadir, the siamang couple, singing another thundering duet from on high to declare their bond.

The keeper beside Carie left for other duties, soon to be replaced by other staff members bending low as they made their way through the crawl space to check the tigers' progress. Just that morning, Dustin had been asking Carie if she planned to light candles for the tigers to set a mood. Now he made his way through the cobwebs, approaching with an evil grin.

"Dustin's coming?" said Carie. She scratched through the dirt, looking for a cockroach to throw.

"I hear you guys used to keep tortoises back here," said Dustin, surveying the cramped possibilities of the crawl space. "I'm going to steal your area."

Carie thought he was joking, but she wasn't sure. She knew that his answer to every problem was to add more turtles. After he left, Carie shook her head in mock dismay. "Freak."

Across the water, the dance spun on. Enshalla was no longer attacking Eric. Instead she resorted to more subtle resistance, leading him in circles, then stopping to present and invite him to climb on top of her. At the last second, every time, she fled. Carie called out advice to the tigers. She told them not to give up. She did everything but play Barry White.

"Sweetie," she told Enshalla, "you just need to relax."

"Eric," she said, "you need to be forceful with her. She *wants* you to be forceful with her."

Carie analyzed Enshalla's and Eric's every move, explaining what was happening in tiger terms and drawing comparisons to human mating rituals. As she spoke, the radio on her belt buzzed with other keepers in other departments reporting their location, asking for a favor, checking on their next work detail. On the boardwalk immediately above Carie's head, children shrieked and roared. Apparently they did not realize any adults could hear them.

"Tiger! Tiger! Tiger!"

Carie sighed. "I don't want kids."

She was amazed at how some visitors acted, the way they pounded on the glass of Enshalla's window and threw things at the tigers, unaware of how rudely they were behaving. She called it "the human exhibit." Soon the children were gone, and it was quiet again. Sometimes, she said, she would go out somewhere—shopping at Target, playing with her dogs at the park—and people would chew her out for working at a zoo.

"I thought you cared about animals," one woman told her.

She defended herself against these slights as best she could. She told them how hard she and the other keepers worked to be good to their animals. She tried to explain the purpose of zoos.

"These animals," she would say, "are ambassadors for animals in the wild."

By now it was past noon. Enshalla had been leading her suitor around for more than two hours. Finally, at 12:25, Eric decided he'd had enough. Directly in front of the viewing window, Enshalla had just presented yet again and was about to wriggle from underneath the male when Eric, obviously frustrated, growled, clamped his jaws onto her neck, and held her down as he mounted her.

Several young children stood wide-eyed at the window. Their mothers shook their heads.

Carie laughed. "Those kids, they learned something today."

Only ten or fifteen seconds after he bit Enshalla's neck, Eric jumped off her. This was to be expected. Tiger sex tends to be rapid-fire and frequent; in the wild, they can mate dozens of times a day. There was no way to know yet if Eric had reached his intended target. Still, Carie was pleased that Enshalla had let him try.

"She did it. She really did it."

Enshalla appeared triumphant as well. After Eric walked away, she stretched her long body, her tail waving back and forth. A few minutes later, she was up and rubbing on Eric, ready for more.

10

The Human Exhibit

Another morning with the chimps. Another sexual request from Herman. In his den, he stood tall and puffed his chest for one of his favorite keepers, Andrea Schuch. From long experience, Andrea recognized that look on his face and knew that it meant he wanted her to show him a little skin. Nothing too explicit. Just a glimpse of her shoulder. Andrea didn't mind. She knew Herman had no control over his impulses. As far as she was concerned, it cost her nothing to make him happy.

"Then we go on with our lives," she said.

How many human females expressed similar sentiments about their husbands? Just let him have what he wants, and everybody can continue with their day. Only, Herman was not human, and not all the female primate keepers were comfortable with a chimp asking them to flash their shoulders.

"It makes me crazy," another keeper told Andrea one day. The other woman was blond. Andrea's hair was long and straight and light brown, but Herman loved her anyway.

Andrea smiled. "It *is* a little crazy."

The other keeper ignored Herman's requests. She knew that if she gave in to him once, he would ask her to repeat the favor more times than she cared to think about.

"I don't like to encourage that kind of behavior," she said.

It was the nature of a keeper's job to wind up almost every day in situations few other people could imagine. They whispered to falcons and flirted with rhinos and learned more than they ever wanted to know about the fetishes of barn owls. If they worked at the zoo long enough, they began to see what looked like human behavior in the animals, and what looked like animal behavior in the humans. It all began to overlap. When keepers were off duty, they would go to restaurants and casually survey the conversations at other tables and be able to tell, within seconds, which person in each group was the alpha. Walking through the mall, they would see adolescent girls strolling slowly in the sunlight, flipping their hair over and over like birds preening in the aviary. Turning the other way, they would see a group of adolescent boys puffing their chests and strutting just like Herman.

The difference was, the boys were still growing up and would soon be transformed into new iterations of themselves. They were going places. Their lives were commencing. But Herman had nothing beyond his exhibit and his den and the ceaseless urgency of his obsessions. He was stuck in every way.

Lee Ann believed Herman's sexual fixation was getting worse as he grew older. She didn't remember him being so relentlessly lustful when she'd first met him. Was it a sign of boredom? Did it mean he wanted something else he could not express? Though she knew Herman as well as any human could know a chimp, Lee Ann understood that there were limits to how much she could fathom of what was happening inside him. In many ways, he and the other chimps remained a mystery. She wished she could talk to them, explain things to them, have them translate their world to her.

She was convinced that Rukiya was easily the most intelligent of the zoo's chimps, much smarter even than Herman. Rukiya's temperament was different than Herman's too. Herman was the patient leader, the one who looked out for all the others, watching out for Alex and even protecting Bamboo from the taunts of the females. Rukiya was more cunning and calculated.

Lee Ann liked to tell a story about Herman and Rukiya—a moment she had witnessed herself. The miracle of the stolen lettuce.

At mealtime in the night house, Rukiya liked to take Herman's food. She waited until he wasn't looking and then grabbed what she wanted. One day, Herman had some lettuce, Rukiya's favorite. When she snatched it, Herman caught her and wrested it away. Then, to Lee Ann's astonishment, he handed it back. Chimps are not known for their social graces. Sharing is not always their strength. Yet Herman, despite his alpha status and superior strength, had let Rukiya have the lettuce and forgiven her for stealing it.

"To me, that's huge," said Lee Ann.

Herman's behavior was revealing, but so was Rukiya's. Although chimps sometimes exhibit altruistic behavior, they also display what primatologists call Machiavellian intelligence. Many species of primates and monkeys have been observed engaging in deception and counter-deception as they compete for power, food, and mating privileges. Chimpanzees rely on numerous tactical ploys. They are capable of hiding, staging diversions, faking tantrums, faking a lack of interest, even feigning a limp. Chimps are particularly known for using such deception as they maneuver to form political alliances and to influence powerful individuals in their social groups.

Lee Ann recognized some of these traits in Rukiya—not just watching her sneak food from Herman, but seeing her manipulate his emotions as well. For instance, when Herman's patience wore thin and he finally grew frustrated with Rukiya, the matriarch would often scream at Bamboo and chase him, acting as though the older male had done something wrong. Bamboo was always an easy scapegoat; Lee Ann had witnessed it many times. Jamie and Twiggy would join her in the chase, and together they would raise such a scene that Herman would forget he was angry with Rukiya. Instead, he would follow her lead and start tearing after Bamboo too. Rukiya and the other females, in other words, were clever enough to redirect Herman's aggression.

"The girls are smart," Lee Ann would say, shaking her head. "I love them, but they can be evil."

Rukiya had a gift for transmitting her mood—contented, upset, playful—to the others. Lee Ann described her as a thermometer for the rest of the group. Rukiya was complex and multifaceted. Along with her cunning, she had a deeply nurturing side that she often displayed with Alex, her surrogate son. Rukiya was often too lenient with Alex when he threw dirt and stomped—like the other adult chimps, she tended to look the other way—but her indulgence did not change the fact that she had accepted Alex as hers and had faithfully protected and raised him for years, preparing the young male for that day when he would almost certainly take over as the alpha. Alex would probably not be mature enough to seize power for a few more years, but the transition was coming. The keepers could see it every day in his increasingly bratty behavior.

Lee Ann identified with the chimps so closely that at times, she almost forgot they were not human. If she was having a bad day, she would go into their night house and sit beside Herman and share her troubles. Through the mesh, across the divide between species, the chimp would listen.

From his perch, Herman watched the approach of the tall man with the light hair and ruddy skin. Herman didn't know the man's name, but he recognized him. The chimp had been given plenty of chances to study this male and notice the easy confidence in his bearing and the way other humans attended to his every word, paying him deference and respect. If the tall man lingered in front of the chimp exhibit, Herman would rock back and forth and throw dirt. He wanted the human to know who was really in charge.

Maybe it would be best to move along, said Lex Salisbury. The CEO did not appear to take offense at Herman's displays. He understood that Herman was attuned to status and power differentials. Besides, Lex hardly needed to prove himself to a chimp. Everyone at Lowry Park knew he was the true alpha. Herman might have been animal number 000001, but in the zoo's hierarchy of walkie-talkie ID numbers, Lex was simply known as 1.

A natural showman, Lex gave the most entertaining and educational tours of Lowry Park. Leading a visitor around the grounds one afternoon, he pointed out the Sarus cranes and talked about how they mated for life. Moving past the river otter exhibit, he described them as aquatic weasels.

"Bloodthirsty little things."

In every corner of the zoo, he could identify every bird and every gecko and charm his guests with details and observations about every species. He talked about the underwater tunnels favored by the moray eels, and how the green tree python hunted for birds by sensing the heat of their bodies. Stopping in front of the manatee pools, he explained how manatees sport vestigial nails on their fins: "Indicative of a terrestrial past." The vestigial-nails observation led him to whales—of which there were none at Lowry Park—and how they happen to have vestigial pelvises.

"They do an eighty-percent air exchange," he said casually.

He was forty-five, but carried himself with the energy of someone at least a decade younger. He lived an hour north of Tampa, on a ranch stocked with zebras and warthogs and other exotic species, and he seemed to constantly be driving them back and forth in his big truck between Lowry Park and his property. Sometimes it felt as though the ranch was merely an extension of the zoo, or as though the zoo was an annex of his ranch. Lex had a habit of blurring the lines, and it made some of the people around him nervous. Lex waved them off. He was always working for the zoo, he said. When was he not working?

Lex was good at drawing other kinds of lines. He would share stories about his upbringing—a childhood in Alaska; his university days in Sydney, Australia; his master's thesis on heat-exchange rates in parrots from New Zealand. But when people asked about his current life outside Lowry Park or inquired about a visit to his ranch, he gently steered the conversation in other directions. His desire for privacy was understandable enough. What was striking was the velvet ease of his deflection. In the spring of 2004, as Lowry Park was gearing up for the grand opening of Safari Africa, he had just gotten married again. Almost no one at the zoo had heard a word. At this point in his career, Lex was as much a politician as anything else. As such he devoted himself to the habits and behavior of his fellow *Homo sapiens*, especially those with the money and connections to help him take Lowry Park into the future. His job relied on grace, discretion, politesse.

"It's a different skill set," he said.

He had to know how to woo mayors and governors. At cocktail parties he needed to be ready to talk about manatees and meerkats with wealthy matrons who could endow another addition to the zoo. From the Swazi court to the Hillsborough County Commission, Lex thrived as an alpha who had to win over other alphas without seeming to challenge their authority. His degree in social anthropology helped. So did his sense of mission and the encyclopedia of species inside his head. Lex understood that the animals were his best marketing tools. The creatures proved irresistible in the jaded halls of power. That was why Lex carried Ivan, the Eurasian eagle owl, on his gloved hand before the Florida Senate. It was why he made sure baby alligators and prehensile skinks and screech owls were on display every spring as bejeweled guests arrived at Karamu, the zoo's annual black-tie fund-raiser.

Perhaps most crucial of all was Lex's evangelism for what zoos can mean to the future of the planet. He was fervent about the promise of Lowry Park as a refuge for endangered species.

"A zoo can be a stationary ark," he would say. "It can be more than entertainment."

The analogy was a bit of a conceit, because it had long been established that zoos—not just Lowry Park, but all the zoos in the world—don't have enough combined space or resources to save more than a fraction of the species that were disappearing. Even so, there was no question that the conservation efforts mattered. Every species given refuge was one fewer wiped out.

Lex's sermons did not always play well among the staff. Some were tired of hearing him brag about Lowry Park's fiscal self-sufficiency. Most U.S. zoos, he pointed out, receive about 40 percent of their funding from taxes. Lowry Park, he said, relied on public funds for only 3 percent. To make ends meet, the zoo had to squeeze the most out of every dollar.

The keepers valued self-reliance too. But a good portion of them worked for a couple of dollars an hour more than minimum wage, while Lex's salary for the 2004 fiscal year would top $200,000—more than the city of Tampa paid its mayor. Why, the keepers wondered, should they get such a small slice of the pie when their CEO's plate overflowed? These complaints were almost always whispered, and for good reason. Outside the zoo, Lex's style was polished, understated, seductive. Inside, he was demanding and not to be crossed. If someone displeased him, he did not hesitate to say so. He punished. He exiled. Employees who differed with him had a way of leaving the zoo quietly under vaguely described circumstances.

Compared with Herman, Lex was a much more aggressive and savvy leader. Unlike the chimp, he understood that being nice was not necessarily part of an alpha's job. He recognized that not everyone liked his style, and did not care. If staff members didn't agree with the way he ran the zoo, then he advised them to look for a new job.

"Because I'm not going to leave," he said. "It's not a democracy. It's a benevolent dictatorship."

Lex accepted that his decision to bring the four elephants from Africa had plunged the zoo into an international controversy. He thought the furor was worth it if it moved Lowry Park forward. He despised inertia. Looking toward the future, he saw the zoo's handful of elephants growing into a mighty breeding herd. They would need more room. He was mulling over the idea of a game park. Maybe in Pasco County, just north of Tampa, or Polk County, to the east.

"In five years, we're going to need to have them on fifty acres or more," he said. "You can't have the biggest vertebrates in the world in a city park."

Lex made this last statement on March 3, 2004, during a lengthy interview in his office that covered his childhood, his parents, his mentors over the decades, and his sixteen-year-old son, Alex. Throughout the conversation he appeared open and relaxed. But he never breathed a word that his wedding would be the very next day.

When he returned to work from his honeymoon, Lex would stand in another ceremony. This one would be as public as it gets. Safari Africa, the child of his hopes and energies and years of orchestration on two continents, was about to be unveiled. Lex had wagered everything to bring the elephants from the African savanna to the center stage of his zoo. This was his moment. The test.

A cool Saturday evening. A fat moon lit the sky. Diamonds sparkled inside augmented cleavage.

All of Lowry Park Zoo was closed and dark, except for the front pavilion and fountain, which were strung with paper lanterns and overflowing with champagne and cocktails and $250 dinners of filet mignon and sea bass. This evening, the zoo was hosting its sixteenth annual

Karamu black-tie gala. This year's theme was Komodo & Kimonos, which explained, sort of, the lanterns, the troupe of performers undulating inside the giant yellow dragon, and the snapdragons and orchids waiting at every table, along with fortune cookies containing a breathless message from a corporate sponsor: *Good fortune smiles on AmSouth customers!*

From their tables, the celebrants gazed into a sea of the wealthy and connected and surgically enhanced. At the zoo, attention was almost always directed toward the behavior of other animals. But on this one night, the spotlight turned to the ruling species. Karamu was the zoo's greatest gathering of alphas. They came to see and be seen, to assert their place in the hierarchy, to show off their jewelry and their curves. Sex, money, and power intersected in a glittering tableau. The hidden currents, churning beneath the civilized veneer, slipped into view. The human exhibit, in full display.

Not everyone was thrilled to be there. At a back table, one of the men—his name was Mike—was complaining between the courses. At his house, he usually decided what to do for fun on Saturday nights. Just this once, he had followed his wife's lead.

"Next thing you know, I'm in a tux," he said, appealing to the other men around him. He turned to his spouse. "Why don't you just kick me in the balls?"

On the far side of the pavilion, Lex shook hands and accepted congratulatory hugs as he introduced everyone to his new wife, Elena Sheppa. The news of their wedding swept through the crowd. Other women appraised the bride, who shimmered in pearls and pink and the aura of newlywed bliss. Someone explained that she was an artist, a sculptor who worked with glass. The consensus held that she was lovely. Unlike so many other men at the gala, Lex looked at ease in his formal wear, hugging Elena close as he smiled and made eye contact with the titans who had come to supply the zoo with cash. An array of CEOs was on hand, along with assorted tycoons, bank execs, law partners, plus one man in a black-on-black tux who was described, again and again, as the orthodontist to all of South Tampa.

A droning buzz arose from the tables. The guests laughed and gossiped and told jokes. They talked so much, at such volume, it was hard to make out what any of them were saying. It did not matter. Just to watch them was far more enlightening. These were primates, after all. Respectable men and women, yes. The highest echelons of Tampa society. But still primates.

What would a field anthropologist, studying this elite sampling of the species, have observed in their behavior? Perhaps the way the males puffed out their chests—no different from the boys at the mall—and swaggered as they approached another alpha. Or the gleam in their eyes as they tested one another with death-grip handshakes. Some skipped the handshake combat and moved directly to mock wrestling, wrapping their arms around one another's shoulders, squeezing and smothering their potential rivals until they surrendered. Once these contests were completed, some of the alphas stood together and surveyed the breeding choices among the crowd.

"I'm hungry now," said one.

The behavior of the women was equally primal. Many had dedicated countless hours and great expense to ensuring that every eye turned their way. Since they were at a zoo, the females had borrowed from nature's palette and showcased themselves with feathers and leopard prints and fur. Even Pam Iorio, Tampa's mayor, had gone wild. Known for her monochromatic wardrobe, she was now wearing a zebra print. "Good to see you again," she said to one well-wisher after another, smiling her official smile. "Good to see you again." A few of the women—not the mayor—were testing the boundaries of how much flesh could be laid bare without inviting the censure of other females in the tribe. One woman wore a shiny black gown, the front of which plunged to just above her navel, revealing her perfectly tanned torso and one hemisphere of each perfectly round breast. Keeping the other hemispheres under wraps was a minor feat of engineering.

The night was all about display. Many of the females towered in stilettos, drawing the attention of men all around. The effect of the heels—the extension of the calves, the raising of their hindquarters—made a statement remarkably similar to Enshalla's presentation to Eric during their mating dance. With their footwear these women were instinctively paying homage to a primal truth that strutted through every cocktail party and late-night soiree. It was no accident that such shoes were called CFM pumps. One man whose wife was among the most provocatively dressed stood guard at her side, watching the other males openly stare. For most of the night, the man kept one hand attached to his wife's body—first her arm, then the small of her back. Then, in front of everyone, he traced his fingers down her spine and cupped his palm around the top of her backside. His claim was clear enough.

Up front, the auctioneer was accepting bids for one of the elephants. "Ten thousand dollars right here," he cried. "Come on, we need eleven!"

The evening was a smash. One couple bid $11,000 to adopt an elephant for a year, calling the pledge a wedding present to Lex and his new wife. Another couple bid $30,000 to adopt three elephants. By the time the proceeds were counted, Lowry Park had raised more than $195,000. Near the end, when the band picked up the tempo and a conga line looped around the tables, Lex approached a dozen or so guests, and whispered, "Come with me."

Lex led them away from the lights and the music and the dancing, but the group did not care. He had promised them a special late-night preview of the elephants. The select few he had chosen included some of the zoo's heavy-hitter donors, as well as Dick Greco—the former mayor who had hobnobbed with Herman at City Hall three decades before. Greco was still a big supporter of Lowry Park. Through the darkened zoo all of them went, past the free-flight aviary and the petting zoo empty now of children and goats, past the warthogs and the giraffes and zebras. Outside the elephant building, Lex bewitched the group with the narrative of the giants waiting inside, telling how they had lost their families as calves and how the zoo had rescued them from another death sentence in Swaziland and how they were flown across the Atlantic in defiance of PETA.

"Did you say the animal-rights groups wanted them shot?" someone asked.

"Yes," said Lex. "Because they feel they're better off dead than in a zoo."

The answer was a little simplistic, yes. But this was not the time for a nuanced discourse on the history and ethics of translocating wild species. The elephant building was the epicenter of Lex's territory. He would tell the story however he saw fit.

He unlocked the front door and escorted everyone into the Africa department's office, where he paused again. The man had a talent for ratcheting expectations. He told the group about Ellie and how her whole family group had been shot in Namibia and how she was brought to the United States as a tiny orphaned calf.

"That's incredible!" a voice called out.

The group was too big to squeeze inside the elephant barn at once, so Lex split them into two groups, reminding everyone to stay behind the yellow line that extended several feet away from the stalls. As the guests stepped inside, their mouths dropped. The elephants were lined up before them, pressing against the bars, trunks waving. Up close, they seemed much bigger. More real. More vivid.

Lex introduced Mbali, who extended her trunk almost to his face.

"Does she want human contact?" someone asked.

"No," said Lex, staying clear. "She's just smelling me."

"This is Ellie," he said, walking to the front of another stall. "Do you see how much bigger she is than the other elephants?"

Ellie, too, reached toward him.

"That's OK, sweetie pie."

The visitors stood transfixed at the yellow line, captivated as they stared up into the elephants' faces and sensed the intelligence and curiosity swirling inside. When Lex turned off the light to leave, the elephants' trunks were still in the air, beckoning.

Sunlight. Bulldozers chugging and beeping, construction workers scurrying. Plumes of dust rising about the five and a half acres that would soon be known as Safari Africa. A few weeks before the May 28 opening, Brian Morrow, Lowry Park's design guru, stood in the middle of the commotion and surveyed his creation. Brian's title was director of capital construction. As a boy, he had designed a model theme park in his family's basement, with a roller coaster and a Ferris wheel. Now he created exhibits at the zoo, studying eroded riverbanks and weathered stones—all so he could heighten the public's sense that they were truly setting foot in Africa.

"Replicating nature," he called it, and he loved the immense scale of what the zoo was attempting. "Africa is big. The exhibits are big. The animals are big."

One of Lowry Park's goals, he explained, was to put visitors as close to the animals as possible without endangering anyone on either side of the fence. That's why the zoo had built a platform where guests could stand at eye level with giraffes and feed them by hand, and a raised viewing area where they could watch from above as the elephants swam in their new 250,000-gallon pool. "It's all about the idea of the juxtaposition of humans and nature," Brian said. "Proximity equals excitement, and excitement will turn into a connection and love for animals."

From another person's mouth, these sentiments might have sounded Orwellian. Bubbling out of Brian, with all his enthusiasm, they made you want to hug a wildebeest. Even Brian, however, would have acknowledged the limits of such artifice. No matter how much ingenuity and delight he and others poured into this project, Safari Africa could never come close to the real thing. Msholo and Mbali and Sdudla and Matjeka must have recognized this better than any of the humans. The Swazi elephants appeared to have adjusted to the new world as well as anyone could have expected. But the acres of the open elephant yards and the accompanying pool were a long way from the landscape they had once roamed. It was true that their former herds in Swaziland were systematically tearing down the trees inside the game parks. Still, what remained was glorious: deep thickets where the red leopard grass grew past the ears of baby rhinos, the watering holes crowded with wildebeests and impalas, drinking deeply as they watched for crocodiles. Some things could not be replicated.

As opening day for Safari Africa drew closer, a sense of momentum could be felt in every department of the zoo. Carie and the rest of the Asia staff exulted in the budding relationship between their beloved Sumatran tigers, who were now peacefully sharing the exhibit almost every day. So far Enshalla showed no sign of pregnancy, but she and

Eric were mating frequently. One day, Enshalla had even allowed the male to join her on the tiger platform—the same one that had been built as her mother's haven when Enshalla was still a cub—and had curled herself at Eric's feet, exuding contentment.

The famously reserved demeanor of the aviary staff had been replaced by tremulous expectation as they awaited the arrival of the zoo's first argus pheasant chick. The female pheasant had laid eggs before, but none had ever hatched. The keepers could tell this time would be different, because they had been candling the pheasant's egg—placing it under a bright beam of light that allowed them to see within and evaluate the viability of the embryo. Under the light, the brown shell became translucent and the embryo revealed itself as a deep crimson form stirring in a web of veins that spidered through the yolk. One of the keepers pointed to a tiny dent in the shell where the embryo was already pushing with its beak.

"This is the pip right here," she said. "We found it this morning."

The aviary staff was keeping the egg inside an incubator, readying a warm new home for the chick. Soon it would make its entrance, chipping its way into the world. The morning after the first pip appeared, the staff could see the tip of a beak, poking from inside. When they returned from lunch, they found the argus chick standing in the incubator, wet and sticky, surrounded by tiny shards of the brown shell.

"When he made his mind up," said one keeper, "he was ready."

In those crucial first hours, they tried not to touch him too much. They didn't want him imprinting on them, mistaking one of them for his mother. The successful hatching made them almost dizzy. Beaming, they led visitors back to the incubator to show off their new arrival. The chick, tiny and brown and fuzzy, stood in the light, softly peeping.

The zoo had entered a streak unlike any it had ever seen before. Safari Africa was going to be a monster hit, Lex and his team could already feel it. All of them, meanwhile, were crowing because the latest issue of *Child* magazine declared Lowry Park the best zoo for kids in the United States.

After months of studying more than 150 accredited zoos, *Child* had rated Lowry Park above the biggest institutions in the country, with the

San Diego Zoo earning the number-two slot. In its article, the magazine saluted Lowry Park for its hands-on exhibits, its array of children's educational programs, and its longstanding commitment to rehabilitating manatees. The judges also commended the zoo's commitment to safety and noted that the staff scheduled Code One drills every month. "The most of our survey," the magazine said.

More good news followed. That same month, attendance hit a historic benchmark as the staff welcomed the ten-millionth visitor to walk through the gates since the new zoo opened in 1988. The lucky guest—a soldier on leave with his wife and children—appeared slightly stunned at the ceremony that awaited him on the other side.

A banner was unfurled. A TV crew hovered. "Congratulations!" someone called out.

Amid the celebrations, there was one more piece of news. No banners were raised for this one. Only a few days after his hatching, the argus pheasant chick died from an infection. The aviary keepers were devastated. To have the chick snatched away, just as they were getting their hopes up, was too hard. The loss, unknown to anyone outside the zoo, was another turn of nature's wheel, a quiet reminder that no matter how hard the keepers worked to care for their animals, there would always be complications that could not be foreseen, outcomes that could not be forestalled.

One morning that spring, Andrea Schuch was giving a talk on chimpanzees when a visitor said something troubling. Andrea had just explained that chimps are humans' closest genetic relative when a little girl, listening on, shook her head.

"No, they're not," said the child. "Because God made us."

Andrea knew there was no point in arguing. But for days, the exchange stuck with her. Even though the girl had obviously been repeating what her parents or another adult had taught her, she had posed an almost timeless question. For centuries, Aristotle and Descartes and other philosophers after them have debated whether animals possessed souls, or reason, or enough sentience to grant them any rights. But for Andrea, the answer was obvious. After her time at the zoo, she could not accept the notion that animals stood outside the sight of God.

"Are you going to tell me that they don't have souls and a place in heaven? That seems very wrong."

Sometimes, when she sat by the window of the orangutan exhibit, Rango would plop down on the other side of the glass, only a few inches away. He would look into her eyes, and she would look into his, and she could feel him gazing into her core.

No, Rango definitely had a soul. So did Herman, and Rukiya, and the others, too.

Andrea was sure of it.

The final days before the debut of Safari Africa were somehow both chaotic and exhilarating. Brian Morrow gave instructions nonstop on both his walkie-talkie and his cell phone. Brian French and the rest of the Africa staff pushed through a stream of last-minute tasks, sweat dripping down their faces. One of the warthogs briefly escaped. The giraffes balked at leaving their barn. A bongo antelope proved so skittish, the staff had to calm him with a small dose of a sedative.

Then, just when it seemed the zoo had been pushed beyond capacity, everything fell into place. At the unveiling, Lex posed for the TV cameras with Mayor Iorio and other dignitaries, all of them holding giant scissors for the cutting of the ribbon draped before the entrance of the tunnel that led to the elephants and the rest of the new animals. Iorio had left her zebra-print jacket at home. Instead she donned a safari hat.

"I think we should celebrate these elephants," she said, turning to Lex in front of the crowd that waited behind the dignitaries. "Where are they? Are they back there?"

Lex grinned. "Yeah."

"Are they happy?"

A bigger grin. "Yeah."

Someone counted to three, and the ribbon fell, and the crowd spilled forward. Emerging from the tunnel into the light, a little girl spied the warthogs and yelled "Pumbaa!" The crowd moved on to the bongo and the hornbills and the crowned cranes and the zebras, and finally to the overlook above the elephant yards, where Ellie and Matjeka were walking together, ears flapping, tails swishing, every giant step and every curlicue of their trunks registering on the faces of all the humans literally gasping with delight.

Lex stood back and studied the reactions and never stopped smiling.

In the rush of that morning, a rumor spread through some of the visitors. When asked if it was true, Lee Ann nodded.

Ellie was pregnant.

11

City and Forest

Now came days of jubilation, months of fiscal glory. A summer of splendor at the ticket windows, of overflowing revenue streams and vaulting growth projections, all fueled by the legions of tots, sun-scorched but happy as they waved at their new best friends, Mr. Warthog and Mr. Giraffe. With the blockbuster opening of Safari Africa, 2004 reigned as the most luminous year in Lowry Park's history.

The news of Ellie's pregnancy only fueled expectations. The nineteen-year-old elephant wasn't due until late 2005. But if she successfully delivered, her baby would draw even more visitors and confirm that Lowry Park could breed its fledgling herd. A calf would solidify Ellie's standing as the matriarch. Brian French and Steve Lefave were increasing Ellie's vitamins and exercising her in the yards and in the pool. They were also brainstorming ways to avert catastrophe during the birth. Calves born in captivity are sometimes stillborn or die within the first twenty-four hours. The mother elephant, usually a first-time mother, can get confused and attack the newborn. Isolated from her species for most of her life, Ellie's inexperience was especially profound. She had never given birth or witnessed another female elephant delivering. She had never even seen a calf.

Somehow, the humans would have to coach her. They had to prepare Ellie for when the contractions traveled through her and then a strange, squirming creature dropped from her womb.

·······

As if to confirm Lowry Park's new prominence, the zoo was invited that December to show off its animals on *Late Night with Conan O'Brien.* Jeff Ewelt and Melinda Mendolusky, the birds-of-prey keepers who led the daily animal shows, were the obvious choices to ferry a sampling of creatures to New York.

They left a couple of days before the show—Jeff and Melinda and their spouses in a van and a truck hooked to a trailer. Since they didn't know which animals Conan would pick to appear on camera, they brought a bounty: a black-headed python, a chinchilla, two New Guinea singing dogs, cave-dwelling spiders from Tanzania, plus Smedley the vulture and Ivan the Eurasian eagle owl. Finally, there was Jeff and Melinda's new favorite, Arnold the show-stealing pig. If a pig could be a mutt, Arnold qualified. He was a mixed breed, only three years old, six hundred pounds and counting. He had been someone's pet, but then he grew so massive that his owner donated him to the zoo. Jeff and Melinda had cast him for the grand finale of their birds-of-prey show. The audience cheered when he lumbered into view. Now he dozed in the back of the trailer, ensconced in hay, bound for stardom. The zoo had even brought him a little blanket to wear while on the air. One side was emblazoned with LOWRY PARK ZOO, TAMPA BAY. The other declared I ♥ NY.

The journey northward played like a hybrid of *The Odyssey* and *Wild Kingdom*, with a dash of *Green Acres*. They drove for two days and most of two nights and got caught in traffic near Savannah and in an ice storm in the Carolinas. When they reached a fresh snowfall outside Rocky Mount, they pulled to the side of the highway and let the singing dogs out to relieve themselves. The dogs, who had never seen snow before, were mystified at first but soon jumped and rolled in the powder, their breath making tiny clouds.

The night before the show, they checked into a Best Western in Hackensack and snuck the menagerie into their rooms. The singing dogs, a nocturnal species, romped through the night in one room with Jeff and his wife; Ivan the eagle owl perched at the foot of Melinda's bed. Arnold was too big to bring inside so they piled more hay around him in the van and wrapped him in a comforter.

The next morning, December 28, they ventured into the jungle of Manhattan, shrouded in blackened icicles and toxic slush and a bone-deep chill. Unbeknownst to the animals, they were headed into one of the cradles of modern civilization—a towering stone temple dedicated to human ambition and pride and the sacrament of the profit motive: Rockefeller Center. Once they found their way to the building and parked in the basement, they ran into an unexpected obstacle. To reach the show's sixth-floor studio, Arnold had to ride the elevator. To get to the elevator, he had to scale a ramp and then walk down a long concrete corridor, an extremely difficult challenge for a giant pig.

"You ready to walk, Arnold?" said Melinda. "This way, Arnie!"

They pushed him up the ramp and then laid out a long piece of rubber matting so he wouldn't slip and urged him on with a trail of marshmallows and powdered doughnuts. The pig hesitated, squealed, tried to turn around. The quest to reach the elevator exhausted him. A crowd gathered just in time to see him evacuate his massive bowels.

"He does what he wants, huh?" said a bystander, backing away from the smell. Jeff and Melinda and their spouses quickly cleaned the mess, then Arnold resumed his slow march, walking in tiny steps like a woman in a tight skirt.

Onto the elevator and up to the sixth floor they rode. Finally they established a base camp on the linoleum floor of the studio's hallway. As extras and crew members hurried back and forth, they all stopped at the sight of Arnold, stretched out in a fresh new bed of hay.

"*Wow.*"

"He's like Jabba the Hutt!"

Nearly everyone was sucked into Arnold's mighty gravitational field. A pneumatic blonde, wearing jeans so tight they could cause gangrene, flirted with him. Max Weinberg, the drummer who led Conan's house band when not on tour with Bruce Springsteen, knew a star when he saw one and stopped to give the pig his regards. Weinberg, a gentleman, made no jokes about bacon, as so many others did. The only person who did not betray the slightest reaction to Arnold's presence was the show's famous host. A thin and almost spectral figure, Conan passed several times without even glancing at the pig sprawled two feet away. The network icon appeared lost inside some preshow fugue state, avoiding eye contact and conversation with everyone in the crowded hallway until he sighted the blonde. Immediately he stopped to chat her up. The prerogative of the alpha, flaunted once again.

The rest of the day zipped by. At rehearsal, the animals were brought onto the set to audition for Conan's consideration. Almost immediately the singing dogs and the vulture were rejected. The others were in, time permitting; Arnold was deemed so spectacular that the show's staff wanted to bring him on last for the segment's climax. To Jeff's and Melinda's dismay, someone suggested that perhaps Conan should ride on Arnold's back during the show. Luckily, the host declined.

"I'm good, thanks."

At showtime, Conan made his entrance to raucous hoots and hollers. Suddenly, the gaunt shadow of the hallway was gone, transformed into another man so electric, he seemed to light the studio on his own. During his monologue, he told the audience that he had some unusual guests waiting backstage.

"There are animals," he said. "They are dangerous. We could all be killed."

More laughter. More approval.

When Jeff and Melinda brought out Lowry Park's animals, Conan knew what to do. He draped the python around his neck and let one of the cave-dwelling spiders crawl up his chest and onto his wrist.

"It's taking my pulse," said Conan.

Through a fortuitous accident, Ivan the eagle owl stole the night. Ivan was supposed to fly from Jeff's wife to Conan—they'd practiced it that afternoon—but the mouse tidbit in Conan's glove fell out, and so Ivan ignored the command. Instead he spread his great wings and circled back over the heads of the audience to rapturous applause. Through it all, Arnold bided his time, in position behind the curtain as he waited to deliver the segment's big finale. But before his moment came, time ran out, and the show went to commercial.

Just like that, it was over. Arnold had traveled the length of the country, shivered through a cold night in New Jersey, and been hauled into a metropolis of honking cabs and strange subterranean smells—the last place on Earth designed for a pig. He had struggled to find his way down a long and perilous hallway, so slippery it made him squeal, endured the condescension of the glitterati, and then been led in and out of a cavernous space that boomed with the roar of humans and burned with the glare of who knows how many tiny suns—all for nothing. In the end, he had been upstaged by an owl.

"Poor Arnold," someone said.

With Melinda and Jeff leading him on a leash, he slowly made his way back to the elevator. By now it was late and the pig was growing restless and cranky. Back in the studio, just before the show ended, someone prevailed upon Conan to give Arnold another chance. A remote camera crew caught up with him in the basement, deep into his plodding retreat.

This was the chance the pig and his handlers had labored toward for so long. At last, Arnold's wet and whiskered snout would appear on national TV and the zoo would cap another triumph. When the show aired after midnight, more than two million Americans would watch Conan's antics with the owl and the chinchilla and the spiders. For many in that vast audience, it would be the first time they had ever heard of Lowry Park. As the remote crew zoomed in, Arnold kept walking in his same short, halting steps away from the camera and the lights, toward the refuge of the trailer. He didn't care about the Nielsens. He just wanted another doughnut.

A second jungle, two thousand miles to the south. Marmosets chirped in the trees. Leaf-cutter ants marched through the underbrush in a winding column.

Dustin Smith was hiking through a tropical forest in central Panama, joining a team of researchers made up of biologists and other herps keepers from other American zoos. They had come to the forest in search of a vanishing species: the Panamanian golden frog. On a cool Tuesday morning in January 2005, Dustin and the others walked in single file, keeping an eye out for boa constrictors. A day or so earlier, in another part of the forest, they had found a fer-de-lance, a deadly viper. Now they climbed a hill scarred with lava flow from an old volcanic eruption, then negotiated their way down the other side, toward a gorge with a rushing stream— one of the last breeding grounds of the golden frog.

Of all the amphibians plunging toward extinction, the golden frog was among the most beautiful. With its bright yellow skin, dotted with deep black chevrons, it had long been Panama's national symbol. The frog was believed to bring good luck; images of it hung on walls in restaurants. In gift shops, the shelves were crowded with tiny golden replicas. The souvenirs far outnumbered the real thing. As the Panamanian countryside had been paved over by developers, a lethal fungus known as chytrid had spread through the streams and rivers. The golden-frog population had been nearly wiped out. Less than two thousand remained in the wild.

"They'll be extinct probably in five years," said Kevin Zippel, the biologist who headed this project. "I don't think there's anything anybody can do to stop that."

In recent years, Kevin and other researchers had gathered small numbers of golden frogs and sent them to zoos and aquariums around the United States. Some would soon be arriving at Lowry Park. Eventually, if a defense against the fungus could be found, biologists hoped to reintroduce golden frogs back into the forest, provided there was any forest left. The odds were not good. Once these last holdouts in Panama died off, the species was almost certainly fated to live out its time on Earth inside tiny rooms at zoos and aquariums.

"Is that right?" Kevin said. "I don't know."

Around the planet, so many amphibian species were headed toward extinction that there was no way to preserve a genetic sampling of them all through captivity. Researchers could not get to them in the wild quickly enough. Even if they could, zoos didn't have room for all the species, leaving Kevin and others to play God. Somehow, they had to decide which amphibian species would be saved and which would be allowed to vanish.

"Is that right?" Kevin said again. "*I don't know.*"

The golden frog had been selected for survival in captivity. Kevin and Dustin and the rest of this team had come to Panama to chronicle the frogs' last stand. They wanted to see how many were still hanging on. If they found any, they would take skin swabs to determine if the frogs were infected with chytrid. In their first two weeks in the forest, the team had encountered a breathtaking array of wildlife—toucans and peccaries and caimans, acacia ants and scorpions, a green parrot snake and a three-toed sloth, a porcupine, even some basilisks, better known as Jesus lizards for their ability to skitter across the top of water. One day, some of the leaf-cutter ants found their way into Kevin's backpack and sliced through his shirt and pants and a belt. But Dustin and the others had found almost no golden frogs.

On this particular morning, they were hopeful. The stream waiting at the bottom of the gorge had historically been one of the best places to find golden frogs. The team called it the Thousand-Frog Stream because in previous years, when the goldens were breeding, the banks were so thick with them that it was hard to step anywhere without risking an awful squish. This morning as the researchers returned to the stream, there was no carpet of gold. Searching under leaves and in the crevices of the stones, they found only a handful of frogs.

Dustin saw one on the side of a mossy rock, then grabbed it. "This is definitely a female," he said, pointing to the frog's feet. She didn't have any pads on the sides of her thumbs. "Nuptial pads," they're called, and only the males have them. They're used to grip the female during breeding. Sometimes the male hangs on for weeks or even longer, waiting for her to lay her eggs so he can be the one to fertilize them. Cupped in Dustin's hands, the female appeared tiny. Someone brought Q-tips to swab her. The samples were secured inside a tiny bottle, and then Dustin let her go.

This site, with the stream rushing over the rocks along the high walls of the gorge, seemed so idyllic, so complete in its hushed perfection, that it felt like an ecstatic vision. Shafts of sunshine, piercing the canopy, fell on the water like light through the stained-glass windows of a cathedral. Vines hung everywhere, bursting with purple orchids. Spiderwebs glistened. A morpho butterfly appeared over the stream. As it fluttered into one of the shafts of light from above, its wings erupted with a metallic, iridescent blue. For a few moments, as the morpho moved from light to shadow and then back into light, the brilliant color flashed on, then off, then on again.

For all the beauty of this place, the researchers were struck by how empty it felt. Dustin, normally joking and talking nonstop, stood at the edge of the stream, wrapped in solitude.

Almost all of the frogs were gone. Erased, seemingly overnight. Nothing would bring them back.

A moment of silence, then an observation.

It had only been a couple of weeks since Lowry Park sent Jeff and Melinda to Manhattan with Arnold and the other animals. Now the same institution had helped send Dustin to the wilds of Central America on behalf of a critically endangered species. In the arc between these two trips, Lowry Park revealed the spectrum of its ambitions—and the difficulty of knowing exactly what to make of those ambitions. The appearance on the Conan O'Brien show might have seemed nothing more than a publicity stunt. But Jeff and Melinda saw it as an unprecedented opportunity for Lowry Park to help millions of Americans connect with wildlife. Jeff pointed to the moment when Ivan the eagle owl took off and spread his wings in front of the camera. Ivan's impromptu flight, Jeff noted, was probably the first time many watching at home had ever seen an eagle owl flying or had even heard of such a bird.

"To see an owl fly around like an owl should fly—that's huge," Jeff said afterward. "There is entertainment value there. There has to be."

The Panama trip was not so easily judged either. What appeared to have been an altruistic act by the zoo was not that simple. Lowry Park did support the trip, but not nearly as much as it might have. The zoo's conservation fund donated about $750—enough to cover Dustin's plane ticket and expenses. But his request to use work days had been denied. Dustin had to devote almost three weeks of his vacation time, nearly his entire allotment for the year, to join the research team in Panama. In the end, it had been Dustin's dedication to the golden frogs, not the zoo's, that made his trip possible. Did that mean Lowry Park didn't care? Hardly. Dustin himself acknowledged the zoo's ongoing support of endangered amphibians. That was why the herps staff worked with the poison-dart frogs; it was why the zoo was bringing in some of the golden frogs. In recent years, Lowry Park's conservation fund had donated more than $3,000 toward efforts to save the golden frogs.

Lex would have said that an appearance on national TV—and any resulting bump in profits—was precisely what made it possible for the nonprofit to fight for the survival of the frogs and other endangered species. The reverse could be argued as well. Critics often said that such conservation efforts were token gestures, designed to legitimize the larger exploitation that zoos perpetrate every day on countless other species in the name of entertaining the masses.

Considered together, the two trips were just another reminder of how at Lowry Park, as at any zoo, the motivation behind every act was open to question. Every decision invited suspicion. Every claim required inspection.

The phone lines kept repeating the mantra: "Thank you for calling Lowry Park Zoo, voted the number-one zoo in America for families."

Lex's vision was materializing. The zoo was winning accolades, drawing bigger crowds, growing almost by the day. A year after the grand opening, Safari Africa was already completing phase two of the expansion, with new exhibits featuring white rhinos and meerkats. A skyride was installed, offering aerial tours. Soon, Ellie would deliver the first calf of what Lex hoped would be many born into the new herd. He frequently checked on Ellie, whose due date was still months away. He and Brian French were disagreeing these days about how to handle Ellie's delivery and what to do with the calf. Brian believed it would be essential to relax the rules of protected contact and allow him into Ellie's enclosure to help her with the delivery and to decrease the chances that she would kill her newborn calf. Lex agreed, but it was clear that their differing views on elephant care were not about to go away. Brian was already lobbying to train the baby elephant with free contact, to encourage the bond between the calf and its keepers. Lex preferred to focus on the bond between the calf and the other elephants. As much as possible, he wanted Lowry Park's herd to live like the herds in Africa. He kept touting his game park plan, describing it as the real future of Lowry Park. The man always had his eye on the next big thing. He breathed ambition.

The never-ending drive to the top was wearing thin among some of the staff. A few keepers still had mixed feelings about the decision to bring over the wild elephants. They'd seen for themselves that the four Swazi elephants appeared to be doing well, and they respected the way Brian French and his staff had worked to help the herd adjust. Even so, Lex's big push had left some wondering, more than ever, about the zoo's priorities and direction. One of the doubters was Carie Peterson. For years, she had been relatively happy working at Lowry Park despite the low pay. By early 2005, though, a growing number of things troubled her. Lowry Park was a nonprofit, but to her it felt as though the place was increasingly being run like a business. She worried that the staff was already overworked and was asked to do too much with too little. Carie didn't understand how Lowry Park could afford the elephants and the other new animals, when as far as she could tell, the budget was already stretched to the limit. If the zoo could find millions of dollars to build a state-of-the-art elephant building, why couldn't it spare a couple thousand to splash some new paint on the walls or fix the damaged doors in the night houses of her department?

Carie tried to be patient. She had voiced her concerns and hoped the problems would soon be addressed. She couldn't imagine walking away from the animals, especially Enshalla. When the tiger finally got pregnant and delivered her first litter, Carie wanted to be there. For Enshalla, she would stay a little longer.

In the elephant building, Lamaze class was under way. Brian French and the rest of his staff had begun to prepare Ellie for labor and delivery. They were teaching her to lower her body by spreading her back legs and bracing them, so that when the baby arrived, it would have a shorter drop to the hard floor. If Ellie stayed in the wide stance, there was also less chance she'd step on the calf when it emerged. With the permission of his supervisors, Brian had begun briefly tethering Ellie's legs—sometimes one, sometimes two—with nylon straps to the bars of her stall. Brian and Steve tethered her before they went into her stall. They wanted Ellie to grow accustomed to the tethers, so that if necessary the staff could restrict her movement during the delivery, offering some safety to both the calf and the humans who would approach to help.

That fall, as Ellie's pregnancy entered its final months, Brian and Steve worked with her every day, practicing the bracing position, teaching her to shift her front legs so the baby could nurse. Brian had wired the night-vision cameras in the barn so that he and the other keepers could call up the video feeds on their computers at home. As the delivery date drew closer, the staff took turns checking the feeds. If Ellie went into labor at night, they wanted to get back to the zoo as soon as possible.

One night in mid-October, it was Brian's turn to take the three-a.m. check. He signed on to his computer at home, scanned the feeds from the night-vision cameras at the zoo, saw that Ellie was doing fine, then went back to sleep. An hour or so later, he was awakened by another keeper calling to tell him that the camera feeds weren't coming up on his computer. Apparently the server had crashed. Brian wasn't worried; Ellie was still a month away from her due date. Besides, he and Steve were scheduled to be back at the zoo before dawn.

At 5:45 a.m., when Brian arrived, he heard an unusual sound from inside the elephant building. A bucket being kicked, maybe. Had someone left it in one of the stalls? He walked into the building and through the kitchen toward the double doors that led into the darkened barn. When he pushed open the doors, a newborn calf ran forward, straight into Brian's leg. It was a male, still bloody, weighing maybe two hundred pounds. Brian's brain raced to catch up. Ellie was still in the barn. Somehow she had given birth on her own. It had to have happened in the past hour, just after the server went down.

The calf was excited and wanted to move. Brian wrapped his arms around him and held him steady. The floor of the kitchen was slick, and if the calf fell or crashed into something, he could hurt himself. Brian looked him over and made sure he wasn't already injured. He stuck his hand into the calf's mouth to see if his airway was clear and pulled out some placenta. He wanted to check on Ellie, but he had to wait until someone else arrived to watch over the calf. Another keeper, someone who worked with the zebras and giraffes, walked in at that moment and found Brian and the calf, locked in their slippery union.

"Oh," the other keeper said. "An elephant."

"Yeah," said Brian. "C'mere and hold him a minute."

He ran out to his car, grabbed his cell phone, called Steve. "We have a little bit of a surprise."

. . . .

The calf was blue and wet and wobbly on his feet. His head was still cone-shaped from being squeezed through his mother's birth canal. His eyes were wide, the black pupils lined with red. His ears appeared pink from the blood vessels under the skin. The umbilical cord had already been severed, but what remained—a short tube—dangled from his belly.

How had his mother delivered the calf on her own? Had she remembered the Lamaze exercises the humans taught her? How had she reacted when she first saw the calf? Brian and Steve and the other keepers had no idea. The only witnesses had been the other elephants, who watched the calf take his first steps before dawn. Lex, who soon arrived to check on the new addition, called it "the virgin birth."

Once the calf was born, he had been small enough to wander between the bars of the stalls. Lex and Brian knew they were fortunate that those first minutes had not careened into disaster. Ellie might have stepped on her baby, or the calf could have roamed into a stall with one of the other elephants and been stomped or kicked and possibly killed. Instead he had found his way into the arms of his human keepers.

The staff moved quickly. Dr. Murphy was summoned. Ellie, in her stall, appeared to have recovered from the delivery, but was obviously unnerved. When Brian and Steve brought the calf back into the barn, Ellie kept her distance. Her ears were pushed out, and she would not look at the baby. She had no idea what to make of him and wanted nothing to do with him. Overcoming her rejection, and soon, was crucial. Already the calf was trumpeting with hunger. If the keepers couldn't get Ellie to let her baby close enough to nurse, the chances were they'd never bond. Brian and Steve moved Ellie to a clean stall and tethered her. They wrapped a harness around the calf's torso and attached it to another strap, so they could pull him back to safety if Ellie became aggressive. Then they slowly led the newborn closer to his mother.

"It's OK," Brian told Ellie. "It's all right."

She was not convinced. Her eyes were wide. When the calf drew near, she tried to shoo him away with her trunk.

"OK, Ellie, hold still," said Brian. "Steady. It's not going to hurt you."

With the human's encouragement, the elephant began to calm down and stopped trying to push the calf away. She reached out with her trunk, touched him briefly, then pulled the trunk away. Brian stood next to her and let her feel his hand on her skin again.

"Brace," he told Ellie, and she obeyed, moving a front leg forward so the calf could nurse. Before the keepers let him get that close, Brian reached under Ellie and massaged one of her nipples to get the first few drops of milk. Soon the calf was underneath her. He was too short to reach his mother, so the keepers gave him a little platform, only a few inches high, to stand on. After several tries, he latched on, and Ellie visibly relaxed. Her milk was flowing. So were her maternal instincts.

"Good girl," Brian told her.

Already, Ellie had shown more fortitude than anyone could have asked. Now she gave a hint of what kind of mother she would be. As her newborn finished his first meal and fell asleep, Ellie reached with her trunk toward the hay scattered around the floor and covered the calf with a makeshift blanket. Then she stood over him, watching and waiting until he needed her again. For the moment, the controversy surrounding Lowry Park's herd had become moot. All the arguments about keeping elephants in captivity temporarily fell away. The baby was here, and would not survive without his mother and human caretakers.

New life insists. It does not debate. It simply appears, trembling and hungry, and will not be denied.

12

Undertow

In those first days after the virgin birth, Lowry Park held its breath. The calf's vital signs looked good, and Ellie allowed him to nurse. But there was no point in tempting fate, so the staff kept him secluded inside the relative quiet of the elephant building.

"We are cautiously optimistic about his survival," said Dr. Murphy.

As the newborn elephant gained weight and grew stronger, Lowry Park prepared to celebrate in earnest. The calf's arrival was another triumph for the zoo, potentially its biggest yet, and the marketing team knew how to capitalize on the moment and maximize exposure. Several weeks after the birth, when the zoo announced the baby's debut, crowds pressed forward. Every time the calf tottered on his stubby legs or raised his tiny trunk or weaved under Ellie's legs to nurse, the gallery erupted with oohs and aahs. Already he had learned to blow bubbles with his trunk, to find shade under his mother's belly, to bond with Matjeka and Mbali, his new aunts, when Ellie stepped away to eat. Behind the scenes, the keepers had already bestowed him with a house name.

"He looks like an Eli," Steve Lefave had pronounced, sizing up the youngster, and Brian French agreed, and so an Eli he had become. But the calf still needed a public name—another marketing opportunity— and so the zoo announced a contest, inviting schoolchildren to suggest African names with special meanings. Once the nominations were in, the zoo picked five finalists and allowed the public to vote online. The

even considered the possibility that t'
tted a certain course for the zoo
ng his mind.

than a zo
with Br
be in t
as he

d man with the thick white hair and the w
ge of the chimp exhibit and grinned. Herma.
saw him and rocked his body and raised his arm 1.
nat's my son," said Ed Schultz, turning to any of the vi.
und him who would listen.

irty-five years had passed since Ed and his family had brou
an to Lowry Park, pausing to let him climb the light pole on the
side. Ed, ninety-one now, was hanging on the best he could. His
Elizabeth, had died years before. Their kids, Roger and Sandy, were
and lived elsewhere with children of their own. Ed was in and out
hospital these days. His hearing wasn't so good. His mind lost
of things. But he had never forgotten Herman, and clearly Her-
ad never forgotten him.

had long since retired, but he still lived in Tampa, and for years
volunteered as a docent at Lowry Park, giving tours and helping
owever he could. Ed's favorite pastime was going to see Herman
lling stories about their life together. At his home, photos of Her-
hung next to portraits of Roger and Sandy and the grandchildren.
d folders overflowing with pictures of Herman and would sift
gh them and hold them with trembling hands as he talked about
ay young Herman joined them at the company picnic or the time
Herman went fishing with the children. For Ed, Herman was the
e between the past and present. At the zoo, whenever Ed looked
s the moat at his old friend, the years fell away, and suddenly he was
in Liberia, holding Herman for the first time. That day so long ago,
Ed had scooped the baby chimp out of the orange crate and into
rms, there had been no way for him to foresee all the implications of
ction. What it would mean for both of them, all the ways it would
e them. How their lives would braid together across the decades.
was difficult to know exactly what Herman made of the relation-
The chimp still felt a deep connection to Ed; that much was obvi-

five nominees chosen by the zoo—Jabali, Jasiri, Kidogo, Moja, and Tamani—were all designed to conjure the wide-open spaces of the savanna, even though the calf was not likely to ever set foot in Africa. They were stage names, selected to perpetuate a larger illusion of wildness.

More than ten thousand votes were cast, some from as far away as France and Argentina, and the clear winner, suggested by a second-grade class at Frontier Elementary in Clearwater, was Tamani:

Tamani means hope in Swahili. We chose hope because elephants are an endangered species and successfully breeding elephants in captivity gives the species hope for survival.

The front office was ecstatic. Lex's plan to build a new and more popular zoo around the elephants was exceeding expectations. Lowry Park had weathered the controversy over the importation from Swaziland and had successfully started a new breeding herd. Ellie, now reigning as the unquestioned matriarch, was turning out to be the devoted mother of the first of what the zoo hoped would be several calves born on the grounds. The other four elephants were already growing old enough to begin breeding as well. As the zoo headed into 2006, attendance topped more than a million visitors a year, hitting a mark that Lex and so many others had worked toward for so long. The animal collection was exploding. The zoo was adding pygmy hippos, dwarf forest buffalo, and scimitar-horned oryxes, all to stock the next phase of Safari Africa. Over in primates, Rango and Josie had delivered another baby orangutan. The Panamanian golden frogs, breeding in a back room of the herps department, had produced more than two hundred tadpoles.

And yet, beneath the waves of exultation, there were unmistakable signs of an undertow. A sense of something approaching its limits. It was there in the exhaustion in the eyes of the keepers, in the way their faces went blank when they heard Lex giving another pep talk about the next round of new exhibits and how they all needed to work a little harder. For those watching closely, the signs declared themselves, too, in the fine print of who was included and who was shut out in the swirl of excitement over Tamani's birth.

Every institution has its hidden workings, quiet shifts in the power structure that are revealed in the smallest ways. When the Soviet Union was still in power, CIA analysts devoted considerable energy to poring over photos showing which commissars were allowed to stand at the dais on May Day, when columns of the empire's weaponry and armies rolled through Red Square. Lowry Park, a nonprofit just named the best children's zoo in the country, was hardly an evil empire, even in PETA's most virulent condemnations. Still, if a team of Kremlinologists had turned their attentions to the hierarchy at the zoo, they might have noted that the only two people who spoke at the press conference announcing the elephant's calf birth were Lex and Dr. Murphy. Brian French, who had shepherded the new herd into existence and coached Ellie through her pregnancy, was nowhere to be seen.

Brian, always camera shy, did not take offense at being excluded from the limelight that day. But he was caught off guard, only a month or so later, when Lee Ann Rottman called him to her office and told him that the zoo was letting him go.

"When?" Brian remembers asking.

"Now."

Brian called Steve Lefave, who was out checking on the rhinos, and told him he needed to come take care of the elephants. Then he gathered his things and drove away, stunned.

Afterward, Lowry Park's spokeswoman declined to comment on the dismissal. "It's a personnel matter that has nothing to do with the animals," she said.

The unofficial word around the zoo was that the firing had grown out of a conflict between Brian and Lex—a conflict that had everything to do with the animals. In interviews, both Brian and Lex confirmed that they'd had a difference of opinion about the protocol for the handling of the elephants. Brian had enjoyed working in the same enclosure with baby Tamani and was eager to continue with free contact. He wanted to move slowly before introducing the calf to the two males. Lex insisted that the keepers stick with protected contact but wanted to see Tamani roaming the yards with the cows and the bulls. "He wanted to put all the elephants together to create a herd environment," Brian said afterward. "He wants to run things a lot more like a game park

o." Asked for his version of the split an's. He preferred the zoo's herd to be e wild. Brian, he said, wanted to return did with the circus elephants.

In retrospect, the collision seemed inevitab d strong temperaments and different notions o he elephants. Once they clashed, there was no d

Brian's departure might not have been so sig isolated incident. But a startling number of staff Park, including three of the six assistant curator terms, in search of a new challenge; Dustin Smit went to Panama to study the golden frogs, took dens. Kevin McKay had accepted a position at drea Schuch had gone back to school to pursue other keepers disappeared amid a cloud of wh the staff roiled with nearly constant turnover.

"Everybody knew that you could get fired at son," one former keeper said.

It was hard to tell what to make of the pattern just the growing pains of an institution redefinin evidence of a deeper problem?

In the Asia department, Carie Peterson debate join the exodus. During her shift, she stayed foc Eric. The two Sumatran tigers were together no cycled into estrus. But still she showed no sign of p was preparing to run some tests to find out wh understood that it might simply be too late for E Even so, it was almost impossible to think of h prime. Ferocious as ever, she still intimidated keep leaps against the mesh. She remained the embodime tyger, her eyes burning in the shadows of her den menace.

"She's beautiful, absolutely beautiful," said C watched her. "And she knows it."

Her attachment to Enshalla was the only thing quitting. She had lost almost all her faith in the zo ous. Still, the keepers had noticed an edge of desperation to Herman's displays, especially as Ed's visits ended. Sometimes the keepers wished he wouldn't stop by so often. Because every time Ed walked away, it seemed to leave the chimp shaken.

Thirty-five years had passed since the Schultzes had brought Herman to Lowry Park. He must have known that his human family loved him, and yet that knowledge must have made his abandonment all the more bewildering. Was it possible that Herman had spent the rest of his life trying to figure it out? Maybe a small part of him still wondered, whenever Ed showed up, if this time he would finally get to go home.

Early in that summer of 2006, the primate keepers were beyond excited. For the first time in years, their chimp group was about to get a new baby.

The young female's name was Sasha. She had been born at the Montgomery Zoo, but her birth mother had rejected her. Lee Ann had arranged for Sasha to be brought to Lowry Park. Knowing Rukiya's strengths as a surrogate mother, Lee Ann and the other keepers were preparing to slowly introduce Sasha to Rukiya and the rest of the group, hoping the matriarch would adopt her, just as she had adopted Alex years before.

Lee Ann, who loved baby chimps more than anything in the world, beamed whenever she got to hold Sasha. In those first weeks, while they prepared to introduce her to the group, Lee Ann and the other keepers allowed Sasha to explore their offices in her diaper. At night they took her home and bottle-fed her formula. She was light and soft and full of energy. She already loved the staff, especially the men. When she saw a human male, even one she'd never met, she would immediately raise her arms for him to pick her up, just as Herman had automatically raised his arms to Ed so many years before.

By early June, the introductions were progressing. Sasha had not yet met Herman or Bamboo. The protocol called for the process to unfold slowly and carefully. So far, the baby had been introduced to both Rukiya and Twiggy. The keepers placed her in a small cage—a "howdy cage," Lee Ann called it—beside the area of the night house that belonged to the females. This gave both the baby and the adults a chance to see and smell one another. It was their way of becoming acquainted, and if it went well, the next step would be to place Sasha in the same enclosure with Rukiya. There was no telling how young Alex would react once he met Sasha and realized he was no longer the baby of the group. It was also impossible to know how Herman and Bamboo would respond. Lee Ann believed Herman would accept Sasha, just as he had accepted Alex, and that his acceptance would guide the others. For the moment, Sasha had been kept away from the males; they might have smelled her scent lingering in the howdy cage, but they had not yet seen her.

As far as Lee Ann could tell, Sasha's arrival had not yet caused any ripples among the other chimps. Except for Alex's obvious ambitions, the group appeared to be as stable as usual. Herman and Bamboo had tangled briefly not long ago. The fight seemed a little more intense than some of their previous squabbles. But afterward they seemed to make up, like always.

Walking past the exhibit a few days later, Lee Ann noticed something odd. Rukiya was sitting behind Bamboo, grooming the hair on his back—a favor Lee Ann had never before seen Rukiya perform for the lowly male. Still, after the bullying the females inflicted on Bamboo, it was refreshing to see him and Rukiya getting along.

That's nice, Lee Ann told herself.

The emergency call went over the keepers' walkie-talkies just after noon on Thursday, June 8. The call was so feverish, the voice on the other end so urgent and strangled with emotion, that it was difficult to make out exactly what was being said, other than the word "primates." The chimps were fighting. They would not stop. The keepers needed help.

Lee Ann happened to be working in the primate area that day. She and the other keepers did not witness the start of the fight, but when they heard the commotion from the exhibit, they rushed out and saw Bamboo and Rukiya attacking Herman. Alex, standing nearby, was trying to defend Herman. The chimps were screaming and their arms were flailing, and Bamboo was chasing Herman and beating him with his fists. Lee Ann and the other keepers were trying to break it up. They coaxed Alex and Rukiya and the other females into the night house. They brought out hoses and sprayed Bamboo. But nothing stopped his aggression. Herman was clearly losing. Even as he defended himself, the keepers could see him fading. Soon Herman was on the ground, sitting cross-legged, slumped over, his head down. He was not moving, even as Bamboo pounded him.

As a security guard ushered visitors away, Dr. Murphy arrived and went around to the high wall of mesh that covered the back of the exhibit. The vet could see that Bamboo was not just upset, but confused and frightened. He kept running up to Murphy and repeatedly making the fear grin, then returning to Herman's fallen body to beat him again. Murphy tried to dart Bamboo, but couldn't get a clear shot. He and one of the primate keepers waited until the chimp moved away, then hurried into the exhibit and dragged Herman into the night house to examine him.

At the clinic, Murphy checked Herman for shock, got an IV running, cleaned him up. The chimp's external injuries—a few puncture wounds on his lip, a torn-up finger and toe—did not appear catastrophic. His pupils and his breathing pattern made Murphy wonder if he had suffered neurological trauma. Maybe during the attack he had fallen. Maybe Bamboo had hit him hard enough to knock him out.

As Murphy continued his examination, Lee Ann and Angela Belcher, the assistant curator in charge of primates, stood nearby and talked to Herman. But he would not wake up. He had slipped into a coma.

Leaving the others to watch over the chimp, Murphy went to the zoo's manatee hospital, where the keepers had brought a sedated Rukiya for a few stitches on her nose. The vet was still working on her when a call came from the clinic not long before seven p.m. Herman had stopped breathing. Rushing back, Murphy found people taking turns performing CPR on Herman's ninety-pound body. Murphy tried for a while, then Lee Ann took over. They kept at it for ten, fifteen minutes.

Lee Ann didn't want them to stop. She didn't understand why this had happened. She couldn't imagine the zoo or her life without Herman. Finally, though, she and the others had no choice but to step back.

The king was dead.

The next day, they allowed Ed Schultz to say good-bye. Lee Ann and Angela escorted him to the clinic and into a corner where Herman's body was waiting. He had been turned onto his side, with one arm stretched across his chest. He had a sheet across the lower half of his body. He looked at peace.

Already Ed felt lost. Tears in his eyes, he took the chimp's hand and felt the leathery palm against his skin. He kissed his forehead, cold now, and spoke softly and called him son. He told him he missed him but that the two of them would soon be reunited on the other side. Again and again, he repeated the name he had given his friend the first day they met, all those lifetimes ago.

than a zoo." Asked for his version of the split, Lex essentially agreed with Brian's. He preferred the zoo's herd to be together, as they would be in the wild. Brian, he said, wanted to return to working free contact, as he did with the circus elephants.

In retrospect, the collision seemed inevitable. Both Lex and Brian had strong temperaments and different notions of how best to work with the elephants. Once they clashed, there was no doubt who would prevail.

Brian's departure might not have been so significant if it had been an isolated incident. But a startling number of staffers were leaving Lowry Park, including three of the six assistant curators. Some exited on good terms, in search of a new challenge; Dustin Smith, the herps expert who went to Panama to study the golden frogs, took a job with Busch Gardens. Kevin McKay had accepted a position at Animal Kingdom. Andrea Schuch had gone back to school to pursue a master's degree. But other keepers disappeared amid a cloud of whispers. By that spring, the staff roiled with nearly constant turnover.

"Everybody knew that you could get fired at any time, for any reason," one former keeper said.

It was hard to tell what to make of the pattern. Were the departures just the growing pains of an institution redefining itself? Or were they evidence of a deeper problem?

In the Asia department, Carie Peterson debated whether she should join the exodus. During her shift, she stayed focused on Enshalla and Eric. The two Sumatran tigers were together now whenever Enshalla cycled into estrus. But still she showed no sign of pregnancy. Dr. Murphy was preparing to run some tests to find out what was wrong. Carie understood that it might simply be too late for Enshalla to have cubs. Even so, it was almost impossible to think of her as old or past her prime. Ferocious as ever, she still intimidated keepers with her snarling leaps against the mesh. She remained the embodiment of William Blake's tyger, her eyes burning in the shadows of her den, radiating a glorious menace.

"She's beautiful, absolutely beautiful," said Carie, sighing as she watched her. "And she knows it."

Her attachment to Enshalla was the only thing keeping Carie from quitting. She had lost almost all her faith in the zoo. Only a small part of her even considered the possibility that things would get better. Lex had plotted a certain course for the zoo's future. She did not see him changing his mind.

The old man with the thick white hair and the weathered face stood at the edge of the chimp exhibit and grinned. Herman, stationed at his perch, saw him and rocked his body and raised his arm in greeting.

"That's my son," said Ed Schultz, turning to any of the visitors milling around him who would listen.

Thirty-five years had passed since Ed and his family had brought Herman to Lowry Park, pausing to let him climb the light pole on the way inside. Ed, ninety-one now, was hanging on the best he could. His wife, Elizabeth, had died years before. Their kids, Roger and Sandy, were grown and lived elsewhere with children of their own. Ed was in and out of the hospital these days. His hearing wasn't so good. His mind lost track of things. But he had never forgotten Herman, and clearly Herman had never forgotten him.

Ed had long since retired, but he still lived in Tampa, and for years he had volunteered as a docent at Lowry Park, giving tours and helping out however he could. Ed's favorite pastime was going to see Herman and telling stories about their life together. At his home, photos of Herman hung next to portraits of Roger and Sandy and the grandchildren. Ed had folders overflowing with pictures of Herman and would sift through them and hold them with trembling hands as he talked about the day young Herman joined them at the company picnic or the time when Herman went fishing with the children. For Ed, Herman was the bridge between the past and present. At the zoo, whenever Ed looked across the moat at his old friend, the years fell away, and suddenly he was back in Liberia, holding Herman for the first time. That day so long ago, when Ed had scooped the baby chimp out of the orange crate and into his arms, there had been no way for him to foresee all the implications of this action. What it would mean for both of them, all the ways it would shape them. How their lives would braid together across the decades.

It was difficult to know exactly what Herman made of the relationship. The chimp still felt a deep connection to Ed; that much was obvi-

five nominees chosen by the zoo—Jabali, Jasiri, Kidogo, Moja, and Tamani—were all designed to conjure the wide-open spaces of the savanna, even though the calf was not likely to ever set foot in Africa. They were stage names, selected to perpetuate a larger illusion of wildness.

More than ten thousand votes were cast, some from as far away as France and Argentina, and the clear winner, suggested by a second-grade class at Frontier Elementary in Clearwater, was Tamani:

> Tamani means hope in Swahili. We chose hope because
> elephants are an endangered species and successfully breeding
> elephants in captivity gives the species hope for survival.

The front office was ecstatic. Lex's plan to build a new and more popular zoo around the elephants was exceeding expectations. Lowry Park had weathered the controversy over the importation from Swaziland and had successfully started a new breeding herd. Ellie, now reigning as the unquestioned matriarch, was turning out to be the devoted mother of the first of what the zoo hoped would be several calves born on the grounds. The other four elephants were already growing old enough to begin breeding as well. As the zoo headed into 2006, attendance topped more than a million visitors a year, hitting a mark that Lex and so many others had worked toward for so long. The animal collection was exploding. The zoo was adding pygmy hippos, dwarf forest buffalo, and scimitar-horned oryxes, all to stock the next phase of Safari Africa. Over in primates, Rango and Josie had delivered another baby orangutan. The Panamanian golden frogs, breeding in a back room of the herps department, had produced more than two hundred tadpoles.

And yet, beneath the waves of exultation, there were unmistakable signs of an undertow. A sense of something approaching its limits. It was there in the exhaustion in the eyes of the keepers, in the way their faces went blank when they heard Lex giving another pep talk about the next round of new exhibits and how they all needed to work a little harder. For those watching closely, the signs declared themselves, too, in the fine print of who was included and who was shut out in the swirl of excitement over Tamani's birth.

Every institution has its hidden workings, quiet shifts in the power structure that are revealed in the smallest ways. When the Soviet Union was still in power, CIA analysts devoted considerable energy to poring over photos showing which commissars were allowed to stand at the dais on May Day, when columns of the empire's weaponry and armies rolled through Red Square. Lowry Park, a nonprofit just named the best children's zoo in the country, was hardly an evil empire, even in PETA's most virulent condemnations. Still, if a team of Kremlinologists had turned their attentions to the hierarchy at the zoo, they might have noted that the only two people who spoke at the press conference announcing the elephant's calf birth were Lex and Dr. Murphy. Brian French, who had shepherded the new herd into existence and coached Ellie through her pregnancy, was nowhere to be seen.

Brian, always camera shy, did not take offense at being excluded from the limelight that day. But he was caught off guard, only a month or so later, when Lee Ann Rottman called him to her office and told him that the zoo was letting him go.

"When?" Brian remembers asking.

"Now."

Brian called Steve Lefave, who was out checking on the rhinos, and told him he needed to come take care of the elephants. Then he gathered his things and drove away, stunned.

Afterward, Lowry Park's spokeswoman declined to comment on the dismissal. "It's a personnel matter that has nothing to do with the animals," she said.

The unofficial word around the zoo was that the firing had grown out of a conflict between Brian and Lex—a conflict that had everything to do with the animals. In interviews, both Brian and Lex confirmed that they'd had a difference of opinion about the protocol for the handling of the elephants. Brian had enjoyed working in the same enclosure with baby Tamani and was eager to continue with free contact. He wanted to move slowly before introducing the calf to the two males. Lex insisted that the keepers stick with protected contact but wanted to see Tamani roaming the yards with the cows and the bulls. "He wanted to put all the elephants together to create a herd environment," Brian said afterward. "He wants to run things a lot more like a game park

13

Freedom

Word of Herman's violent overthrow quickly spread throughout the zoo and beyond the front gates. Normally, the death of a chimpanzee would not have merited the slightest notice in the outside world. But Herman was one of the most famous animals in Tampa Bay history, adored by generations of local residents who had grown up marveling at his displays, and his loss was all the more newsworthy because it had exploded out of nowhere.

The evening of the attack, an anonymous caller tipped off the *St. Petersburg Times* even before the zoo had a chance to publicly announce that Herman was gone. For the next two days, the coup was splashed across the front page. Noting Herman's prominence as "a beloved fixture" at the zoo, the newspaper pieced together an early account of the assault that was largely accurate, except for one significant detail: The newspaper reported that Rukiya had been injured after she "intervened" in the battle. The assumption tucked inside that verb—that Rukiya had tried to break up the fight—was easy enough to understand, given that primate males are often viewed as inherently violent and females as implicitly more gentle. In this case, however, the assumption was wrong. Lee Ann and the other keepers who witnessed the fight saw Rukiya not trying to stop the violence, but teaming up with Bamboo against Herman.

The necropsy report was released several weeks later. Dr. Murphy found that Herman had died from acute head trauma and had also suffered from heart disease. The vet's examination of Herman's injuries also revealed a clue as to the extent of Rukiya's involvement in the attack. Although Bamboo had beaten the alpha severely, it would have been difficult for him to have inflicted the bite on Herman's lip. Bamboo, old and relatively feeble, had virtually no teeth left. It was one of the reasons he had trouble defending himself when the females bullied him.

The most disturbing question about the attack—the mystery that confounded almost everyone—was why Bamboo had gone after Herman with such blind fury. In the years since Bamboo had arrived at Lowry Park, Herman had been his closest ally and defender. By all appearances, the two of them had developed a bond as close to friendship as chimps could get. In news interviews afterward, Dr. Murphy talked about how he had often seen the two males romping together in the dirt.

"Everybody considered them buddies," said the vet. "They were like two old gentlemen, rolling around on the ground, laughing and tickling each other."

For many, Herman's passing seemed almost impossible to accept. Herman had been the embodiment of Lowry Park's history, good and bad. He was the zoo's witness, its elder ambassador. Even Lex was a newcomer compared to him. In the mid-1980s, when Lex had arrived, Herman was already fifteen years into his reign. How could he be gone?

As with the deaths of so many legends, rumors circulated, both inside and outside the zoo. Some wondered if Bamboo had sensed that Herman's powers were waning, that he was ailing or vulnerable in some way the staff had not yet detected. Other theories suggested that baby Sasha's arrival had somehow altered the group's power dynamics and spurred Bamboo to plot an assassination. Some implied that greed had led to Herman's death. This line of argument was based on the well-documented fact that baby animals were good business for zoos and on the supposition that a hunger for more profits might have been the real motive for acquiring Sasha, thereby triggering the attack. Intriguing as it sounded, the theory seemed implausible to anyone who knew Lee Ann and how crazy she was about chimps. It was she, not the zoo's front office, who had pushed for Sasha to be brought in. The infant chimp had needed a home and a mother, and Lee Ann thought Lowry Park could give her both. Her lifelong devotion to chimpanzees was well established. She was obsessed with protecting the species, especially the handful who lived at Lowry Park. The notion that she would have agreed to put Herman or the other chimps at risk, just to pull in a few more dollars, was ludicrous.

A few people whispered that the true cause of Herman's death was Lex and his ceaseless ambitions. If the staff had not been decimated by so many resignations and firings, if they hadn't all been so consumed with the new exhibits and the next expansion, then maybe there would have been more staffers in the primate section on the morning of the attack. Maybe a keeper would have seen what was happening more quickly and sounded the alarm, and then they could have separated Bamboo and Herman before things got so out of hand.

Lee Ann, still a true believer, did not give any credence to that particular theory. The curator certainly did not blame Lex for what had happened. The truth was, she did not know what to think about Herman's death. She was so heartbroken that she could not summon enough calm to reflect on what had happened. For weeks, she had trouble mentioning the chimp's name, even with friends.

Outside the zoo, some wondered out loud if Bamboo should be punished. Hadn't he murdered Herman? Lee Ann heard these questions and shook her head. The law was another human construct. Among animals, there was no such thing as murder, or even right and wrong. Herman was gone. Bamboo and the others remained. That was all.

After Herman's death, Ed Schultz didn't go to the zoo much anymore. He couldn't bring himself to look out into the chimp exhibit and not see his friend waiting for him.

"I just can't put myself together on that," he said.

Ed railed at the injustice of Herman's overthrow. Even though he knew chimps should not be judged by human standards, Ed was appalled and believed that Bamboo had betrayed Herman. One day, Ed went into the zoo and made his displeasure known by standing in front of the chimp exhibit with his back turned toward Bamboo and the others. He refused to look at them.

At home, Ed gave himself over to grief.

"Half of my life with that little fella," he said, fighting back another wave of tears. "Didn't we ever love him."

Bamboo was suffering as well. In the days after the attack, he was seen searching for Herman in the exhibit and the night house. When his companion did not reappear, Bamboo lost much of his appetite. He and the other chimps seemed unsure what to do next. They were quiet and appeared confused. They were all waiting for Herman's return.

In the depths of that summer, the distress inside the zoo grew palpable. With all the turnover, the remaining keepers were working extra hours and were busy training new hires. More animals seemed to arrive every day; new directives from management appeared on staff bulletin boards. Safari Africa was preparing to expand. The Asia section, home to Enshalla and Eric, closed to the public while construction crews moved in to renovate the exhibits.

The frustration that had been building quietly inside the staff bubbled over when Lowry Park's supervisors embarked on a quest to identify the caller who had leaked the news of Herman's death to the *St. Petersburg Times.* Several keepers, including Carie Peterson, were being summoned into offices for questioning. Word spread that Lex and his team had assembled a list of suspects, made up primarily of those who had dared to complain about their work conditions and the care of the animals. There were rumors the zoo was checking phone and e-mail logs and even considering the use of polygraphs.

For Carie, the leak investigation was the final indignity. She had no idea who'd tipped off the newspaper. But to her, the zoo's hunt for the tipster smacked of an obsession with control. Had they expected to keep the death of their most beloved animal a secret?

In mid-July, Carie finally quit. She'd found another job working with animals—this time at the Humane Society of Tampa Bay—but even as she started the new position, she could not stop thinking about Enshalla. At night, she was haunted by guilty dreams that took her back to the zoo and into the tiger night house. She would see Enshalla's face turned toward her, wondering where she had gone.

. . . .

The departure of Carie, yet another veteran, opened a huge hole in the staff. Another keeper in the Asia department, a veteran who had repeatedly suggested improvements in animal care, was fired only a few days after Carie left. Recognizing that the Asia staff required more help, the zoo hired a new keeper, a man who had just graduated from a zookeeper program in Gainesville. He was learning the protocols but had a long way to go.

The rest of that summer, Lowry Park tried to regain its footing. The staff needed to stabilize—and soon, because that September, the zoo would co-host the annual convention of the AZA. In just a few weeks, hundreds of zoo officials would descend on Tampa and tour Lowry Park, appraising every exhibit, mentally noting whether the zoo measured up. For Lex, it was another chance at the national spotlight. For the staff, it was just one more pressure. Already the keepers were scrambling to prepare for the distinguished guests.

Then, on Tuesday, August 22, as closing time drew near, the staff heard three words crackling on their walkie-talkies.

"Code One, tiger."

Enshalla was out.

Late that afternoon, the new keeper found himself alone with the tigers.

Chris Lennon, thirty-three, and only a month into his job, would normally have had another keeper watching over him. But Carie was gone, and the other experienced keeper had been fired. Pam Noel, the assistant curator who supervised the Asia department, had been on duty earlier that day, but she'd been called away when one of her children suffered an asthma attack at school. Chris was on his own with Eric and Enshalla.

By four thirty, he was ready to feed the tigers and shift them from the exhibit into the night house. He placed their dinner in separate dens, then pulled a lever that allowed Enshalla to enter the building. As always, a barrier of thick mesh stood between him and the tiger. And as was her habit, ever since she was young, she waited for him to walk past her den and then leaped toward him against that mesh.

Chris continued with his routine. He was standing in a little corridor, preparing to shift Eric from the exhibit into his den, when something made him turn around. A sound, maybe. First he saw a chunk of meat in the hall where it should not have been. Then he saw Enshalla. She had left her den and had passed through a door he had accidentally left unlatched. Now the tiger was loose, only a few feet away, and eyeing him.

If she wanted to attack, there was no place for Chris to go. The only exit was a door that led out into the exhibit, where Eric was still waiting to come inside.

For reasons that no one would later be able to explain, Enshalla did not pad toward him. For almost fifteen years, she had displayed unremitting hostility toward humans. But on this day, she ignored the new keeper and kept moving. Chris hurried to the end of the hall and threw shut the night house's mesh door, so Enshalla could not reach him if she changed her mind. He got on his radio and declared the Code One.

Enshalla walked calmly out of the building and into the sunlight. For the first time in her life, she was free.

This was the moment the staff had prayed would never come.

Once the warning sounded over the walkie-talkies, the zoo went into emergency lockdown. By now it was approaching five. The few visitors who remained on the grounds were hurried to safety behind closed doors. The front gates were blocked off. The weapons team grabbed rifles and shotguns.

From inside the night house, Chris told them Enshalla had gone into an area that until recently was the home of Naboo. The rhino had been moved because his exhibit was being remodeled. Even over the radio, the distress in Chris's voice registered clearly. He sounded shaky, but was holding it together, reporting Enshalla's movements. He watched the tiger as she lingered in Naboo's former exhibit, now turned into a construction site.

Years ago, before Naboo had arrived, this had been the Asian elephant exhibit. The night house through which Enshalla walked had once been the barn where Tillie the elephant had killed Char-Lee Torre. The exhibit beyond, where Enshalla had wandered, was ringed by a muddy moat filled with elephant grass. The moat was deep but not wide. It was designed to keep in elephants and rhinos, not an animal that could leap.

Enshalla's position put her a few strides from the front gates, near the manatee fountain so popular with small children on warm August days such as this one. If the tiger had escaped earlier, when the zoo was more crowded, she could have easily cleared the moat and gone hunting among toddlers.

Following the Code One protocol for tigers, the weapons team surrounded the area. An assistant curator climbed with his rifle to the top of the Komodo building. Someone else took position behind the tiger night house. The protocol suggested that the team first attempt to lure the tiger back into her den with food, but that was not likely to work this time. Enshalla didn't appear hungry; in fact, she'd walked past her food as she'd slipped out. Even so, she remained dangerous and was likely to defend herself if cornered.

The weapons team waited for Dr. Murphy to arrive with his tranquilizer gun. Until then, they trained their weapons on Enshalla. Most of the team's members had known the tiger for years. Several remembered her as a cub. Lex had known Enshalla since she was born at the zoo fifteen years before. Late that afternoon, when she escaped, the CEO was driving north on I-275 toward his Pasco County ranch when his cell phone rang.

"Come back right away. There's a Code One tiger."

Lex got off at the first exit and turned his truck around and sped back toward the zoo. By then Dr. Murphy was ready with his darts. The rest of the weapons team had Enshalla in its sights. Every time she moved, rifles followed. So far she had done nothing aggressive. She lay down for a few minutes, got back up, chewed grass, rested in the sun. She did not roar or growl. She was quiet.

When Lex returned to the zoo, he took cover in a car parked on the sidewalk between Enshalla and the fountain. Inside the car were Lee Ann and a primate keeper armed with a 12-gauge shotgun. The team was trying to decide on the best vantage point for Dr. Murphy to dart Enshalla. They considered putting the vet on the zoo's skyride—a safe position, but too high and far away. They also considered having him climb to the top of the tiger night house, but they didn't want Enshalla to see him and become agitated. Like so many of the animals, Enshalla did not like Murphy, because she associated him with the jab of a tranquilizer. Just recently, he had immobilized her to perform the tests to determine why she hadn't become pregnant.

"This cat hates me," Murphy told Lex.

Knocking out Enshalla would be dangerous. Tranquilizers don't always work instantly, as in the movies. Their effects depend on unpredictable variables—the animal's emotional state, the exact place the dart enters the body. In 1974, at the Knoxville Zoo, a veterinarian had fired a tranquilizer dart into an escaped Bengal tiger. The tiger, approximately twenty-five feet away, leaped onto the vet and mauled him.

"It happened so fast," one witness said, "he didn't have time to move."

News of the Code One was out. A guest, herded inside a building, had apparently phoned the media. Reporters were calling. In the sky, a news helicopter hovered. The weapons team hoped the chopping sound would not set the tiger on edge. Soon Enshalla was moving again. She walked to the edge of the exhibit, then jumped down into the tall grass inside the moat, making it harder for the weapons team to see her. She had found the perfect place to disappear.

By now it was close to six o'clock. Enshalla had been out for roughly an hour. Dusk would be falling soon. If the team was going to tranquilize her, they knew they had to do it fast, or they risked losing her in the darkness. Murphy stepped onto the boardwalk that lined the exhibit, trying to stay out of the tiger's sight. Lex got out of the car, armed with the shotgun, to cover the vet.

Enshalla was still in the moat. Unable to get his shot with the tranquilizer gun, Murphy climbed to the top of a platform draped with ivy—a platform where, many years earlier, children had climbed onto the backs of elephants for rides. The platform was roughly seven feet high, giving Murphy the angle he needed. He aimed and fired. The dart hit Enshalla's neck, but the drugs did not knock her out. Instead Enshalla was enraged. She lunged toward the vet, clawing up the ivy. She was only a few feet from Murphy when Lex fired.

Enshalla dropped into the elephant grass, but was still moving. Lex fired three more times.

Finally the tiger was still.

14

Conspiracy Theory

That Tuesday evening, as Carie finished her shift at the animal shelter, strange messages from friends at Lowry Park flooded her cell phone's voice mail.

"I'm sorry," they told her. "You need to watch the news."

Then they hung up.

The lack of any explanation was unsettling enough. But even worse was the urgency that Carie detected beneath the voices. On her drive home, when she finally had a moment free, she phoned someone at the zoo.

"What's wrong?" Carie asked. "What happened?"

"I'll tell you," said the friend, "but you have to pull over first."

At first Carie didn't want to stop, but her friend insisted. She stopped the car on the shoulder, her sense of dread growing. "What is it?" she said. "Is Enshalla dead?"

The friend paused, then said yes.

Carie began to scream.

The next morning, Lowry Park was all over the front page again. Even so, the zoo was open, and the canned jungle drums were beating their familiar message, and couples and families were lined up at the ticket windows. A bloody death, it turned out, was a good draw at the front gate.

Despite the attempts at normalcy, the staff was visibly reeling. The deluge had already begun: news conferences, tearful interviews, petitions for Lex Salisbury's firing. The furor grew when Lowry Park confirmed that Chris Lennon was new to the zoo and had apparently never before worked with large carnivores. By all accounts, Chris was so devastated by Enshalla's death that he was holed up at his apartment, not even answering the phone. Lowry Park placed him on leave, then promptly fired him. A state wildlife inspector recommended that the young keeper be charged with improper handling of captive wildlife, a misdemeanor. Ultimately, though, the Hillsborough County state attorney's office declined to press charges, saying there was no evidence of criminal intent.

Lowry Park itself was reprimanded. The Tampa Police Department expressed frustration that the zoo had not immediately called 911 to report the escape of a dangerous animal. An inspector from the U.S. Department of Agriculture, who visited the tiger night house after the shooting, declared the zoo's training and safety procedures inadequate. The new keeper's inexperience had been a safety hazard, the inspector said. So was the policy that had allowed one keeper, working alone, to shift dangerous animals from their exhibit into their dens. The inspector's report concluded:

Correct: Immediately.

Outside the zoo, Enshalla's shooting was more fodder for the endless debate over the ethics of keeping animals captive. Many were incensed at the CEO, calling him "Wild West Lex." Others wondered why the zoo hadn't found another way to pacify the tiger. Couldn't someone have thrown a net?

When asked these questions by reporters, several current and former keepers from Lowry Park all agreed that the zoo had done the only thing it could in an impossible situation. They explained how long it could take tranquilizers to kick in, how a net would not have contained an angry tiger's teeth or claws. Once Enshalla leaped, they said, Lex had no choice but to pull the trigger.

"That's his only option," said Brian Czarnik.

Brian was the keeper who had been fired from the Asia department not long before Enshalla's death. He was more critical of the events that had led up to the tiger's escape. Like Carie, he believed the zoo had been stretched too thin for too long. To him, Enshalla's escape as a result of a new keeper's mistake only proved it. In interviews with the *St. Petersburg Times* and other news outlets, Brian listed his complaints. He didn't understand why the zoo had only one staff veterinarian for approximately eighteen hundred animals—a question many others had asked as well. He believed Lex's constant push for expansion had worn people down and driven a wedge between the keepers and management. And he was critical of the zoo's eagerness to market the arrival of new baby animals such as Tamani.

"If it's nice and fluffy," he said, "they'll use it."

Brian said he'd been fired because he spoke up about problems and pushed for change. Other keepers, he said, had been dismissed after they protested. All of these firings, combined with the departures of Carie and Dustin and others who had left on their own, had created a vacuum of experience.

At a news conference after Enshalla's death, Lex was asked about Czarnik's firing.

"Our policy is not to go into employee matters," said the CEO. "But the guy was fired for good reason."

Still, Lex confirmed that his reputation as a tough boss was well-deserved. "I am demanding, and I want this place to be the very best," he said. "If people don't perform, they generally are unable to stay here."

Looking into the news cameras, Lex maintained the calm exterior that had served him so well with mayors and governors and kings. A day after facing an escaped tiger, he was more than ready to stare down a room full of reporters. He said that Lowry Park hadn't reported Enshalla's escape to Tampa police because the zoo's weapons team had the situation under control. He pledged that the zoo would call 911 more quickly, should such an emergency ever arise again. But his comments about the police were far from apologetic.

"We don't call them unless we need them," he said. "We really don't want people storming in with guns who don't really understand animal behavior."

Someone asked Lex why he had insisted on being the one to put Enshalla down. Why hadn't he let a member of the weapons team take the shot? Lex explained that he saw it as his job. He hadn't wanted somebody else to be forced to gun down the tiger. Throughout the press conference, Lex tried to dial down the emotions of what had happened. Though he had known the tiger all her life, he avoided referring to her by name. The effect was disturbing. Suddenly Enshalla was no longer the fierce beauty who terrified and enthralled the public and her keepers and even her lethal suitors. Now she was simply the animal in question. It felt as though she were being erased.

Lex acknowledged that her untimely death was unfortunate. But as the press conference went on, he did his best to move the conversation from the dead tiger to the ongoing mission of Lowry Park.

"The thing that makes us want to keep going on is that we feel like we have a moral purpose, that we're making a difference," he said. "And I think we are."

The high-minded words did not stem the torrent of criticism. On the Internet, Lex was accused of murdering Enshalla. Lee Ann was stunned. She had seen Lex moments after he shot Enshalla, and no matter how controlled he'd appeared in front of the cameras, she knew how much the incident had shaken him. What was he supposed to have done when Enshalla attacked? she wondered. Just let the tiger kill Dr. Murphy? If anything, Lee Ann was grateful to her boss for taking on such an awful responsibility.

"Lex did us a favor," she said. "This is his zoo, and he cares about this place, and he had to make a difficult decision."

What almost no one noticed, in the fog of questions, was the way Lowry Park's history had circled back on itself. But Lex saw it.

On the afternoon of the press conference, Lex guided two reporters to the boardwalk above the rhino moat to show them exactly how he had ended up shooting Enshalla. He was not being boastful or defensive. The reporters had asked him to walk them through the complicated sequence, so they could describe it more accurately in their coverage, and he was simply granting their request.

Away from the glare of the TV lights, Lex let down his guard. Enshalla's death, he said, was the second most heartbreaking moment he had ever known at Lowry Park. The only thing worse had been the morning in 1993 when the elephant killed Char-Lee Torre. Both tragedies had unfolded in this corner of the zoo. When Lex fired at Enshalla, in fact, he had been standing beside a plaque memorializing Char-Lee's death. He pointed to the plaque now, so the reporters would see it. Not to linger on the coincidence. Just to note it.

In the years to come, as generations of new visitors strolled through the zoo, they would have no idea that a keeper and a tiger had both died in this spot. Once the exhibit was remodeled, it wouldn't look remotely the same. But the history would still roil underneath.

Two terrible days, thirteen years apart, now framing everything in between.

In the primate department, there was talk of a statue. The keepers wanted some way to remember Herman, and the zoo was considering a plaque or perhaps even a bronzed figure to be erected in front of the chimp exhibit. Something respectful that honored his decades in this place and would allow him to reign on.

The surviving chimps, meanwhile, had not fully recovered. They were still in transition, waiting for the next alpha to declare himself and take power. The primate keepers crossed their fingers, hoping it would not be Alex. Since Herman's death, the adolescent male had been stirring things up. He had even claimed Herman's throne, staking out the former alpha's station beside the waterfall. Bamboo, content to sit on the rocks one level below, didn't bother trying to knock Alex off the perch. But as summer turned into fall, it became clear that Bamboo had accepted the mantle of the alpha. Bamboo wasn't as self-assured as Herman, but he seemed reasonably comfortable with his new role. The chimps seemed to have stabilized again, at least for the time being. Sasha's introductions with the rest of the group had continued since Herman's death. Rukiya had accepted the role of the infant's surrogate mother; Sasha had bonded with Rukiya and now followed her everywhere. Sasha was also extremely attached to Bamboo. One night, she had climbed into his nest in the night house and slept beside the new king.

Those who loved Herman were still trying to decipher why he had been overthrown by Bamboo, the lowest member of the hierarchy. Clearly something had shifted in the group, something the keepers had not seen coming. But what had been the catalyst? Why would Bamboo have gone after Herman, who had treated him with respect? What had Bamboo stood to gain that wasn't already available to him? He had a steady supply of food, and Herman had never tried to stop him from mating with the females. What could have set him off?

Now that some time had passed, Lee Ann was able to talk a little about Herman's death. She admitted she was still mystified by what happened. But she had arrived at a theory. Whatever had transpired, she believed that Rukiya had been at the center of it. Lee Ann thought back to the earlier fight between Bamboo and Herman, not long before the fatal attack. She remembered Rukiya grooming Bamboo and how unusual that had seemed. She thought about the many times she had seen Rukiya manipulating Herman and Bamboo, redirecting the males' aggression. Somehow, she believed, Rukiya had quietly orchestrated the coup.

"I think Rukiya instigated," said Lee Ann. "I love her dearly . . . but I think she had a very big hand in starting the fight."

To her, it seemed unlikely that Bamboo would have made a power grab on his own, without encouragement. Lee Ann didn't believe that either he or Rukiya had meant to kill Herman. She thought it more likely that the attack had been launched to intimidate the alpha and force him to surrender, just as he had done years before when challenged by Chester. But then Herman had apparently hit his head, or the level of necessary violence had been miscalculated.

Lee Ann wasn't even sure Bamboo had understood what he was doing. She remembered his fear grins that day, his obvious confusion. Somehow, Rukiya must have found a way to set him off. But why would Rukiya have shifted her allegiance away from Herman? Over the years he had been unusually kind to her. What could have been her motive for getting rid of him? Lee Ann had heard the rumors that Sasha's introduction had triggered the attack, but to her that explanation seemed implausible. At the time, Sasha hadn't even met any of the male chimps and had never even been in the same enclosure with any of the females.

Lee Ann's theory was that Rukiya was clearing a path to the throne for her adopted son. She wanted to make it easier for Alex to eventually become the king. Rukiya was smart enough to have calculated the odds. It was predictable that Bamboo would assume alpha status once Herman was pushed aside; he was the only other adult male in the group. But Bamboo was old and weak and not likely to hold on to his throne for long, especially in the face of a serious challenge. Alex was young and strong and growing stronger.

Lee Ann's scenario was eerily reminiscent of *I, Claudius*, Robert Graves's classic novel about the first Roman emperors. In the book, the Empress Livia, wife to Augustus, poisons and murders and plots against any rivals who stand between her son Tiberius and his succession to the throne.

Even if Lee Ann's theory was wrong and Rukiya had nothing to do with planning the attack, it was not hard to imagine Alex taking over soon. Whatever happened, the old king would not be forgotten. At her desk, Lee Ann kept a framed photo of Herman and an urn with some of his ashes. In his honor, she had made a list of all the things she loved about him. To name a few:

> He was a gentle soul.
> He liked to have his nails done.
> He loved to flirt with pretty girls in tank tops.
> He always made up after a fight.
> Even when he was mad he always gave warning
>   and was never sneaky.
> He was a good judge of character.

That fall, the battle between the zoo and its critics escalated.

More former staff members stepped forward with criticisms, including Jeff and Coleen Kremer. Jeff had worked in security and visitor services; Coleen had worked in the education department and then outreach. Both gave interviews to news organizations, saying they loved Lowry Park but had quit out of frustration with the zoo's direction. The Kremers echoed the complaints that Lowry Park's staff was overworked and had become demoralized under Lex's tyrannical management and his constant push for expansion. They insisted that Enshalla's escape had not been the only serious Code One. From his stint as a security guard, Jeff reported that Tamani, the baby elephant, had gotten loose twice during his shifts. To the Kremers and others, these incidents—combined with Enshalla's death—raised a serious question about how well the zoo was maintaining its growing animal population. To make sure their concerns were heard, the couple had launched a Web site called TampasZooAdvocates.com and had dedicated the site to the memory of Herman and Enshalla.

The Kremers were particularly concerned about several African penguins that Lowry Park had brought in for a new exhibit. The penguins, a warm-weather species from South Africa, had been held in a back area of the zoo while their exhibit was under construction. In the meantime, two of the penguins had died.

"You think this place is about education or the animals. You're dead wrong," said Jeff. "It's about one thing and one thing only: money."

The zoo fired back, tackling these charges one by one. Greg Stoppelmoor, the zoo's assistant curator for the aviary, confirmed that two of the African penguins had died. Greg, who had previously worked with this group of penguins for years in Dallas, reported that the birds had both suffered from asper, a respiratory ailment common to the species. Their deaths, he said, had nothing to do with the move to Lowry Park.

Lee Ann and others confirmed that on a couple of occasions Tamani had briefly slipped out through openings in the cable fence around one of the elephant yards. He had never wandered far, they said; usually he stayed within a few feet of his mother, on the other side of the fence. As for the maintenance issues in the animals' night houses, Lee Ann confirmed that repair schedules had been a bit hectic during the construction of Safari Africa. Since then, she said, the animal department had been given its own maintenance worker and was having no problem keeping up with work requests. Either way, she pointed out, the zoo's facilities had always been safe. She noted that the USDA inspection immediately after Enshalla's escape had found no problems with the locks or latches or anything else in the tiger night house.

"The zoo was not in disrepair," said Lee Ann.

Lex, meanwhile, did not buy the argument that Enshalla's death had anything to do with Lowry Park being overextended.

"We are not understaffed," he said. "Enshalla got out because of human error."

Lex remained unbowed. Late that September, when Lowry Park co-hosted the AZA convention in Tampa, he gave a triumphant speech summarizing the zoo's efforts on behalf of endangered species. The audience was filled with his peers, men and women who understood what it was like to preside over the fate of so many creatures. There were no critics in the room, no reporters waiting to pounce. It was his moment, not theirs. Knowing this, he flashed the charm that had won over so many other alphas, and delivered a sermon of inspiration. He talked about how the Florida legislature had designated Lowry Park as a refuge for the state's threatened species, recognizing its longstanding efforts to preserve whooping cranes and red wolves and Florida panthers and Key deer and Key Largo woodrats and, of course, manatees. Since the zoo's manatee hospital opened more than fifteen years before, Lex pointed out, the staff had worked with 181 manatees and had returned 84 to the wild.

He talked about how the zoo was fighting for the preservation of thirty-three species managed by the AZA's species survival plans, including orangutans and Komodo dragons. He talked about the project to save the Panamanian golden frogs, the zoo's financial support for chimpanzee research in the wilds of the Congo, and its contributions to the survival of black rhinos and other endangered species in the game parks of Swaziland.

"This," he said, "is what we should be doing."

Waves of applause rose toward the ceiling. Engulfed in the validation of his tribe, Lex shook hands, accepted congratulations, waved to old friends. A month earlier, when the zoo had been staggering in the wake of both Herman's and Enshalla's deaths, he had seemed, for the first time ever, on the verge of losing control and possibly losing his job. Now he had regained his equilibrium and appeared more invincible than ever. For the foreseeable future, the zoo was Lex's to rule. He would take it in whatever direction he saw fit.

15

Winning

The storm lost its thunder. Months went by, then a year. Lex ruled on. The keepers, seeing how it was, either quit—knowing they would be replaced soon enough—or they stayed and made whatever peace they could with the pay and the hours and the weight of someone else's ambitions.

The zoo grew and grew, like a creature unto itself, insatiable. A stream of new animals poured through the back gates in vans and trailers and flatbed trucks to be unloaded and examined and duly logged into the registrar's files. The collection was surging so quickly that it seemed as though Lowry Park was gathering all of creation.

The critics pounded away. On its Web site, PETA kept up their campaign against elephants in captivity. On their site, the Kremers chronicled every health-code violation at Lowry Park, every USDA citation, every lawsuit filed in circuit court, every news article on the zoo's failings. They made no money from their efforts, but they thought it was important, and so they persisted.

Carie Peterson stayed out of it. She now preferred to concentrate on her job at the shelter, finding foster homes for abandoned cats and dogs. It didn't pay much either, but the work felt right. Her home overflowed with a menagerie of her own—at last count, four dogs, four cats, three turtles, two chinchillas, two snakes, two blue-tongued skinks, one hamster, and one tarantula, not to mention assorted creatures she fostered on the side.

She tried not to think too much about her time at Lowry Park, about Enshalla and Naboo. But sometimes she couldn't help it. Somewhere along the line, something had gone deeply wrong. In her view, money became more important than the animals. She wasn't sure when the balance shifted. Maybe it was when they flew in the elephants from Swaziland. Maybe even before.

Whenever the subject of the zoo came up, Carie became a ghost. She avoided conversations about it, would not return phone calls from people who wanted to ask her about it. She refused to even drive past the place anymore.

Lex had learned not to worry about the missiles fired at the walls of his kingdom. He paid little heed to the critics, the petitions calling for his firing, the blogs that still described him as a murderer. Zoos, he pointed out, had been a part of human culture since ancient Mesopotamia. They weren't likely to go away anytime soon. Especially his zoo.

In the past five years, from 2003 to 2008, Lowry Park had become one of the fastest growing zoos in America. With annual attendance topping 1.2 million, the transformation that Lex had pushed for had become a reality. When he'd arrived in 1987, he said, Lowry Park had thirty-two animals. Now the collection contained approximately two thousand, representing more than three hundred species from around the world.

His blueprints called for more growth, more animals, more ways to put visitors close to as many species as possible. In a move that proved his ambitions had not dimmed, Lex had hired Larry Killmar, the deputy director of animal collections at the San Diego Zoo and San Diego Wild Animal Park. Already, Larry was talking about filling Lowry Park with more species, including gharial crocodiles, an endangered species from India.

The centerpiece of Lex's reinvention of Lowry Park remained its fledgling elephant herd. Elephants were now the zoo's official emblem and appeared on the cover of its annual reports, on the staff's business cards, on the big sign out front that welcomed visitors. In recent years, several zoos around the country, especially in northern cities such as Detroit and Chicago, had closed their elephant exhibits, citing concerns about the animals' well-being and the zoos' inability to provide them a suitable habitat. In an online explanation for their decision, Detroit Zoo officials said they believed their elephants belonged in a warmer climate and that elephants would need, at a minimum, ten to twenty acres to roam. Without explicitly mentioning Lowry Park or San Diego, the Detroit officials questioned the practice of placing wild elephants in captivity.

It is unclear if the capture of wild elephants for exhibition in zoos is in fact a "rescue" if the elephants' needs cannot be met by the captive facility.

The warmer temperatures of Florida were well suited to the elephants. But Lex acknowledged that Lowry Park's growing herd would someday need more room. For now the elephants seemed to be doing well. Sdudla had been loaned to the Montgomery Zoo for breeding, and Ellie reigned as the matriarch. After those first shaky moments immediately after the birth, she had proved to be an excellent mother. Tamani was now two years old and weighed fifteen hundred pounds. He still nursed, but spent much of his time outside in the care of his aunts, Mbali and Matjeka. He swam in the elephant pool. He chased after guinea fowl.

Despite the critics' jabs, the zoo's conservation credentials were touted to be as strong as ever. An AZA spokesman said that the zoo's conservation program "puts them among the best in the country." The manatees still swam in front of the huge picture windows, surfacing like leviathans. The blue poison-dart frogs and Panamanian golden frogs were still breeding to the wailing of Led Zeppelin. Dan Costell, the hulking wrestler who had once waged war with Carie Peterson and other bunnyhuggers, still tenderly cared for the frogs, adjusting the mist and temperature in their small room, encouraging them to breed, stemming the tide of extinction. Dan and others in the herps department had also begun working with another endangered amphibian species, the Puerto Rican crested toad. Recently the toads had produced tadpoles. Some stayed at the zoo. Others were sent back to Puerto Rico to be reintroduced into the wild.

Even as the staff fought for threatened species, Lowry Park was evolving into a hybrid of a zoo and a theme park. Ten years before, almost the only ride offered had been the merry-go-round. Now there was the skyride, a pony trek, and an area where children could take spins in flying bananas. In an area once reserved for a herd of five bison, a water flume called Gator Falls had just opened. The bison were gone, replaced by screaming children.

Like any institution, Lowry Park had the right to move in new directions and seek new revenues. But the line between entertainment and conservation was growing increasingly fuzzy. The latest situation with the tigers was emblematic. Eric, the male Sumatran, still lived at Lowry Park. But with Enshalla dead, he had no mate. Zoo officials said they'd searched for another female Sumatran for him to breed with, but since they couldn't find one, they were now talking about moving him elsewhere. Until they found him a new home, Eric was spending a great deal of time confined inside his den in the night house, because the zoo had brought in two white tigers who took turns with Eric sharing the exhibit. The available space had grown even more crowded when the female white tiger gave birth to three cubs. One was stillborn. The other two, now a year old and growing, wrestled and chased each other.

The white tigers were unquestionably beautiful, and there was no doubt that the public loved them. But they were also a genetic aberration, their coloring the result of a recessive gene. Even ardent supporters of zoos were scathing in their criticisms of institutions that exhibited white tigers. There was no conservation value to them, said the critics; the only reason for showing the species was because they're a moneymaker.

Lex did not agree. He argued that the white tigers deserved the zoo's attention, that the increased revenues they brought in would help fund the conservation efforts with manatees and other species. Besides, he said, there was nothing wrong in engaging the public with such captivating animals. Before you can educate people, he said, you had to get them through the front gates.

This much was certain: Lex got results.

Repeatedly he had set his sights on something and then found a way to pull it off. As he entered his second decade at the zoo, his will never seemed to waver. He was one of those people who created his own weather. When he was having a good day and felt benevolent, he radiated a joy that enveloped everyone around him. He would beam, and they beamed with him. When he felt misunderstood or grew angry, he made it rain.

He dismissed his detractors with a story. One day, years before, he said, he had given a tour of Lowry Park to George Steinbrenner. As they walked through the zoo, the Yankees owner talked about how he was known as a sore loser.

"You show me someone who's a good loser," Lex remembered Steinbrenner saying, "and I'll show you a loser."

Lex smiled.

"Damn right," he said. "I'm used to winning, and I don't like not winning."

Herman was gone now, but the true alpha of Lowry Park was still standing, mapping the zoo's path into the future. He had survived every challenge and had outflanked the adversaries who demanded his removal. He had shrugged off their attacks, slipped through their nets. As usual, he made no apologies. If anything, he was bursting with bravado. *Maddux Business Report*, a local magazine, was interviewing him about Lowry Park's runaway success under his leadership. He posed for the cover—the picture showed him in his safari hat, next to a giraffe—and boasted again about how the zoo relied on almost no tax dollars. Zoo execs who weren't financially prudent, he said, never lasted. Part of his excitement stemmed from the fact that he was planning a new venture, something even more audacious that promised to make him more controversial than ever. A year and a half before, he had joined forces with another partner, a local veterinarian, and purchased 258 acres outside Lakeland, just north of the I-4 corridor in the center of Florida. Now he was quietly building a massive game park called Safari Wild.

One Friday morning that December, when the project was still a closely guarded secret, unknown even to most of Lowry Park's board of directors, Lex invited a *St. Petersburg Times* reporter—the author of this book—to the park for a sneak preview of his latest work in progress. Accompanied by his wife, Elena, and by Larry Killmar, Lex steered a Land Rover through sprawling fields of thick green Bahia grass, where waterbucks and kudus and wildebeests already roamed. An Indian rhino twitched his ears beside a mud wallow. Watusi cattle, crowned with great curving horns, clopped heavily toward the vehicle, their throat flaps swaying in time with their steps, their tails flicking in the sun.

If all went as planned, Safari Wild would open the following year and would offer tours to small groups of visitors, no more than five hundred a day. Lex wasn't sure yet what mode of transport would carry them on these safaris—maybe something solar-powered—but the guests would get close to the animals and be able to admire them in the open.

"It's a little edgy," he said.

From the backseat, Elena listened closely, petting a Welsh terrier named Pippi who sat in her lap and panted happily, pink tongue lolling.

As Lex laid out his plans, Elena frowned and leaned forward and said this conversation needed to remain off the record, at least for now. Lex glanced back at Elena and shot her a look. For a split second, his face went dead, and time seemed to stop inside the vehicle. Then he softened. Calmly, with only a hint of impatience, he told his wife that the interview was very much on the record and that he was excited about Safari Wild and wanted the public to know what he was doing. Elena crumpled into her seat and gazed into the distance. Larry held still and acted as though he hadn't heard a word. Pippi looked back and forth at the humans, reading us with her shiny brown eyes.

Pushing onward, Lex explained that eventually the park would be stocked with close to a thousand animals, representing dozens of exotic or endangered species. He wanted to bring in giraffes and ring-tailed lemurs and even cheetahs, a species that he pointed out had once roamed this land. The fossil record, he said, showed that cheetahs had first evolved in North America before they migrated to Asia and Africa.

"Their main prey was the prong-horned antelope. That's why the prong-horned antelope runs as fast as it does."

He was talking more quickly now, growing more animated as he spun down the list of all the creatures he was gathering from other institutions and other countries. Sable antelopes and scimitar-horned oryxes. Sandhill cranes, black-and-white ruffed lemurs. An aviary populated by oscillated turkeys, wooly-necked storks, and crested screamers. As he reeled off the species, his face glowed with a mixture of both childlike wonder and ravenous lust. He wanted primates from Asia. Some orangs, maybe a few gibbons. Just that morning, he said, the park had received a shipment of Barbary sheep, a species originally from the mountains of northern Africa. He was raiding his own collection at the ranch, bringing in fifty axis deer, astonishingly beautiful animals, with a blizzard of spots blowing through their fur. Even though they were native to Sri Lanka, the bucks had antlers that looked like something invented by the Brothers Grimm.

Lex was cutting a deal with Lowry Park to bring three white rhinos to Safari Wild. The zoo was rapidly outgrowing its current space, he said. It needed an off-site facility where surplus animals could be housed, and he was ready to help by boarding the rhinos and other animals. Safari Wild was already looking after the bison that had been displaced by Gator Falls. At the moment, he was finalizing plans to fly in some patas monkeys, an African species famed for their speed and shyness. His workers were constructing an island for the monkeys and a wide moat to hold them. The key, he said, was in picking the right species. You needed a discerning eye to build a strong collection. A willingness to make choices.

"We're not averse to taking risks," said Larry, chiming in from the backseat.

Despite all the turmoil that had surrounded the importation from Swaziland, Lex longed to acquire a few more elephants. He didn't know where they would come from, or how he'd hack his way through all the red tape to get the permits. He just knew he wanted them, and what he wanted, he usually got.

"I'd *love* to have elephants here," he said, as though it were the easiest thing in the world.

He was showing his range now, deploying all his weapons. Just a few moments ago, he had offered a glimpse of his steely side, silencing his wife with a flash of his eyes. Now he had become Noah incarnate, open-hearted guardian of the world's wonders. His confidence filled the Land Rover with light.

Larry, so quiet before, grew positively expansive on the subject of how useful Safari Wild would be to Lowry Park, offering the zoo a safe and affordable haven for its collection. Typically, he said, zoos worried too much about overbreeding and what to do with surplus animals. Larry advocated boldness in these matters.

"We should have sustainable populations at the ready," he said. "You manage the surplus. If you're afraid of surplus, *then get out of the business.*"

Elena, rejuvenated by the outpouring of bravado, was smiling again. She described the game park as a place where wildlife could be wild, a place where animals would have room to move, where they could simply *be.* Clutching Pippi, she railed against humanity's attempts to manipulate nature.

"The more we interfere, the more we muck it up," she said. "Nature does it better than man ever could."

Coming from the wife of a zoo director, the argument was startling Lex had devoted his career to arranging and rearranging the natural world. He was the man who made elephants fly. Safari Wild was itself a radical reconstruction of nature. The game park was spacious, yes. But it was still a glorified zoo that would ultimately be filled with animals seized from every corner of the globe, species that would never end up within ten thousand miles of one another, were it not to fulfill the whims of humans. Wasn't the little dog nestled in Elena's lap a classic example of manipulated nature? Hadn't Pippi once been a wolf?

If either Lex or Larry noticed the oddity of Elena's arguments, neither of them showed it. Maybe such contradictions were almost too much for two zoo executives to contemplate. Instead they just kept smiling as Lex drove past cypress woods where dwarf buffalo peered from the shadows, past lush green meadows where zebras kicked and snorted. It was a beautiful day, with a crystalline blue sky stretching above and a cool breeze whispering through the magnolias. A perfect day for showing off their new kingdom, teeming with new multitudes.

Others at the zoo, hearing about Safari Wild, had warned Lex that he was flying too close to the sun. Just because his other gambles had paid off did not mean he was untouchable. They warned him that there was no way to pull off the venture without tangling the interests of the zoo and the game park. This time, they said, his best intentions might not be enough to protect him. As usual, Lex had brushed away the questions. Just a couple weeks before, he had signed a memorandum of understanding with the executive committee of Lowry Park's board, pledging that Safari Wild's relationship with the zoo would be noncompetitive. He planned to present the memorandum to the full board at next month's meeting. Talking it through now, he insisted that he would not profit from any relationship between the zoo and the park, that great care would be taken to guard against conflicts of interest. The arrangement would be good for both Lowry Park and Safari Wild.

"We've run it by the zoo's auditors," he said. "There has to be a very careful accounting."

"It's not the money that's driving this," said Elena.

"It's a real benefit for everybody," said Larry.

It was hard to tell if the three of them truly had no doubts about Lex trying to run both a nonprofit zoo and a for-profit animal attraction. Couldn't any of them see how messy it could get with animals traveling back and forth between the two institutions? Could they not imagine how it would play in the newspapers?

Lex showed no such uncertainty. As he finished the tour of Safari Wild, he stopped the Land Rover in a meadow and called Fassil Gabremariam, the chairman of the zoo's executive committee, and put him on speaker phone so they could talk about the arrangements. Gabremariam was a distinguished figure, a banker and businessman who had served as commissioner of the Tampa Port Authority and who was now a director of the Jacksonville branch of the Federal Reserve Bank of Atlanta. On the phone, he talked about Lex's expertise and his love for animals and the excellence of his leadership. He explained that the relationship with Safari Wild would carry Lowry Park into the future.

"We need to continue to change, to grow, to maintain the quality of the product," he said. "In order to do that, we need some extra land."

When Lex described his plans for the zoo and the park, he sounded like an adventurer. Fassil, who had signed off on the deal, sounded more like a diplomat. Speaking quietly and with understated self-assurance, he talked about Lowry Park's strategic design and the integrity of its assets and the delicate balance needed to perpetuate its mission.

"I want it to be the best zoo in the nation and maybe the rest of the world," he said.

Near the end of the conversation, Fassil paused. The relationship between Lowry Park and Safari Wild was still in its early stages, he said, choosing his words carefully. Developing that relationship would be sensitive. He thought it best, he said, if this conversation—indeed, any reference to Safari Wild—stayed out of the newspaper until Lex and the executive committee had a chance to present their proposal to the zoo's full board. Lex listened respectfully and did not overrule the request immediately, as he had with his wife. Instead, he thanked Fassil and said something noncommittal about how he would figure it out. Then, after hanging up, Lex said it was fine, he'd smooth it over with Fassil and make sure the board was up to speed before the news hit the paper.

In the space of an hour or so, Elena and Fassil—two people he trusted—had counseled a modicum of caution. But Lex was undeterred. If anything, he was exuberant. Safari Wild, he said, was just one step in his own strategic design. Within five years, he hoped that the zoo would acquire an even bigger parcel of land, possibly as much as two thousand acres, somewhere outside of Tampa. He saw this larger game park—which would serve as an extension of the existing zoo—as the next stage in the zoo's evolution.

"We're not done," he said, grinning. "We're just getting started."

He hit the accelerator and pushed on.

16

Not Winning

The real trouble began when the monkeys decided to take a swim.

Their mass plunge, an act of defiance that would soon acquire the shimmer of legend, took place on April 19, 2008. The fifteen patas monkeys had arrived at Safari Wild and been exiled on the island only two days earlier. Up to that point, they had been kept in cages. The only reason they escaped was because Lex wanted to let them out of the cages and give them a chance to enjoy the open space of the island. A couple people had warned him the species could swim, but he believed that the sixty-foot moat would hold them, even if they could.

That Saturday morning, one of Lex's employees freed the monkeys from their cages. Given the uncertainty of the species' abilities, there had been some debate about whether to introduce them onto the island one at a time, or all at once. The staffer settled the debate by letting them out together. As he watched, one of the females promptly jumped into the water and began paddling, with the other fourteen quickly following.

The staffer immediately called Lex.

"The introduction," he said, in a massive understatement, "has gone very badly."

It's not clear if the monkeys had a leader or a plan, or if they just spontaneously decided it was time to go. There were two babies in the group, both of whom presumably clung to their mothers' necks to avoid drowning. Possibly the others held paws or even tails. Somehow, all fifteen made it safely across, climbed an eight-foot wall on the other side, then fled into the surrounding swampland.

"They outfoxed me," Lex said afterward. "I think they're more street smart than a zoo monkey."

Patas monkeys are native to Africa, but these fifteen had come from Puerto Rico, where their species had been introduced into the wild and allowed to multiply beyond human control. They raised such havoc, raiding pineapple and plantain crops, that the government had insisted some either be killed or be sent away to new homes. Lex, already familiar with the death-or-captivity equation, had seen a good opportunity to rescue some monkeys and stock his game park with a fascinating species.

To human eyes, patas monkeys appear somewhat comical. They have a rusty-colored coat, but their cheeks sport swaths of white hair that look like Prussian sideburns, which gives them a remarkable resemblance to those grumpy, grizzled colonels who sport muttonchops in old movies. They have a habit of bouncing up and down, which is why they're sometimes called dancing monkeys. They're not particularly big—the males typically weigh about twenty-seven pounds and the females roughly fourteen—but they have elaborate defenses to keep them out of the jaws of predators. Able to run at thirty-five miles per hour, equipped with the thin and elongated bodies of greyhounds, they are officially the fastest monkey on Earth. Though they are a social species and tend to live in groups, they are extremely skittish and tend to bolt. When chased, they rely on evasive tactics, often splitting into two groups. Sometimes one patas will act as a decoy and lead the threat away from the others. At night, they sleep one monkey to a tree to avoid detection.

None of this deterred Lex. Flashing his famous confidence, he promised that the fifteen escapees would be captured and back in custody at Safari Wild within a week. The monkeys were easy enough to find, at least at first. But every time one of Lex's trappers crept toward the monkeys' hiding places, the animals fled. The trappers attempted to lure them into crates baited with apples and bananas and monkey chow. But the monkeys were too smart.

Soon reporters were calling Lex, calling the zoo, calling the Florida Fish and Wildlife Conservation Commission. TV news vans hurried down quiet country roads, headed for Safari Wild. One day a news helicopter appeared in the sky above the park, presumably in pursuit of an aerial sighting of one of the escapees. The noise only made the situation worse, scaring the monkeys and driving them deeper into the swamp. In early May, the trappers caught the first two of the fifteen, a female and a baby. In mid-June, they got three more. But ten monkeys remained at large. Sightings were reported as far as Dade City, twenty-five miles away. A woman who lived on the other side of the swamp called her sister one night after seeing what she believed to be three of the escapees lurking in the trees outside her house, chirping.

"I have monkeys in my yard," she said.

On the other end of the line, her sister paused. "Really? Monkeys?"

"Yes."

The sister searched online for information about patas monkeys and read about them stealing the crops in Puerto Rico.

"Give them some fresh pineapple," she advised.

"I don't have any fresh pineapple!"

The woman searched her kitchen and found a banana and placed it on a branch. A little while later, when she looked back outside, the banana was gone.

People who lived near Safari Wild scanned the woods through binoculars, hoping for a glimpse of the fugitives. Others saw them by chance in the distance and wondered if they were hallucinating. The monkeys were seen sprinting across pastures, peering out from trees, foraging for food. They snuck onto a ranch and fiddled with the switches and knobs on two tractors until the batteries went dead. The rancher figured out what had happened when he discovered tiny paw prints in the dust. His grandson offered to shoot the monkeys, but the rancher didn't want to hurt them. Too pretty, he said. When corn began to vanish from the rancher's deer feeders, he set up a motion-sensitive camera, just to see them up close. He'd spied the monkeys before, out on his property, but had never gotten within a hundred yards before they disappeared.

The monkeys didn't mind the camera. Soon the rancher had dozens of photos that showed them climbing all over his corn feeders, reaching inside a cage to spin the mechanism that released the grain, staring at a raccoon that had been caught inside a trap intended for them. He was struck by how relaxed the monkeys seemed, how brazen.

"They're smart," he said. "Very smart."

The newspapers and TV stations ate all of it up. The monkeys' mass breakout was irresistible to the journalists' sensibilities, even more so than Enshalla's surprising death. The tiger's escape had been big news, without question. But the whole thing was over in less than two hours, and with no further developments, the outrage had quickly faded. The monkey caper lingered on and on and got better with every new twist. In those first months, everything about the story—the Prussian sideburns, the way the monkeys evaded the trackers—was funny. Just the word "monkey" had a power all its own. It energized any headline, made any newscast more zany.

Something else was driving the coverage as well, something that had started out underneath but was now surfacing. With every new update, readers and viewers were reminded that a zoo director—the same man who had gunned down Enshalla—was now being outwitted by a gang of wayward monkeys. Tracing the narrative arc between the two events engendered a certain smugness, a satisfaction that only grew as the coverage continued. Soon the story wasn't really about the monkeys anymore. It was about the spectacle of watching Lex finally getting his comeuppance.

The second act of the public shaming opened that fall.

The reporters intensified the pressure. The escape of the patas monkeys had drawn their attention to Safari Wild, which had received almost no prior coverage. They started asking questions about Lex; the ties between Lowry Park and Safari Wild; and how anyone could possibly be running a nonprofit zoo and building a for-profit game park, both within fifty miles of each other. These were the questions that Lex had been warned about, and now they were being posed almost every day in the newspapers and on TV newscasts.

Revelations tumbled forth with dizzying speed, chronicling an ever-growing list of conflicts of interest. There were articles about Lex trading animals back and forth between the zoo and the game park and his ranch, about Lex selling animals to the zoo at one price and buying them from the zoo at another, and about how a giraffe and an antelope that had been transferred from the zoo to Lex's ranch had died there. It turned out that Lowry Park employees, their salaries paid for partially by tax dollars, had built two barns at Safari Wild, and that the five bison who had been nudged out of the zoo to make room for Gator Falls were not only staying at the game park, but the zoo was paying the park six hundred dollars a month to house the animals.

On and on it went.

For a time, Lex defended himself. He insisted that he'd never profited from any of these dealings and that he had only wanted to help the zoo grow by allowing them space for their surplus animals. He said he had nothing to hide, but allowed that there had been misunderstandings and errors in judgment.

"I should have had better political instincts," he said. "But I'm not a political person."

The statement was curious. It felt disingenuous, because over the years Lex had proved to be a skilled politician, someone who knew the system and had the judgment to manipulate it to Lowry Park's advantage. He could never have carried out the zoo's transformation had it not been for his gift for wooing county commissioners and mayors and governors and legislators, not to mention corporate executives and society mavens and assorted multimillionaires. And yet the statement essentially proved that whatever political instincts he once possessed had slipped away. To suggest that his mistakes had been merely political, not substantive, was guaranteed to raise the eyebrows of even those who wanted to keep faith in his best intentions.

Early on, when he was still giving interviews, Lex pointed out that his dealings with the zoo had been vetted for any potential impropriety. After all, he had signed the memorandum of understanding with Lowry Park's executive committee to avoid the very accusations he now faced. True enough. But then it came out that the zoo's board had reviewed the memo over the summer and had been concerned enough to dissolve the agreement.

It did not advance Lex's case when Fassil Gabremariam, who had approved many transactions between the zoo and the game park, turned out to be listed in Safari Wild's incorporation papers as an officer in the game park's conservation fund. The water grew even muddier when it was revealed that two of the white rhinos that Lowry Park had loaned Safari Wild were pregnant, and that the original agreement had called for the first rhino calf to be given to the zoo and the second to the game park. It was roughly at this point that Pam Iorio, Tampa's mayor, got mad enough to jump in. Iorio publicly reminded Lex that the zoo operated under the oversight of the city of Tampa; according to a lease, both the land under the zoo and the animals were owned by the city. She ordered an audit of Lowry Park's dealings with Safari Wild, insisting that the zoo and the game park sever all ties and that the park return any of the zoo's animals it was still holding.

At first Lex tried to argue with the mayor—more proof that his instincts were failing him. But then he learned to be quiet and agreed to most of the mayor's demands. He announced that he would take a leave of absence from the zoo while the city conducted its audit.

A couple of months later, the audit came back loaded with bombshells. The report said that Lex had charged the zoo almost four thousand dollars in reimbursements for a three-day trip to Paris that he and Elena had enjoyed on their way back from an international conference in South Africa. It also cited Lex's divisive management style and confirmed, after interviews with the staff, that he had created a climate of fear where employees hesitated to speak out. But the most damning findings detailed the rampant conflicts of interest. The bottom line, the report said, was that Lex's pattern of improper dealings had cost the zoo more than $200,000.

> Fundamentally, Mr. Salisbury appeared to treat the operation
> at Lowry Park Zoo, his for-profit venture Safari Wild, and his
> residence ranch as one. . . . He seems unable to differentiate
> between his role as CEO of the Zoo and the role he plays with
> his business and his ranch . . .

The audit was sixty pages long. Once Mayor Iorio heard what it contained, all restraint fell away. She demanded that Lex be fired and that he repay the $200,000. She also seconded the audit's recommendation that the case be turned over to law authorities to decide if criminal prosecution was warranted.

Lex, no longer willing to be silent, returned fire with a statement released through his attorney. He blasted the city auditors for ignoring his side of the story and called them "minions" of the mayor. He said that in reality, the zoo owed *him* $403,117 for housing their animals for free or at discount and for loaning his own animals to the zoo. And he vowed to fight for his job at an upcoming meeting of the zoo's board.

Ultimately, it was up to the board and not the mayor whether Lex stayed on. Judging from the reactions of board members to the audit, his chances did not look good. One member offered him a piece of advice: "Plead for mercy."

The debacle was already tarnishing both Lex and the zoo itself. As the revelations mounted, the AZA temporarily suspended Lowry Park's accreditation, which it had held for twenty years. Without the AZA's seal of approval, the number one family zoo in America tumbled toward disgrace. It stood to lose its lease with the city, which required that it maintain the accreditation, and as long as the suspension held, it could not trade animals with other accredited institutions. The AZA had also suspended Lex's individual membership. He was officially persona non grata.

Lex made an easy target. For years he had reveled in the scorn of others and nurtured a cult of his own oversized personality. It was obvious that he loved the zoo, but his love had brought not just increased revenues but devastation. He was both creator and destroyer. Even so, whatever had gone wrong at Lowry Park was not his fault alone. Though he had perpetuated an illusion of limitless authority, in reality he served at the discretion of Lowry Park's board. The thirty-some directors on that board were hardly powerless. Among them were a former governor of Florida and a former mayor of Tampa, plus an assortment of other public officials, corporate execs, and high-powered lawyers. Not exactly a timid bunch. Surely a few of them had heard some of the alarming reports on staff morale. It must have penetrated their consciousness that two of the zoo's most famous animals had died bloody and unnecessary deaths. Any of these directors could have stepped outside their comfort zones and wandered the zoo on their own and talked quietly to the staff. And if they didn't like what they learned, the board members had the authority to fire the CEO whenever they pleased.

Obviously Lex had a talent for dazzling this council of alphas who held his future in their hands. He knew when to listen respectfully, when to bathe them in praise, and when to inspire them with another sermon about an independent zoo fighting against the tide of extinction. Over the years he had invited many of the zoo's most crucial supporters to join him on trips to Kenya and Tanzania. He had taken them to Swaziland to see the elephants eating their way through the trees. He had taken them to the palaces of Ethiopia and introduced them to what remained of the royal lions. Until now, it had worked. Even the deal with Safari Wild had been approved by Fassil Gabremariam and the rest of the board's executive committee. Lex had asked for their blessing, and they had granted it. Now he had been cast as the scapegoat. It was hard to feel sorry for him, given how much damage he'd caused, but still it made no sense. Fassil had already resigned quietly, and it was difficult to understand why the rest of the executive committee hadn't resigned with him. If the memorandum of understanding with Safari Wild was the font of all outrage, how did those who voted for it keep their positions?

The truth was, many of the audit's findings about Lex should not have shocked anyone. His plan to build Safari Wild—and the likelihood of it generating controversy—had been reported in the *St. Petersburg Times* months before the monkeys escaped or the scandal broke. His intimidation of keepers had been reported as well. His habit of transferring animals back and forth between his ranch and the zoo, meanwhile, had not been a secret. He'd talked about it openly for years; the staff routinely saw him driving a trailer onto the zoo grounds, carting zebras or warthogs from his ranch. He had not acted as though he thought any of this was wrong. As the audit had noted, he seemed to view the zoo's animals and those on his ranch and at the game park as part of one big traveling collection.

Even the transfer of the white rhinos had been conducted in the open. Iorio had dubbed it Rhinogate. But months before the scandal broke, the transfer had been featured on *The Mayor's Hour*, Iorio's own cable TV show. An episode that had aired in April showed a city Parks and Recreation crane lifting a crate holding one of the white rhinos onto the back of a flatbed truck in preparation for the move to Safari Wild. Lex smiled and waved at the camera as he drove the truck away, taking the rhinos to their new home.

Now that Lex was cornered, Iorio was giving interviews saying she couldn't understand how so many things could have gone wrong without someone raising a flag. But in the years before, the flag had already been publicly raised on the Kremers' Web site and in news reports published after the deaths of Herman and Enshalla. Clearly, Iorio had not been paying attention, even to what was happening with the zoo on her own TV show. For years, the mayor and a long list of other public officials and local luminaries had cozied up to Lex, rejoicing as he brought in the elephants, dancing in the conga line with him at the black-tie fund-raisers, standing beside him and cheering for the TV cameras when it was time to cut the ribbon on another new wing. At Karamu, Iorio had even worn her zebra-print jacket.

Only a few months before the scandal, the rich and powerful had treated Lex like a prince of the city. Then, in an instant, they had turned on him. Whether or not he deserved their scorn, there was something savage about the reversal. It was a primal reckoning that had nothing to do with audits or memoranda of understanding. Lex had been strong once. He had been useful to their purposes. Now that he was wounded and trailing blood through the grass, the pride was ready to finish him off.

That September, just as the onslaught against Lex was beginning, five of the monkeys were still at large. The others had been captured alive and returned to human custody. The island at Safari Wild obviously was not a good idea, so instead they were shipped to Lowry Park for safekeeping. At the time, that fact did not yet seem ironic.

The next chapter was chronicled by *St. Petersburg Times* reporter Ben Montgomery. A rancher who lived near Safari Wild told Montgomery that he'd been in his truck one morning, headed out to feed his cows, when he caught a glimpse of an unidentified animal in the distance. It was big and reddish, and Trent Meador thought maybe it was a coyote. He stopped his truck, grabbed his rifle, and studied his prey through the scope. The animal, hiding behind a wild palmetto, seemed to be looking back at him. Meador saw white fur on the animal's face and decided it was not a coyote but a raccoon. He pulled the trigger and went to retrieve the body and picked it up by its tail. Then he stuffed the carcass into a feed sack and put it in the back of his truck and called his wife.

"Shot a what?" she asked.

"Shot a monkey," he said.

"You didn't either."

Once Meador showed his wife the proof inside the feed sack, he wondered if it might have been a mistake to kill the monkey. Without giving his name, he called the Fish and Wildlife Conservation Commission.

"If I saw one of those monkeys, and I shot it, would I be in trouble?" he asked.

The answer was no. Patas monkeys were a non-native species and were not protected. No charges would be filed.

Afterward, Meador kept the carcass in a freezer. Sometimes he took it out and snapped photos with his cell phone. He showed them to so many friends that people began to call him, asking to see his dead monkey.

Someone asked if he felt any remorse.

"Not at all," he said. "You seen the teeth those jokers got on 'em? Teeth an inch and a quarter long."

Eventually, he took the monkey's body to a taxidermist to have it stuffed. He wanted it on the wall of his game room.

The final four fugitives remained on the loose. They were the most elusive and presumably the smartest. By now their exploits were legendary. Through all of that summer and fall they had made fools out of every human who pursued them—and a mockery of human ascendancy over other species. Their subversive freedom had even managed to bring infamy upon the man who had sought to imprison them. Sightings grew so rare that they began to seem like puckish phantoms, haunting the shadows at the edge of the swamp.

Lex Brown, a sod farmer, initially dismissed the reports he kept getting from his foreman, who insisted the famous runaways were lurking in the field behind his back porch.

"Señor!" cried the foreman. "The monkeys! The monkeys!"

"You're loco," Brown said. "They're raccoons."

The man would not budge.

"No," he told his boss. "Monkeys, monkeys, monkeys."

Finally the farmer drove over to the foreman's house and peered across the meadow and glimpsed a quartet of monkeys bobbing. The farmer still didn't quite believe it—maybe his eyes were wrong—and so he and the foreman started leaving out oranges and other fruit, just to see what happened. When the fruit disappeared, Brown was finally ready to believe. Monkeys? On his farm? That was new. It was funny, his having the same first name as the guy who'd accidentally let the monkeys out in the first place. But no matter. Through binoculars, he saw them taking cover in clumps of cypress trees and chasing one another across his sod fields and climbing on his corn feeders. He noted that there was a big male and a smaller male and a mother with a baby, and that the big male was the lookout. Whenever Brown drove toward them, the male would let out a warning and they would all scatter. It was a primitive alarm system, but effective. The farmer's truck never got within a quarter-mile before they fled.

At first all of it was entertaining. Then came the Sunday morning in December when he discovered that one or more of the monkeys had defecated on his John Deere tractor. He realized that the monkeys were potentially serious pests. If somebody didn't stop them, they would reproduce, and suddenly there would be all these new monkeys, just as hard to catch and just as ready to befoul his beloved John Deere and cause all other manner of minor havoc. "It was war," he said. He was neighbors with Trent Meador and knew that Meador had shot one of the monkeys. But Brown didn't want to kill them. Instead, he determined to build a better monkey trap, outfitting a big dog kennel with a trapdoor and dangling a bunch of purple grapes inside as bait. If a monkey entered, he'd have to stand on a pipe to reach the grapes, and the weight would release the trapdoor with a loud hiss and a bang. As he welded the pipe into place, his four targets huddled together on a motor grader off in the distance and studied his handiwork.

"You're not going to catch those monkeys," said his wife, Deana.

Brown set the trap later that day. The next morning, the big male was dancing inside the kennel, chirping angrily as he scrabbled along the walls to find a way out. Triumphant, Brown texted Deana:

GOT MONKEY #1

They named him Clarence and left him there to lure in the others. The next day they caught Casper, the other male. Then they caught Hazel and Hazel's baby, Lola.

Containing the four of them in the kennel was a challenge. The monkeys had already proven to be good swimmers. Now they turned out to be restless diggers, as well, continually trying to claw their way out. Brown and his workers patched the damage, but the monkeys kept at it. Meticulous, they searched every square inch of the mesh, testing the wire for weak spots where they might push through. Repeatedly, Clarence hurled himself against the door with the operatic fervor of a professional wrestler.

Deana devoted herself to making sure the monkeys were well cared for. When it rained, she draped ponchos over the kennel so they wouldn't get wet. She emptied her kitchen cabinets in search of Craisins and other morsels. She allowed the monkeys to reach through the mesh with their slender fingers and take the food from her palm, gentle as babies. She loved feeding them so much that she made special trips to the grocery. Usually she shopped at Publix, but on the monkey runs she went to Winn-Dixie, not wanting anyone she knew to see her and ask why her cart was filled with bananas and grapes. Enthralled with her new charges, she would sit beside their kennel and chat with them, delighting in the way they mimicked her expressions. She even let them hold her fingers.

"It's different looking in a monkey's eyes than in a cat's or dog's eyes," she said. "There's a connection."

The love that Deana felt for the monkeys was overpowering. It was exactly the kind of bond that zoos hope for—that moment of recognition when an animal and a guest recognize something in each other. Deana wanted to keep the monkeys or else turn them loose again. But her husband said no.

"They're not our monkeys," he told her.

So on December 15, a trapper backed his truck up to the kennel and loaded the four monkeys up for their transfer. Eight months after they swam to freedom, the last handful of runaways was returned to Safari Wild.

The board meeting to decide Lex Salisbury's fate was three days away.

17

Cull

That Thursday broke bright and clear and unseasonably warm, even for Florida. A sense of karmic justice shimmered in the sunlight. After a lifetime of consigning other animals to captivity, Lex had become the hunted. Newspaper editorials demanded his firing. Letter writers recited the litany of his alleged crimes against nature, from the murder of Enshalla to the heartless removal of the wild elephants from the savanna. Now the mayor had raised the possibility of criminal charges, a suggestion that evoked the remarkable image of a zoo director ending up caged.

Lex felt as though he had been invited to his own execution. Even so, he was not about to surrender. That morning, as he dressed and shaved and steeled himself to face the judgment of the other alphas, he believed he still had a fifty-fifty chance—a testament either to the strength of his character or the depth of his denial. There was no reason to stand before the board and make his case unless some part of him thought he could work his magic one more time and escape the trap in which he'd become so thoroughly enmeshed. It did not matter that he had laid the trap himself. He insisted that the audit was a sham that would never stand up in court. He saw himself as wrongly accused, misunderstood, persecuted. He wanted his moment.

He and Elena drove into Tampa together in their '92 Nissan Pathfinder, so old and faded it was hard to tell it had once been gold. They had brought Pippi along for the ride, as well as another little terrier mix named Grub, possibly because he and Elena longed for the comfort of two creatures who still loved them. Lex was not about to explain such choices. He was in no mood for trifling questions. He no longer answered reporters' phone calls, except to tell them never to call again. Whatever he had to say was for the board alone.

A swarm of TV news crews awaited them at a hotel near the airport. Usually the board meetings were convened at the school attached to the zoo, where young children attended classes and camps, but the board chairman had decided he didn't want the kids being disturbed by the stampeding media.

There had been a debate over whether the zoo should allow the press and public to attend the meeting. Pointing out that Lowry Park relied at least partially on public funding, Mayor Iorio and other officials argued it was only right that the meeting should be open. Instead, Lowry Park stonewalled. In a move that would make it clear that the zoo's image problems could not be blamed solely on Lex, the zoo had hired five uniformed Hillsborough County sheriff's deputies to keep reporters under control and away from the boardroom. The decision reinforced the impression that Lowry Park had a great deal to hide and offered fodder to critics who pointedly asked how the zoo could justify spending tax dollars to hire guards to keep the public out.

Even before the meeting began, the scene at the hotel descended into farce. A spokeswoman, with a smile pasted on her face but with panic behind her eyes, waded into the crowd of reporters and photographers, trying to herd them into an upstairs room. The journalists, who knew a cage when they saw one, ignored her. They planned to maintain their vigil until Lex made his grand entrance—they needed the footage—and now they called out questions at board members who were trying their best to slip into the hotel unnoticed.

The savage nature of the moment kept surging to the surface. As the journalists grew more impatient with the efforts to corral them and more frustrated with how long it was taking Lex to arrive, their aggression mounted. *We are sharks*, one reporter told herself, *waiting to be fed.*

. . . .

Lex and Elena were en route when word reached them about the mob out front. So they swung around to a back entrance. Lex got out and strode inside, ignoring the one or two reporters covering that door. Any thought of following him was rendered moot by the uniformed deputies.

With nothing else better to do, some of the journalists reluctantly retreated to the confinement of the media room and poured themselves coffee. A deputy stood outside the door, making sure they didn't get close enough to the meeting to snoop. A couple of reporters drifted back toward the parking lot, hoping Elena would make an offering to the beast of their daily news cycle—a quote, a denial, even a muttered insult. Anything was better than the nothingness of the hotel corridors.

Elena parked the Pathfinder and hurried past them without a word, looking angry and disheveled. The reporters walked over to the SUV and noticed the vehicle had a bumper sticker in front: EAT MORE BEEF. Peering inside, they saw one of Lex's safari hats on the backseat, along with Pippi and Grub, who clamored by the window, barking at the strangers.

"Oh my God," said one reporter. "There's dogs in the car."

By now it was midday and sweltering, with the sun bouncing off windshields. The reporters, sweating, looked at the terriers and knew they had a story. In Florida, dogs left in hot cars died all the time. Surely the wife of a zoo director would know that.

Someone inside the hotel warned Elena that reporters were lurking near the Pathfinder, so she came back out and moved it to a parking lot a couple of blocks in the distance. She wanted to hear Lex's speech to the board, and she thought Pippi and Grub would be fine, because she'd left the SUV in the shade of a live oak and rolled the windows down a few inches. Undeterred, the reporters hiked over and kept an eye on the dogs. They called their editors, and soon the news appeared online. A reader, worried about Pippi and Grub, called Hillsborough County Animal Control.

"You can't possibly be serious," a spokeswoman for the agency said when she heard the news.

Inside the hotel, Elena was frustrated because she had been blocked from hearing Lex's defense or even sitting with him outside the meeting. Like the journalists, she wasn't allowed near the proceedings. Finally she gave up and made the long walk back to the Pathfinder and the dogs. An animal control investigator was waiting. By this point Pippi and Grub had been locked inside for anywhere from an hour to two hours. They were panting, but did not appear in serious distress.

The investigator confronted Elena.

"Would you leave your baby in a car with the windows cracked?"

Elena was tempted to reply that she wouldn't put a dog collar on her baby, either, or have her baby neutered. Instead she looked at the investigator and said, "You're absolutely right. I'm sorry."

The investigator, Elena recalls, told her she was lucky not to be on her way to jail. If Elena had left the dogs in the heat any longer, the investigator said she would have been forced to break into the car and rescue the animals and have her arrested. Around them, the craziness kept escalating. A sheriff's deputy pulled up, ready to take Elena into custody if necessary. Reporters hovered. A TV cameraman recorded Elena's moment of shame. Pippi and Grub barked and barked.

"Welcome to my world," Elena told the investigator.

Using a thermometer, the investigator determined that the temperature inside the SUV had climbed to ninety degrees. The investigator told Elena the dogs needed water. But when she brought some back, Pippi and Grub were more interested in declaring themselves to the cameraman. The investigator wrote Elena two tickets for improper confinement of animals, and two more for failure to have tags or vaccination records. Elena took the tickets, took the dogs, and drove away. Somehow, while her husband was inside fighting for his job, she had managed to get herself charged with animal cruelty.

The journalists scattered to call their editors again. Lowry Park's efforts to muzzle the press had backfired. The whole thing was an embarrassment not just for Lex and Elena, but for the institution that had employed Lex for the past twenty years. Already, news of the cruelty charges was attracting hits on the news sites and spreading to animal lovers and zoo haters around the world.

The glee was unmistakable.

The afternoon dragged on. Inside the media room, the captive journalists bristled. One reporter had to ask for permission to use the bathroom. The others kept poking their heads into the hall, watching for board members coming or going. They texted officials inside the meeting, begging for updates.

Whatever transpired in the room—the arguments and counterarguments, the vote itself—was supposed to remain a secret. Inevitably, though, details trickled out. The city auditor delivered a detailed accounting of Lex's manifold sins, an indictment so scathing that it rattled at least one board member who had been inclined to think favorably of the CEO. The mayor, through a representative, made ominous suggestions about the dire consequences that would rain upon the zoo if Lex was not driven from their midst. One board member, a retired president of an insurance brokerage firm, defended the accused and cautioned against rushing to condemnation. As the man spoke, he had the impression that none of his fellow board members was paying him the slightest attention.

Through it all, Lex waited in a nearby room, sequestered from the general proceedings—an odd requirement, given that even defendants in criminal trials are allowed to sit in court and hear the testimony and evidence arrayed against their future. When the board finally allowed Lex entrance into the inner sanctum, he was confronted by rows of faces, many appraising him with a detachment that caught him off guard. Others appeared livid. In the past, some of the directors had called him their friend, and before he entered the room, he had hoped that at least a few would remember the world they had created together at the zoo.

Lex tried to make his case. He had prepared a bound volume of documents refuting the charges in the city audit and had made sure that a copy was placed before every board member. He was ready to demolish the audit, line by line. But as he stood there, he realized most of the board had not even glanced at his documents and had no intention of doing so. Looking them in the eye, he apologized for his part of what had happened, but insisted that the blame was not entirely his to shoulder. All he'd ever wanted to do, he told them, was build a zoo that mattered.

"Don't judge me completely by the past year," Lex said. "Judge me by all twenty-one years I've given."

One of the board members, a woman he'd danced with at Karamu, aimed a dagger of a question at his jugular.

"Did anybody ever tell you no?" she asked.

"Sure," said Lex.

When they were done with him, he was shown the door. By then all of his cautious hopefulness was gone. The hearing had been a well-designed piece of stagecraft, but the outcome had obviously been decided long before. Making matters worse, the news of Elena's debacle with the dogs had spread through the hotel. If there had truly been hope of Lex holding on to his job, surely the animal cruelty charges had shattered it. Here was a man allegedly incapable of protecting his own pets. Could the board really trust him at the helm of an ark?

No. Lex would either step down, or they would fire him. The vote was unanimous. Even Lex's defender went along with the motion, since it allowed his friend a measure of dignity. The board chairman went to the room where Lex was churning and laid out his options. Lex agreed to resign. Afterward, he emerged from the hotel, stony-faced and silent, and caught a ride to a friend's house where Elena awaited with the dogs and the citations and her new infamy.

It was unlikely that they would ever be invited back to the garden again.

Dusk

In the year that followed Lex's exile, Lowry Park fought to remove itself from the shadow of all that had gone wrong. The acting CEO—Craig Pugh, who had served for years as deputy director—oversaw a revamping of the zoo's policies. By the following spring, the zoo had regained its accreditation with the AZA, a crucial first step back toward respectability.

In September 2009, the zoo embarked on what could only be described as a halfhearted search for a new executive director. The search, such as it was, was announced with a classified ad on the AZA's Web site. Curiously, the ad did not mention Lowry Park's name or even that it was a zoo. Instead, it described the institution in question as simply a "West Central Florida nonprofit committed to education and species conservation."

Why did Lowry Park word the ad so strangely? Were they afraid that no one would want to apply to a zoo that had seen so much trouble? Were they trying to keep the search quiet so that relatively few candidates would apply, therefore making it more likely for them to promote someone from within? The zoo wouldn't say. In fact, the zoo's management no longer wanted to talk about the events of the past several years. Even in off-the-record conversations, they acted as though Lex had never existed. A few months later, the board unanimously voted to appoint Craig Pugh as the fulltime CEO. In the press release, the board chair praised the new leader's ability "to move this organization forward." Pugh talked about how Lowry Park was both an animal attraction and an institution devoted to conserving nature. "A business with two brands," he called it.

Given all the turmoil Lowry Park had endured, the desire to push on was understandable. But the zoo had become a place where certain chapters of the past were all too easily swept away. Nowhere on the public grounds was there any mention of Enshalla and all the years she'd ruled, bringing beauty and wonder to the masses. No statue of Herman had been erected. Instead a plaque was affixed to a rock near the chimp exhibit, commemorating the fallen king as "a gentle soul and friend to many." The words, written by Lee Ann, were a true summation of Herman's life. But most visitors walked past without noticing. The zoo was much more interested in drawing attention to the births of new animals. A map handed out at the front gates showed every exhibit where newborns awaited—marked with the word "Baby!" The marketing of new life had reached perfect clarity.

The greeting on the phone lines had been refined as well. No longer did the recording allude to any magazine's ranking of the zoo's suitability for children and families. The new message was simpler:

"Thank you for calling Tampa's Lowry Park Zoo, voted the number one zoo in America."

Lee Ann remembered. Sometimes, it seemed as though she carried the entire zoo inside her. At the end of the day, when she rubbed her eyes from exhaustion, all of it was written on her face. The weight and hopes of this institution she loved beyond reason. Its past and present, its best moments and its worst. Countless keepers who had come and gone. Generation after generation of animals who had been born and died inside these walls. Their ghosts lived within her, and when she talked about them, it became clear that she was a captive in the garden, too, and could never let go of its endless joys and sorrows.

Her voice grew especially quiet when she told the story of what had happened to the chimps after Herman was overthrown.

"I swore I wasn't going to talk about that," she said.

Bamboo ruled as the alpha for three years. Old and frail as he was, he prevailed. He did not let Alex's displays fluster him. He got along with Rukiya and the other females and was especially close to Sasha. The young female, growing rapidly, still relied on Rukiya, her adopted mother. But in Bamboo, Sasha found a father. Many nights, she still climbed into his nest and slept beside him. Bamboo and Rukiya took turns watching over her. Entranced with Sasha, Bamboo would offer her fruit and entice her to climb onto his lap. He doted on her, and she adored him back. In their bond, Bamboo found his best self.

One summer day, the keepers discovered the king's body curled in the nighthouse. The years had caught up with him. He had struggled with congestive heart failure; his lungs had filled with fluid. Afterward, the other chimps paid their respects. One by one, they ventured inside his den and reached out to touch him and confirm he was truly gone.

Bamboo's death, so soon after Herman's, was difficult enough. But even more painful was the unexpected collapse of Sasha. She was three years old and appeared healthy. One Friday, she was playing and running. The next day, the keepers noticed that she wasn't eating and seemed a little off. The following morning, when she lost consciousness, the staff took her to the clinic. Murphy tried to revive her, but it was no use. Suffering from a viral heart infection, she never woke up.

Lee Ann, who had taken such pleasure in cradling Sasha as a baby, made herself carry the female's body into the nighthouse so that the other chimps would understand she was dead. The staff did not yet know what had killed her, because Murphy had not yet performed the necropsy. Worried that Sasha might be infectious, Lee Ann did not place her inside any of the dens. Instead she walked up to the mesh, holding the body for the others to see. The group exploded with grief. Rukiya whimpered and wailed. Then she grew angry and stomped back and forth, showing her disbelief. Finally she became silent. As the others approached the mesh and reached their fingers through the openings to touch Sasha's body, Rukiya retreated to the back of her den and sat facing the wall. She could not bear to look at her daughter, lifeless in Lee Ann's arms. She couldn't look at any of them.

For days, Rukiya had trouble accepting Sasha's death. When Lee

Ann came back to the nighthouse to check on her, Rukiya would grow excited. It was obvious that the matriarch clung to the hope that the humans who had taken Sasha away could also bring her back.

The combined loss of the group's oldest and youngest members devastated the others. Bamboo had been their leader; Sasha's youth had graced them with new energy and purpose. Afterward, when Lee Ann watched the remaining chimps, she was struck by how subdued they were. Sometimes, they seemed lost inside an almost eerie stillness.

Nearly a year later, Alex was still not quite mature enough to become the alpha. He acted like the king, strutting along the rock wall. But when his displays grew too annoying, Rukiya quickly put him in his place. The chimps remained unfocused. They needed a spark. Lee Ann was considering bringing in an older male who could take control. Or maybe another baby.

Deciding the future of the chimps was only one of the many projects filling Lee Ann's every waking minute. Seventeen manatees, a record number, were swimming in the rehab pools. Naboo and Jamie, the Indian rhinos, had a young calf. In Safari Africa, a pair of shoebill storks guarded a brand new chick, the first ever hatched in North America.

Lee Ann had not forgotten Lex. She wished him well, hoped he found his way. But she had little interest in theorizing about whatever had gone wrong under his tenure. She had a zoo to watch over. An imperfect zoo, yes. Sometimes glorious, sometimes maddening. But for better or worse, it was hers to worry about now.

El Diablo Blanco stared into the flames. The wind rustled through the live oaks. In the distance, across the rolling fields of his private ranch, zebras grazed and warthogs strutted. High above, vultures circled in a flawless sky.

"Turkey vultures," said Lex, identifying the species with a glance. He leaned toward the campfire he'd just stoked to ward off the chill of an unseasonably cool Sunday afternoon. He took off his safari hat and removed his work gloves, one finger at a time, and explained how his enemies and supposed friends had brought him down.

"I'm not a political guy," he said, repeating a familiar theme. "I'm an operations guy, and that was part of my problem. That's why I got bitch-slapped the way I did."

A luxuriant pause.

"I thought if I did everything under the rules and regulations, then I would be fine."

Elena, sitting close by, joined in. "He was doing his job. He's never been interested in politics as a full-contact sport."

It was the last day of February 2010. Several months before, Lex and Lowry Park had reached a financial settlement. Originally he had been told he owed $200,000. But the zoo, clearly weary of the whole affair, had agreed to accept $2,212. And just the other day, the Florida Attorney General's Office had removed another cloud with a letter to Lex's attorney.

> After a review of police reports, evidence, and witness statements, it has been determined that further prosecution is not warranted. While it is clear Mr. Salisbury's actions presented a conflict of interest, there is a lack of evidence to support any criminal intent.

So much for the mayor's suggestion that Lex was a crook.

As Elena and Lex relaxed in front of the fire, they were accompanied by the two dogs who had been locked in the Pathfinder on the day of the final board meeting. Grub, worn out from sniffing lemurs and barking at giraffes, napped nearby. Pippi had climbed into Elena's lap. The little terrier was still ailing from a nasty encounter with a *Bufo* marine toad in the yard. The toads secrete a toxic milky substance—a classic revenge of an ectotherm—and when Pippi got too close, she'd swallowed enough of the poison to nearly choke her.

"She's deaf as a post now," said Lex.

"She's gotten otherworldly," said Elena.

The little terrier was fascinating in her ability to survive anything—toxic toads, hot cars, hordes of journalists. But even more improbable was Lex's claim that he had never been a politician. Before everything went sour, hadn't he seduced half of City Hall?

Lex shrugged. What he meant, he said, was that he had never learned to wear the mask of a politician.

"I was myself. I wasn't trying to *be* anything. I was able to get people enthusiastic about what I did." That passion, he said, was always genuine. "I guess I'm a good politician if I believe in something. But I don't consider myself a salesman. . . . I never had to be fake."

With the dropping of the criminal investigation, Lex insisted that he had been exonerated. He pointed out, again, that Lowry Park's relationship with Safari Wild had been blessed by the zoo's executive committee—a fact that neither the mayor nor the zoo's board had cared about when they went after him.

"I never tried to hide anything, and everything I did, I got approval for."

To him, the whole thing was a witch hunt. He believed that the mayor wanted him fired because she was angry that he made more money than she did and because she needed to flex some muscle. The case against him sounded bad, no question. Ultimately, Lex said, that perception had trumped reality. He was still stunned that so many had turned on him so quickly. But he had no desire to seek retribution.

"People have to live with what they did, and if they have consciences they're going to be harder on themselves than anything I can say or do."

Leaving the zoo was hard. But he still worked with animals, both at his ranch and at Safari Wild. He was fighting bureaucrats and licensing issues, but hoped to open the game park within a year. Also, he and Elena were set to begin tours showcasing the animals on the ranch.

By now the sun had begun its descent toward the treetops. Sandhill cranes, their great gray wings whooshing, sailed overhead and landed in the shallows of an ephemeral wetland behind the house. On many evenings, two hundred of the cranes roosted along the shore. The air filled with their warbling calls.

Pippi, who could no longer hear the cranes, had fallen asleep on Elena's lap. The terrier clearly held no grudges about the day she was left behind in the heat of the parking lot.

"We weren't thinking straight," said Lex.

"We were really stupid," said Elena.

And yet, Lex said, Elena was now "a nationally recognized pet abuser."

Elena explained that she hadn't wanted to leave Pippi and Grub at home all day and that she hadn't expected to stay inside the hotel as long as she did. Lex was in crisis mode. She wanted to be supportive. She lost track of the time. As for the dogs not having tags, she thought they'd been licensed through the zoo. What bothered her most, she said, was the idea that she might have somehow hurt her husband's chances to stay at Lowry Park. Lex acknowledged that the incident hadn't helped. But he was more upset for Elena, knowing how awful it must have been to be charged with mistreating the dogs—especially on TV.

"It was a day from hell," he said.

The campfire was dying. The chill was deepening.

What had Lex learned from all of this?

He did not hesitate to answer. He had given the city a priceless gift, he said—a zoo with a national reputation and a world-class animal collection and revenues that had increased a hundredfold. In return, the ruling class had sought to ruin him and throw him in jail.

"Tampa," he said, "eats its young."

No one could accuse Lex of modesty. His perpetual defiance was precisely what made some people love him and so many others loathe him. But just because he was unrepentant did not mean he was completely wrong.

Looking back on his downfall, it was hard to deny that the whole thing was driven, at least in part, by an orchestrated hysteria. Over the years, Lex had supplied his enemies with plenty of ammunition. Considering the dismal morale of the zoo's staff after Herman's and Enshalla's deaths, the board might have had grounds to force him out long before the patas monkeys escaped from his island. But the outrage over Safari Wild had nothing to do with the well-being of the animals at the zoo or the game park. Despite the thunder of the audit, the scandal wasn't about misappropriated funds, either. Otherwise, the city and the zoo would have pressed harder to recoup their alleged losses.

In the end, it was about the balance of power—who would guide the zoo into the future, who got to decide what was acceptable and what was out of bounds—among a select handful of primates. Watching the official blustering and posturing was similar to standing in front of the chimp exhibit and seeing Herman and the other drama queens shriek and pound their chests and chase one another, round and round.

All of it was a sideshow that distracted attention from the deeper questions of what kind of zoo Lowry Park should be and how it should evolve and what role it might play, along with other institutions, in the future of life on Earth. How much in legal fees did the city of Tampa devote to its crusade against Lex? Imagine what those sums could have meant for any one of the species disappearing into oblivion every year.

Whatever offenses Lex committed, they pale in comparison to the damage the human species is currently inflicting on the wildlife of this planet. In his book *The Future of Life*, the famed biologist E. O. Wilson surveys the waves of extinction wiping out species around the planet and calls Homo sapiens "the serial killer of the biosphere."

Global warming. The melting of the polar ice caps. The poisoning of the seas and skies. The fires burning through the Amazon. Millions of us, driving our children to school, driving to the grocery, driving to work. For these and a hundred other reasons, many of the species at Lowry Park are on the brink of extinction in the wild. Some have already been pushed over the edge of that cliff.

In the forests of Panama, the golden frogs have all but vanished. None has been sighted in any of the breeding grounds that used to teem with their numbers, even inside the gorge the researchers called the Thousand-Frog Stream.

"I would say they are relics," says Kevin Zippel, the biologist who is leading efforts to save the golden frog and other amphibian species around the world. "They're on their way out."

That morning in January 2005, when Kevin and Dustin and the other researchers climbed down into the gorge, was one of the last sightings of golden frogs in the wild.

• • • • • • •

Even in Africa, time is running out.

Mick Reilly and his family are still watching over the elephants and the black rhinos and the lions and all the other species that have been given sanctuary inside the game parks of Swaziland. Mick's father, Ted, has been preserving the country's wildlife for four decades. Mick has been at his father's side, wading among the animals since he could walk. There's a picture of him standing in the bush as a toddler, staring down a rhino.

Mick is thirty-nine now. All his life, he and his father have worked with the Swazi king to protect the animals. They have fought the politicians, the poachers, the killers who came into the parks in the early 1990s and mowed down the rhinos with machine guns, then cut out their horns and left their carcasses bleeding in the dirt.

At Mkhaya, the park reserved for Swaziland's most endangered species, there are rows of great bleached skulls from those slaughtered rhinos. Bullet holes are still visible. Spend an afternoon with Mick and Ted, riding in a Land Rover through the twisting trails, and they will show you all that they have fought for, all that the rest of us are losing. Weaver nests, hanging from trees like paper sacks. Eagles turning in the blue dome of the sky.

Mick does not romanticize the savanna. He often hears tourists, wide-eyed, waxing on about the balance of nature.

"There's no such thing," says Mick, sitting at the wheel of the Land Rover. "There never has been. There's no balance, because it's always in a state of change."

He talks about the swath that nature cuts through animal populations, wiping them out with a drought or a flood or disease. Not to mention the destruction wreaked by humans. As he says these things, a herd of zebras gallops along the horizon behind him, followed by a herd of wildebeests.

"Nature," says Mick, quoting his father, "plays no favorites."

Today, seven years after the eleven elephants were sent to San Diego and Tampa, the herds they left behind still threaten to overrun the game parks of Swaziland. More calves have been born. Poachers have been kept away. There are now thirty-seven elephants in the parks—almost the same number as in 2003, when the eleven were sent to the United States. As before, the herds are tearing down almost every tree in sight. Some of these trees are three centuries old. When they die, they are not easily replaced.

"In the span of a man's lifetime," says Ted, "that vegetation will never come back."

The Reillys are back to the same quandary. They know they can't let the elephants continue to destroy so many trees. But they don't want to be forced to kill off any of the herds. They are experimenting with contraception; there have been recent advances in elephant vasectomies. Just last year, a specialist from Disney's Animal Kingdom worked with a team of other veterinarians to surgically sterilize seven bulls from Mkhaya and Hlane. The Reillys are cautiously optimistic about this development. They are also open to the idea of sending more elephants to an American zoo where they will be well-treated.

Mick and his father don't want to be dragged into another controversy. They just want to find an answer that makes some kind of sense.

Late one afternoon, the two of them are together as a ranger drives them along another dirt road inside Mkhaya. The elephants are nowhere in sight. The question of what should be done with them seems far away. Mick and Ted are content to enjoy the last golden hours of the day. They pass warthogs hurrying through the bush. They find a female rhino who has just given birth in the grass.

At dusk, they stop at a watering hole where the hippos float and bellow in the purple water. In the gathering darkness, father and son listen, enveloped in silence. Then it's time to go.

"*Chubeka,*" Mick tells the driver. *Carry on.*

"Let us chase the sun," says Ted.

··· Acknowledgments ···

My thanks to Yann Martel, whose beautiful novel *Life of Pi* made me want to chronicle daily life inside a zoo. I read *Life of Pi* in the summer of 2003, just as Lowry Park was preparing to transport the elephants from Swaziland, and when I saw news accounts of the court battle and the marathon flight, I knew the zoo was ripe for exploration.

I am indebted to Lowry Park's administration and staff, past and present, for allowing me to wander inside their world for so long—especially Lex Salisbury, Craig Pugh, Heather Mackin, Rachel Nelson, Trish Rothman, Larry Killmar, Andrea Schuch, Kevin McKay, David Murphy, Jeff Ewelt, Melinda Mendolusky, Brian French, Steve Lefave, Dustin Smith, Virginia Edmonds, Bob Scheible, Brian Morrow, Dan Costell, Kelly Ryder, Pam Noel, Brian Czarnik, and Carie Peterson. I am also indebted to many others outside the zoo, including Ed and Roger Schultz, Maggie Messitt, Monica Ross, Elena Sheppa, Don Woodman, Ian Kruger, Kevin Zippel, David Gardner, and Jeff and Coleen Kremer, and to the family of Char-Lee Torre. I thank Peter Wrege and Katy Payne at Cornell's Elephant Listening Project for lending me their expertise as they read over my sections on elephant communication and behavior. I am especially grateful to Mick and Ted Reilly for helping me understand how they got elephants to fly and for showing me Mkaya and Hlane. My heartfelt thanks to Lee Ann Rottman for her unwavering patience with a reporter who, in the beginning at least, was afraid of animals. By the time we were done, she had me cradling a baby chimp.

This book is based on a series originally published in the *St. Petersburg Times*, and I would like to thank everyone in that remarkable newsroom whose support made that work and this book possible, including Paul Tash, Neil Brown, Stephen Buckley, Patty Cox, Patty Yablonski, Nikki Life, Dawn Cate, Lane DeGregory, Kevin McGeever, Tim Nickens, Desiree Perry, Boyzell Hosey, Gretchen Letterman, and Jill Wilson, gone but not forgotten. I am deeply grateful to Alex Zayas, Ben Montgomery, Don Morris, and Kelley Benham, whose reporting on the escape of the patas monkeys and on Lex Salisbury's downfall informs so much of the book's final chapters. Special thanks to Kelley for her patience, advice, and ferocious line revisions. She remains the Enshalla of editors. Also to Stefanie Boyar, who snapped hundreds of startling images during all those years I was taking notes, including the cover photo of Rango, and to my editors Neville Green and Mike Wilson, whose insights and sensibilities shaped my reporting from start to finish.

Special thanks to my agent, Jane Dystel, and my editor at Hyperion, Gretchen Young, as well as her assistant, Elizabeth Sabo, all of whom helped me reimagine this work and coax it into a book. Also to Bridget Nickens at the University of South Florida, who graciously assisted me with research; to Patsy Sims and the rest of my colleagues at Goucher College's creative nonfiction MFA program, who indulged me with their enthusiasm through six summers of my working on this project; and to Brad Hamm, the dean of Indiana University's journalism school, whose support and vision kept me going during the home stretch. Also to Stephanie Hayes and Mallary Tenore for their eagle eyes as they read over the manuscript. And to Anne Hull and David Finkel for decades of listening and prodding.

I am grateful to the Poynter Institute for Media Studies, which gave me a quiet home where I could write and pace, and thoughtful colleagues who offered friendship and guidance. My humble gratitude to Karen Dunlap, Butch Ward, Keith Woods, Chip Scanlan, Jeff Saffan, and finally David Shedden, who tracked down hundreds of articles for me. I am indebted, as always, to my mentor and brother Roy Peter Clark, who was writing his own book down the hall at Poynter and who urged me on every step of the way, often materializing at my office door with a few words of encouragement just as the sun was rising over Tampa Bay.

Deepest thanks and love to my sons, Nat and Sam, and my wife, Kelley, for their inspiration and neverending support. I owe them everything.

··· Notes ···

For further details on the sources listed in these notes, see the Bibliography on page 281.

1 THE NEW WORLD

1   *Eleven elephants. One plane:* The scene from the 747 was reconstructed from the author's interviews with Mick Reilly and Chris Kingsley, the only two humans in the cargo hold with the elephants as they traveled from Johannesburg to Tampa.

4   *elephants loom like great gray ghosts:* The author was in the Land Rover, reporting in Mkhaya in April 2007, when this incident occurred with the elephants and the bushwillow.

6   *The conflict unfolds in miniature inside Swaziland:* The history of the Reilly family and of the reintroduction of wildlife to Mlilwane, Hlane, and Mkhaya are based largely on author interviews with Ted and Mick Reilly.

6   *an old jeep named Jezebel:* Cristina Kessler, *All the King's Animals: The Return of Endangered Wildlife to Swaziland*, page 21.

7   *Their armored captive was groggy:* Cristina Kessler, *All the King's Animals*, page 21.

8   *miles of dead trees:* From the author's firsthand reporting in Swaziland in 2007.

9   *"Kahle mfana":* Mick Reilly recounted this dialogue to the author, writing out both the original lines in siSwati and the English translations.

10   *so corrosive it can eat through metal:* Holly T. Dublin and Leo S. Niskanen, editors of "IUCN/SSC AfESG Guidelines for the *in situ* Translocation of the African Elephant for Conservation Purposes," page 38.

12   *elephant culls had long been a reality:* This chapter's lengthy description of the history and methodology of culls in different African countries is gathered from numerous sources, including "Lethal Management of Elephants," a chapter written by Rob Slotow and others for *Elephant Management: A Scientific Assessment for South Africa,* by R. J. Scholes and Kathleen Mennell; *Elephants and Ethics: Toward a Morality of Conscience,* edited by Christen Wemmer and Catherine A. Christen; Dale Peterson's *Elephant Reflections;* Raman Sukumar's *The Living Elephants: Evolutionary Ecology, Behavior and Conservation;* Iain and Oria Douglas-Hamilton's *Battle for the Elephants;* Katy Payne's *Silent Thunder;* and Cynthia Moss's *Elephant Memories.*

12   *The brutal choreography evolved:* To describe the history of elephant culls inside Kruger National Park, the author also relied on the chapter on elephant management, authored by Ian J. Whyte, Rudi J. van Aarde, and Stuart L. Pimm, in *The Kruger Experience: Ecology and Management of Savanna Heterogeneity* edited by Johan T. Du Toit and Kevin H. Rogers, pp. 332–348; numerous sections of Salomon Joubert's massive *The Kruger National Park: A History,* especially volumes one and two; and "Assessment of Elephant Management in South Africa," a powerpoint presentation authored by dozens of elephant researchers, delivered on February 25, 2008.

13   *the use of Scoline was prohibited:* "Elephant Culling's Cruel and Gory Past," an article posted on the International Fund for Animal Welfare's Web site.

13   *"Don't ask me if I enjoyed it":* This quote and the description of vultures and hyenas waiting for the disposal teams to finish are taken from Fred Bridgland's article, "5,000 Elephants Must Die. Here's Why," *Sunday Herald,* October 24, 2004.

14   *drawn to the remains of their kin:* Cynthia Moss, *Elephant Memories,* pp. 73–74, 270–271.

14   *elephants pushed their way into the shed:* Mary Battiata, "The Imperiled Realm of the Elephant: Africa's Thinning Herds, Locked in a Struggle for Survival," *Washington Post*, March 15, 1988.

15   *as though they were investigating:* Dale Peterson, *Elephant Reflections*, p. 244.

15   *elephants ninety miles from a cull:* Cynthia Moss, *Elephant Memories*, pp. 315–316; "Lethal Management of Elephants," p. 298; also Battiata's "The Imperiled Realm of the Elephant," *Washington Post*, March 15, 1988.

15   *believed to be capable of hearing storms:* This description of elephants' ability to communicate over great distances is based on numerous sources, including Katy Payne's *Silent Thunder*; Joyce Poole's *Elephants;* Caitlin O'Connell's *The Elephant's Secret Sense*; Cynthia Moss's *Elephant Memories*; W. R. Langbauer Jr.'s "Elephant Communication" in the journal *Zoo Biology*; "Unusually Extensive Networks of Vocal Recognition in African Elephants," by Karen McComb and others, in *Animal Behaviour*; "African Elephant Vocal Communication I: Antiphonal Calling Behaviour among Affiliated Females," by Joseph Soltis and others in *Animal Behaviour*; and "Rumble Vocalizations Mediate Interpartner Distance in African Elephants, *Loxodonta Africana*," by Katherine A. Leighty and others, also in *Animal Behaviour*. Two of the most helpful sources I discovered on this subject were the Web site for ElephantVoices, an organization run by Joyce Poole and Petter Grannli, and the site for the Elephant Listening Project at Cornell, founded by Katy Payne and now directed by Peter Wrege.

15   *"a throbbing in the air":* Katy Payne, *Silent Thunder*, p. 20.

16   *ears stiffened and spread wide:* Elephants have exhibited this behavior while listening to low-frequency calls, as has been chronicled in "African Elephants Respond to Distant Playbacks of Low-Frequency Conspecific Calls," an article by William R. Langbauer Jr., and others, from the *Journal of Experimental*

Biology; and "Responses of Captive African Elephants to Play-back of Low-Frequency Calls," by Langbauer and Payne and others, in the *Canadian Journal of Zoology*, among other sources.

16   *orphans had wreaked havoc:* This phenomenon has been repeatedly chronicled in multiple sources, including Charles Siebert's "An Elephant Crackup?" *New York Times*, October 8, 2006.

17   *then San Diego and Lowry Park made sense:* Author interviews with Ted and Mick Reilly, as well as Lex Salisbury.

18   *a helicopter crew darted every elephant:* This description of how the elephants were darted, assessed, and moved to the boma is based on the author's interviews with the Reillys, Lex Salisbury, and Brian French.

18   *performed field sonograms:* Based on author interviews with the Reillys, also "Reproductive Evaluation in Wild African Elephants Prior to Translocation," by Thomas B. Hildebrandt and others, from the proceedings of a 2004 joint conference of the American Association of Zoo Veterinarians, the American Association of Wildlife Veterinarians, and the Wildlife Disease Association, pp. 75–76.

18   *Two of the females were pregnant:* Andrea Moss, "Elephant Pregnancies Spark New Concerns," *North County Times*, July 15, 2003.

18   *protesting and organizing letter-writing campaigns:* The opposition of the animal-rights coalition has been documented in numerous articles, including "The Swazi 11: A Case Study in the Global Trade in Live Elephants," a paper presented by Adam M. Roberts and Will Travers at the XIXth International Congress of Zoology in August 2004 in Beijing; Kathy Steele, "Experts Oppose Importing Elephants to American Zoos," *Tampa Tribune*, July 3, 2003; and Graham Brink, "4 Elephants from Africa Arrive at Zoo," *St. Petersburg Times*, August 23, 2003.

18   *"If the elephants are euthanized":* From a transcript of a hearing on August 6, 2003, in front of U.S. District Judge John D. Bates.

19   *"consider them as sentient beings":* from an open letter written by Dr. Cynthia Moss and eight other researchers, sent on June 24, 2003 to San Diego Zoo and Lowry Park Zoo.

19   *PETA offered to pay:* The efforts by PETA and the rest of the coalition to stop the elephant importation have been chronicled in numerous articles, on the Web sites of some of these groups, in public statements by their representatives, and in various court documents, including a Memorandum Opinion filed on August 8, 2003 in the United States District Court for the District of Columbia, Civil Action No. 03-1497; and in the Plaintiffs-Appellants' Emergency Motion for an Injunction Pending Appeal, filed in the United States Court of Appeals for the District of Columbia Circuit, Case No. 03-5216.

20   *thronged together to push her through the fence:* Author interview with Mick Reilly.

2   THE AUDACITY OF CREATION

22   *thumping fists on steering wheels:* The author witnessed this scene repeatedly throughout 2003 during morning rush hour traffic jams on I-275 at the Sligh Avenue exit.

23   *The zoo was a living catalogue:* My thoughts on this point were guided by the introduction to Eric Baratay's and Elisabeth Hardouin-Fugier's *Zoo: A History of Zoological Gardens in the West*, pp. 7–13.

24   *whimpered like a puppy:* Author observation during reporting with Pam Noel, assistant curator in charge of the zoo's Asia section.

24   *bestowing the animals with* Star Wars *names:* Author interviews with Kevin McKay, Pam Noel, Lee Ann Rottman, Virginia Edmonds, and Andrea Schuch.

25   *frogs and toads were dying off:* Author interviews with Kevin Zippel.

25   *A parade of raptors:* This scene, including the details on Myrtle's release and the dream of her return, are based on the author's reporting inside the birds of prey building and his interviews with Jeff Ewelt, who released the dove behind his home, and with Melinda Mendolusky, who shared her dream.

27   *unloaded a large mound of horse manure:* James Steinberg, "Heavy Security Awaited Elephants," *Los Angeles Times*, August 23, 2003; also "PETA Protests Pachyderms with Poo," 10News.com, posted to Web site on August 22, 2003.

28   *living proof that visionaries can be hell:* This description of Lex Salisbury is based on the author's several years of observing and interviewing Salisbury, as well as the author's interviews with multiple members of Lowry Park's staff, past and present. Also based on an audit the city of Tampa ordered in 2008 to assess Salisbury's leadership.

29   *bush khakis and a safari hat:* Salisbury wore this garb in many issues of Lowry Park's *Zoo Chatter*, in the zoo's annual reports, and on the cover of the *Maddux Business Report*, in the fall of 2008, beside the headline "A WILD THING."

29   *"resembles the great white hunter":* Jeff Klinkenberg, "Wolf Pact: Endangered Red Wolves Find a Haven at Lowry Park Zoo," *St. Petersburg Times*, March 11, 1990.

29   *"El Diablo Blanco":* The nickname was shared during several author interviews with Lowry Park staffers and was confirmed during an author interview with Lex Salisbury.

30   *a tiny menagerie:* Account of zoo's early history based on information from the zoo's Web site, as well as numerous news articles over the years.

30   *undisputed star in those early years:* "Animal Parade a Fun Idea," *St. Petersburg Times*, June 23, 1965.

30   *threw food over a fence:* "Lowry Park Safeguards Its Guests," *St. Petersburg Times*, July 5, 1966.

30   *stoplights on Happy Drive:* "Kids Do Driving on 'Polite Boule-
      vard,'" United Press International article, published in the *St.
      Petersburg Times*, November 28, 1966.

30   *"a children's paradise":* "Nature Trail: Stark Contrast," *Evening
      Independent*, May 31, 1965.

30   *Sheena the elephant was shipped off:* "Elephant Dies of Heart
      Attack," *St. Petersburg Times*, January 30, 1986.

30   *"It was a rat hole":* Christopher Goffard, "Zoo Will Add a World
      of New Life," *St. Petersburg Times*, May 29, 2001.

32   *Disney's armies of Imagineers:* Some readers may be aware that
      the publishing house for this book is also owned by Disney. The
      author wishes to note that he included the description of the
      theme park entirely on his own, long before his publisher had
      any idea such a passage would be part of the manuscript. The
      author included this section not as an endorsement of Animal
      Kingdom but because it would be virtually impossible to chron-
      icle Lowry Park's recent history without discussing its place
      among other major animal attractions in central Florida.

34   *"See the big monkey?":* The author repeatedly witnessed the same
      exchange between Herman and various moms, with the moms
      uttering almost exactly the same words every time.

34   *His early life had unfolded:* These sections on Herman's life and
      history are based on the author's observations of the chimp over
      the years, plus his interviews with Ed and Roger Schultz as well
      as with multiple members of Lowry Park's primate staff and
      other employees, including Angela Belcher, Kevin McKay, David
      Murphy, Rachel Nelson, Lee Ann Rottman, Andrea Schuch, and
      Heather Mackin.

35   *"We better move":* The author observed this scene firsthand.

36   *Enshalla appeared, cloaked in a calm:* These sections on Enshalla
      and Eric are based on the author's observations of the two Suma-
      tran tigers between 2003 and 2006, plus interviews with multiple

members of Lowry Park's Asia staff and other keepers and employees who observed and worked with the tigers over the years, including Ged Caddick, Brian Czarnik, Rachel Nelson, Pam Noel, Carie Peterson, and Lee Ann Rottman.

37　*Her favorite was Obsession:* Author interview with Pam Noel.

37　*"wildernesses of freedom":* Ted Hughes, "The Jaguar."

40　*peat swamp forests where she belonged: Tigers of the World*, edited by Ronald L. Tilson and Ulysses S. Seal, p. 86.

40　*"core of the zoo's conscience":* Phillip T. Robinson, *Life at the Zoo*, p. 59.

41　*to live with ambivalence:* Author interviews with Brian Czarnik and Carie Peterson.

41　*many keepers had reacted with quiet unease:* Author interviews with multiple members of the Lowry Park staff, including Brian Czarnik, Brian French, Carie Peterson, and Lee Ann Rottman. Some were describing their own ambivalence; others, including French and Rottman, were simply attesting to the ambivalence they had witnessed among others on the staff.

3　NIGHT DELIVERY

43　*Swazi Eleven arrived in America:* This scene is based on author interviews with Brian French, Lee Ann Rottman, Lex Salisbury, and Heather Mackin, all of whom were at the airport and rode in the convoy. Also Kathy Steele, "Elephants Are Slipped into Zoo After Dark," *Tampa Tribune*, August 23, 2003.

43　*caller threatened to burn down the zoo:* James Steinberg, "Heavy Security Awaited Elephants," *Los Angeles Times*, August 23, 2003.

43　*police had escorted the trio away in handcuffs:* Author interview with Heather Mackin; Tampa police report 03-359730; Tamara Lush, "Trio of Protesters Arrested at Zoo," *St. Petersburg Times*,

August 15, 2003; Kathy Steele, "Importation of Elephants Protested at Zoos, Embassy," *Tampa Tribune*, Aug. 15, 2003.

43   *a lead indicating that activists:* Based on an author interview with Larry Killmar and also an FBI memo, written on August 20, 2003, and obtained by the American Civil Liberties Union. The memo is posted online at http://www.aclu.org/spyfiles/jttf/288.pdf.

44   *Lowry Park's curator:* In the fall of 2003, Rottman was actually the zoo's acting curator because at that time the previous curator was on extended medical leave. Soon afterward, Rottman was officially named curator. For all intents and purposes, she was already serving in that capacity on the night the elephants arrived from Swaziland.

44   *one of the zoo's true believers:* Description based on years of the author observing and interviewing Lee Ann Rottman.

44   *as though she were a baboon:* Kari K. Ridge, "I'm just one of the mandrill troop now," *St. Petersburg Times*, December 23, 1996.

44   *three wallabies had died:* Amy Herdy, "Wallabies Die after Trip in Ryder Truck," *St. Petersburg Times*, July 2, 2002.

44   *the animal's trunk dangling underneath:* Murray Fowler, *Restraint and Handling of Wild and Domestic Animals*, pp. 7, 73; also Fowler and Susan Mikota, *Biology, Medicine and Surgery of Elephants*, pp. 86–87.

45   *braced herself for the possibility:* The author observed Lee Ann Rottman discussing these fears during a meeting of Lowry Park's docents on October 15, 2003.

45   *convoy turned east:* Scene based on author interviews with Lee Ann Rottman, Lex Salisbury, Brian French, and Heather Mackin.

46   *"Learning to read the animals":* Details from the elephants' first days at the zoo are based on author interviews with Brian French.

46   *Born into a family of circus performers:* Author interviews with French.

48 *a fatality rate three times that of coal miners:* John Lehnardt, "Elephant Handling: A Problem of Risk Management and Resource Allocation," the *Journal of the Elephant Managers Association*, 1991.

48 *an Asian elephant killed Char-Lee Torre:* The account of the handler's death is based on author interviews with the Torre family and Lex Salisbury; also Marty Rosen, "Elephant Kills Young Trainer at Tampa Zoo," *St. Petersburg Times*, July 31, 1993; and Marty Rosen, "Elephant Had Challenged Her Trainer Before," *St. Petersburg Times*, August 7, 1993.

48 *elephants were not dominated:* The descriptions of free and protected contact are based on numerous sources, including Eric Scigliano, *Love, War, and Circuses: The Age-Old Relationship Between Elephants and Humans*, pp. 280–286; Fowler and Mikota, *Biology, Medicine, and Surgery of Elephants*, pp. 52–55; "Welfare Implications of Elephant Training," an article published by the American Veterinary Medicine Association's Animal Welfare Division; Gary Priest, "Zoo Story," *Inc.*, October 1, 1994; and Jennifer Orsi and David K. Rogers, "No Rules on Handling Elephants," *St. Petersburg Times*, July 31, 1993.

50 *"She doesn't really know how to be an elephant":* Account of Ellie's history and behavior based on author interviews with Lowry Park staff, including Brian French, Steve LeFave, and Lee Ann Rottman.

50 *Night-vision cameras:* Description of the elephants' first days is based on author interviews with Brian French, Steve Lefave, and Lee Ann Rottman.

52 *"Even if a lion could speak":* Wittgenstein, *Philosophical Investigations*, p. 241.

52 *a lexicon that catalogues:* Based on information from the Web sites of ElephantVoices and of the Elephant Listening Project at Cornell University's Bioacoustics Research Program.

55 *named by rangers inside Mkhaya and Hlane:* Author interview with Mick Reilly.

4 SIREN SONG

57   *manatees did tussle occasionally:* Jennifer Young Harper and Bruce A. Schulte, "Social Interactions in Captive Female Florida Manatees," *Zoo Biology*, 2005, pp. 137–139.

59   *" 'I wish they didn't have to be here.' ":* Several of Lowry Park's keepers expressed such ambivalence during interviews with the author.

59   *sixty-four manatees back into the wild:* Posted in Lowry Park's Florida mammals office in October 2003.

59   *"We take 'em in":* Author interview with David Murphy.

59   *keepers would drape themselves:* The author witnessed many manatee exams over several years and accompanied the staff on several manatee releases.

60   *newborn calves whose mothers had abandoned them:* These sections on the orphaned manatee calves are based on the author's interviews with Virginia Edmonds and Lex Salisbury, as well as e-mails from Edmonds, and the author's firsthand reporting.

61   *the staff dubbed him Buttonwood:* The description of the staff's attempts to save the calf are based on the author's interviews and e-mails with Edmonds. Also, Shari Missman Miller, "Newborn Manatee Rescued, Coddled," *St. Petersburg Times*, May 15, 2003; and Rob Brannon, "Orphaned Manatee Delights Fans," *St. Petersburg Times*, May 26, 2003.

61   *different combinations of formula and Pedialyte:* "Zoo Puts Foundling Manatee on Display," *St. Petersburg Times*, May 26, 2003.

61   *hoping she would let him nurse:* "Despite a Couple of Setbacks, Buttonwood Is Getting Better," Shari Missman Miller, *St. Petersburg Times*, July 6, 2003.

61   *his small gray body floating:* Cory Schouten, "Facing Long Odds, Buttonwood Dies At Zoo," *St. Petersburg Times*, July 12, 2003.

62   *a second abandoned manatee calf:* Details on Loo's life and death are based on the author's interviews with Virginia Edmonds and Lex Salisbury, as well as e-mails from Edmonds. Also, the author saw Loo in one of the medical pools, in between feedings, not long after the calf was brought to the zoo.

62   *faint calls of the adult manatees:* Author interview and e-mail exchange with Dustin Smith, who first told me that the Lowry Park keepers could hear the sounds. Background on the vocalizations was found on a Web site put together by the University of Rhode Island's Office of Marine Programs in partnership with Marine Acoustics, Inc. The page that describes the vocalizations can be accessed at http://www.dosits.org/gallery/marinemm/31.htm, and it includes an audio clip of a vocalization provided by David Mann at the University of South Florida.

63   *each new wave of visitors:* During his years of reporting at the zoo, the author witnessed these behaviors many times.

64   *an institution custom-made for families:* Sue Carlton, "Renovated Zoo Will Roar with Excitement," *St. Petersburg Times*, October 18, 1987.

65   *replica of a raccoon dropping:* Lex Salisbury displayed the dropping during a tour he gave the author in October 2003.

65   *"We call him Pee Goat":* Author interview with Carie Peterson.

66   *The curator and the defiant monkeys:* The author witnessed this scene.

67   *the ultimate troubleshooter:* This description of Lee Ann Rottman's history and duties is based on the author's many interviews with Rottman and years of watching her do her job.

67   *a hippo surfaced directly beneath her boyfriend:* Author interview with Rottman.

68   *"He's very handsome, I think":* Author witnessed this moment with Rottman and Rango.

69   *"the Berlin boys":* Based on author interviews with Brian French and Lex Salisbury, also "Inseminating Elephant Takes 2 Germans, an Ultrasound and a Very Long Wait," by Tom Paulson, *Seattle Post-Intelligencer,* March 2, 2005.

69   *raised the height of Lowry Park's perimeter fence:* Author learned this while listening to Lee Ann Rottman's talk in front of the docents in October 2003.

69   *red paint and paint thinner:* Jane Fritsch, "Animal Activists Deface Homes of Dunda's Keepers," *Los Angeles Times,* October 15, 1988.

70   *a compelling example:* "On the Brink of Extinction: Saving the Lion Tamarins of Brazil," *The Encylopedia of Mammals,* pp. 342–343.

70   *none had ever been selected:* Author e-mail exchange with Lex Salisbury.

71   *not even attempt to climb into the trees:* Vicki Croke, *The Modern Ark,* p. 195.

71   *Bornean orangutans were so endangered:* Michael Casey, "Orangutans on 'Fast Track to Extinction,' " *Independent,* July 6, 2008.

71   *"not all it's cracked up to be":* Author interview with Lee Ann Rottman.

5   ROYALTY

72   *Liberia, December 1966:* Account of Herman's early life and history are based primarily on the author's interviews with Ed and Roger Schultz. The details of the baby chimp's purchase, including the thumbprint, are also based on a copy of the original receipt, provided to the author by Ed Schultz.

74   *tumbled into a snow bank:* Scene based on a family photo taken by Roger Schultz and shared with the author by Ed Schultz, as well as the author's interviews with both the father and son.

75	*incident in Stamford, Connecticut:* This account is compiled from several news reports, including Andy Newman, "Pet Chimp Is Killed After Mauling Woman," *New York Times*, February 16, 2009; Stephanie Gallman, "Chimp Attack 911 Call: 'He's Ripping Her Apart,'" CNN.com, February 18, 2009; Anahad O'Connor, "Woman Mauled by Chimp Has Surgery, and Her Vital Signs Improve," *New York Times*, February 18, 2009; and John Christoffersen, "Brothers: Victim of Chimp Attack Feared Animal," Associated Press, June 28, 2009.

77	*sued the city for discrimination:* Shannon Behnken, "Tuskegee Airman Demanded Equality," *Tampa Tribune*, August 14, 2007.

77	*Razor blades were flicked:* David Smith, *Evening Independent*, August 31, 1976.

77	*Sea lions collapsed:* "Kindness Kills Old Sea Lion," Associated Press article published in the *St. Petersburg Times* on June 6, 1963.

77	*Two Bengal tigers died:* "Youth faces charges for tossing Tylenol tablets to otter at zoo," United Press International article published in the *St. Petersburg Times* on May 29, 1983.

77	*"I didn't even want to talk about it":* Richard Danielson, "Lowry Park Zoo Has Record Number of Visitors," *St. Petersburg Times*, December 6, 1966.

77	*stole one of the zoo's lions:* "3 Charged in Lion Theft," *St. Petersburg Times*, February 19, 1976.

78	*the chimp hurled away:* "Mayor Greco Gets a Hand," Associated Press article published in the *St. Petersburg Times*, Sept. 27, 1972.

78	*Herman read the nonverbal signals:* Author interviews with Kevin McKay, Lee Ann Rottman, and Andrea Schuch.

78	*staff left Schultz a key:* Author interviews with Ed Schultz. This detail was confirmed by Lowry Park staff.

79	*"Wonderful," she called him:* Details of Jane Goodall's affection for Herman and Lowry Park are taken from Mary Dolan's "Noted

Expert on Primates Visits ChimpanZoo Site," *St. Petersburg Times*, May 7, 1987; and Sue Carlton's "Primate Expert Touts Zoo Project," *St. Petersburg Times*, May 9, 1990.

79   *a wild chimpanzee call:* Dong-Phuong Nguyen, "A Girl's Curiosity Nurtured Expertise," *St. Petersburg Times*, March 23, 2005.

79   *just as Gombe's chimps did in the wild:* Jane Goodall, *In the Shadow of Man*, pp. 35–36.

80   *termite mound was not real:* Vicki Croke, *The Modern Ark*, page 39.

80   *distaste for seeing animals in cages:* Eric Baratay and Elisabeth Hardouin-Fugier, *Zoo*, p. 237.

80   *simulated bird droppings:* Phillip T. Robinson, *Life at the Zoo*, p. 90.

80   *"imitation freedom.":* Baratay and Hardouin-Fugier, *Zoo*, p. 244.

81   *In one gruesome case:* Frans de Waal, *Chimpanzee Politics*, pp. 211–212.

81   *"an assassination":* Richard Wrangham and Dale Peterson, *Demonic Males*, p. 128.

81   *waging war on other chimp groups:* Jane Goodall, *Through a Window*, pp. 98–111.

81   *eating their flesh:* Jane Goodall, *Through a Window*, p. 108.

81   *while others dismember him:* Jane Goodall, *Through a Window*, pp. 104–108; also Wrangham and Peterson, *Demonic Males*, pp. 17–19.

81   *"so naturally aggressive":* Author interview with Andrea Schuch.

81   *just to maintain his dominance:* This account of Chester's dominance, and of Herman's confusion during that time, is based on author interviews with Lee Ann Rottman.

83   *play through the scenarios:* Author interview with Rottman.

83   *a hand on his daughter's shoulder:* Author witnessed this scene.

84   *their protector and leader:* This account of Herman's reign in the renovated Lowry Park, including his reaction to Dr. Murphy's dart, is based on author interviews with Rottman.

84   *imbued with ruthless purity:* This account of Enshalla's history and behavior is based on the author's interviews with multiple members of Lowry Park's staff, including Brian Czarnik, Pam Noel, Carie Peterson, Lee Ann Rottman, and Lex Salisbury, as well as interviews with Ged Caddick and Don Woodman, who worked with the tiger in earlier years, and from the author's own years of observing her at the zoo and shadowing her keepers as they cared for her.

85   *Tigers have distinctive personalities:* Lee S. Crandall, *A Zoo Man's Notebook*, p. 133.

85   *"true to her species":* Author interview with Pam Noel.

85   *"tofu shaped to look like their prey?":* Ibid.

86   *she treated him as an intruder:* Mary Jo Melone, "Tigers Take Time Breaking the Ice," *St. Petersburg Times*, June 28, 1989.

86   *Shere-Khan struggled and suffocated:* Kathleen Ovack, "Tiger Kills Rare Cub as Visitors Watch," *St. Petersburg Times*, May 6, 1990.

87   *"she wasn't seeking human companionship":* Author interview with Ged Caddick.

87   *walked into the Bengal tiger exhibit:* "Fatal Mauling a Metrozoo Mystery," *Miami Herald*, June 7, 1994; and "In the Zoo World, a Mistake Can Be Lethal," *Boston Globe*, June 11, 1994.

87   *lion bit down on her hand:* Logan Mabe, "Lion Bites Off Worker's Arm," *St. Petersburg Times*, May 13, 2002; and Kathryn Wexler, "Zoo Keeper Put Fingers in Lion's Cage," *St. Petersburg Times*, May 14, 2002.

87   *nothing like holding a housecat:* This description is based on the author's firsthand experience at the home of Don Woodman, a

veterinarian who worked with Enshalla as a young tiger. At the time of our interview, his family was foster caring for a litter of ten-week-old tiger cubs orphaned after they were confiscated from a facility where they were being neglected. During our interview, one of those cubs kept climbing into my lap and trying to gnaw on my notebook.

88   *cubs were an instant hit:* Marty Rosen, "Tiger Kittens Make Debut," *St. Petersburg Times*, November 27, 1991.

89   *the explosions startled him:* Author interviews with Don Woodman.

89   *they found Rajah dead:* Ibid.

89   *something set them off:* Janet Shelton Rogers, "Zoo's Female Tiger Dies after Fight with Mate," *St. Petersburg Times*, March 12, 1994; also "Crushed Windpipe Killed Tuka," *St. Petersburg Times*, March 16, 1994.

90   *trained to check and recheck every lock:* Author interviews with Pam Noel, Carie Peterson, Brian Czarnik, and Lee Ann Rottman.

90   *answered with a half-roar, half-snort:* Author witnessed this scene.

91   *"All our girls are like that here":* Author interview with Carie Peterson.

91   *chasing his minders:* Author interviews with Kevin McKay, Andrea Schuch, and Lee Ann Rottman.

92   *race toward her, running on all fours:* Author interviews with Pam Noel and Lee Ann Rottman.

6   COLD-BLOODED

93   *died in Virginia's arms:* Author interviews and e-mail exchanges with Virginia Edmonds.

94   *"They're good at birthing":* Author interview with Dan Costell.

95   *calculus of life and death:* Author interviews and observations of the herps staff.

95   *"Whoever hatches first, wins":* Details on frog eggs and mortality rates among K-selected and r-selected species based on author interviews with Dan Costell, Dustin Smith, and Kevin Zippel.

95   *running catalogue of stereotypes:* The author heard these stereotypes constantly bandied among the zoo staff during his years of reporting.

96   *Dustin and Dan—as they were invariably called:* The portraits of the two herps keepers' personalities are based on many interviews with them and other keepers, as well as years of observing them both at the zoo and outside the zoo.

97   *the minor god who held sway:* The author followed Dan Costell many times as he nurtured the frogs and their artificial rain forest.

98   *a Komodo dragon coiled itself:* Author witnessed Dan Costell getting this tattoo.

98   *"Loser," he would say, smirking:* Author witnessed this exchange, and many others like it, while following Dustin Smith on his rounds.

98   *hurled her droppings at him:* Author interviews with Dustin Smith. Lee Ann Rottman confirmed the orang's general dislike of men.

99   *Gabremariam had visibly shuddered:* Author witnessed this moment on the elevator while following Gabremariam and Lex Salisbury to a Tampa city council meeting.

99   *Dustin could quote the studies:* These studies were confirmed in Vicki Croke's *The Modern Ark*, p. 97.

100   *a cluster of howler monkeys:* Author witnessed these keeper scenes, including Kevin McKay's comment on Grimaldi, Carie Peterson's

encounter with the geese, and Dan Costell's fascination with the frogs.

101   *Led Zeppelin wailed on:* The author noticed that Zeppelin songs almost always happened to play on the radio inside the venomous snake room. ZZ Top also serenaded the snakes regularly.

101   *"I'm no bunnyhugger":* This section on keeper culture is based on the author's numerous interviews and months of reporting with Costell, Carie Peterson, and many other members of Lowry Park's staff.

103   *especially fond of Bamboo:* Author interviews with Costell, Carie Peterson, Dustin Smith, and Lee Ann Rottman.

7   FRONTIER

104   *Code One drill, again:* Author witnessed the scene.

105   *Lowry Park's Code One protocols:* Based on author interviews with Lee Ann Rottman, Lex Salisbury, and many other keepers.

105   *At the Ueno Zoo in Tokyo:* Phillip T. Robinson, *Life at the Zoo,* p. 77.

105   *most likely to kill humans:* Vicki Croke, *The Modern Ark,* page 105.

105   *rainstorm flooded the polar bear moat:* Ibid.

106   *Hurricane Andrew roared:* Tai Abbady, "Miami's Zoo Teems with New Life 10 Years after Hurricane Andrew," Associated Press, 2002; also, the Miami zoo's Web site describes the devastation of the hurricane at http://www.miamimetrozoo.com/about-metro-zoo.asp?Id=93&rootId=8.

106   *Lowry Park . . . had never taken a direct hit:* In the decades prior to 2003, the worst hurricane to come close to Tampa Bay was Hurricane Elena, a Category 3 storm that stalled just off the central Florida coast in 1983 before turning northward.

107   *a Siberian tiger named Tatiana:* This account is based on numer-
        ous *San Francisco Chronicle* articles and on a fifteen-page report
        compiled by several AZA inspectors in the wake of the attack.
        The inspectors interviewed many of the San Francisco zoo em-
        ployees who were on the grounds the evening of the attack, and
        together their accounts offer a comprehensive and detailed time
        line of the incident. The inspection report was completed in
        March 2008 and was accessed by the author on the *San Francisco
        Chronicle*'s Web site at http:www.sfgate.com/ZCTQ.

107   *"My brother's going to die":* The excerpt of the 911 call is taken
        from a transcript published in the *San Francisco Chronicle* on
        January 16, 2008.

109   *alerting him to the bad news:* Justin Scheck and Ben Worthen,
        "When Animals Go AWOL, Zoos Try to Tame Bad PR," *Wall
        Street Journal,* January 5, 2008.

109   *dismissed zoos as wretched prisons:* "Zoos: Pitiful Prisons," article
        on PETA Web site, accessed July 10, 2009, at http://www.peta
        .org/mc/factsheet_display.asp?ID=67.

110   *first time a zoo escape had resulted:* Scheck and Worthen, "When
        Animals Go AWOL," *Wall Street Journal,* January 5, 2008.

110   *" 'I am the lion now!' ":* Lawrence Wright, *The Looming Tower,*
        p. 231.

111   *tried to approach Knut:* "Lonely Man Jumps Into Cage With
        Polar Bear Knut," Associated Press, December 22, 2008.

111   *teacher despairing over her inability:* "Woman Is Mauled by
        Polar Bear after Jumping into Berlin Zoo Enclosure," Associated
        Press article published in the *Los Angeles Times,* April 15, 2009.

111   *into a pit with a pride of ten lions:* "Lioness Kills Man Who
        Jumped into Zoo Pit," Reuters, January 25, 2002.

111   *a keeper discovered her body:* This description is based on several
        Washington Post articles, including Avis Thomas-Lester's "Au-

topsy Says Lion Attack Killed Woman; Police Try to Establish Identity of Woman Found in Lion's Den," March 6, 1995; Phil McCombs' "In the Lair of the Urban Lion," March 7, 1995; and Toni Locy's "Lion Victim Spent Final Day at Court; Clerk Says Woman Wanted to File Suit for Custody of a Daughter," March 10, 1995. In addition, Kay Redfield Jamison provides a haunting summary and analysis of the case in "The Lion Enclosure," a chapter of her book *Night Falls Fast: Understanding Suicide*, pp. 154–159.

112 *zoo's most serious Code One:* This brief history of animal escapes at Lowry Park is based on author interviews with Dan Costell, Rachel Nelson, Lee Ann Rottman, and Heather Mackin. The author observed the guinea fowl on the loose and heard the "code one, chicken" call.

112 *Lex called to Rudy:* Salisbury's success in safely retrieving the orangutan was reported in the *St. Petersburg Times* on June 28, 1991. In addition, Salisbury shared some details of the incident in an e-mail exchange with the author.

112 *orangutans are known as escape artists:* Eugene Linden, *The Octopus and the Orangutan*, p. 96.

113 *a set of Code One recommendations:* The author saw this advice on a bulletin board in the herps building and wrote it down.

114 *"The night before she died":* This account of Char-Lee Torre's last weeks and her death is based on the author's interviews with Torre's family and with Lex Salisbury; on the Tampa police report on the attack, #93-050287; and on several *St. Petersburg Times* articles, including Marty Rosen's "Elephant Kills Young Trainer at Tampa Zoo," July 31, 1993, and Rosen's "Elephant Had Challenged Her Trainer Before," August 7, 1993.

115 *Asian elephants typically show more patience:* M. Gore, M. Hutchins, and J. Ray, "A Review of Injuries Caused by Elephants in Captivity: An Examination of Predominant Factors," *International Zoo Yearbook*, 2006, p. 60.

115   *New trainers . . . particularly vulnerable:* Same study as above; also Amy Sutherland, *Kicked, Bitten, and Scratched,* p. 270.

115   *Tillie had spent three decades in captivity:* Details on the elephant's history are available in *The North American Regional Studbook—Asian Elephant,* p. 51.

116   *a particularly ugly scandal:* This account of the elephant controversy at San Diego is based on a series of articles by Jane Fritsch published in the *Los Angeles Times* between May and December of 1988.

116   *Protected contact . . . showed another way:* The section chronicling the development of protected contact is based on numerous sources, including Gary Priest's "Zoo Story," published on the Web site of *Inc.* in October 1994; an article by Priest and others titled "Managing Elephants Using Protected Contact," *Soundings,* First Quarter 1998, pp. 21–24; and a collection of pieces written by Tim Desmond, Gaile Laule, and Margaret Whittaker, three consultants who worked on the new protocol with Priest. One article, "Protected-Contact Elephant Training," was presented by the consultants at the 1991 AZA conference. The other articles are available online at http://www.activeenvironments.org.

116   *caring for an elephant's feet:* Gary Priest, "Zoo Story," and Ian Redmond, *Elephant,* p. 16.

117   *rearing up like Godzilla:* Tim Desmond and Gail Laule, "Protected-Contact Elephant Training," pp. 4–5.

117   *they vandalized his car:* Amy Sutherland, *Kicked, Bitten, and Scratched,* p. 271.

118   *"one of the very best zoological parks of its size":* Jennifer Orsi, "Tampa's Lowry Park Zoo: From Bad to Best," *St. Petersburg Times,* March 3, 1994.

118   *risk was minimal and manageable:* E-mail exchange between author and Salisbury.

118   *Tillie's warnings began almost immediately:* Larry Dougherty, "Zoo Cleared in Elephant Handler's Death," *St. Petersburg Times*, April 3, 1997.

119   *"Don't hurt the elephant":* Lex Salisbury recounted this detail in an interview with the author.

120   *Mourn not for us:* Torre's family showed the paper and its handwritten verse to the author. The lines are from "The Star," a *Twilight Zone* episode based on a short story by Arthur C. Clarke.

120   *photos of Char-Lee Torre still hung:* Observed by author during his reporting.

8   BERLIN BOYS

121   *Msholo weave his trunk:* Scene described to author during interview with Brian French.

121   *Elephants are skilled tool-users:* A detailed list of their abilities, and an account of them blocking the cull roads, is available in "Tool Use by Wild and Captive Elephants," an article by Suzanne Chevalier-Skolnikoff and Jo Liska, published in *Animal Behaviour*, Volume 46, p. 210.

122   *their abstract works have been auctioned:* Hillary Mayell, "Painting Elephants Get Online Gallery," *National Geographic News*, June 26, 2002. To view or buy examples of elephant artwork, go to http://www.novica.com/search/searchresults.cfm?searchtype=quick&txt=1&regionid=1&keyword=elephants&keywordsubmit=. The paintings are accompanied by articles about the artwork and discuss the differences between paintings where a handler guides the elephant's brushstrokes and where the animal has been allowed to move the brush across the page however she likes.

122   *large rocks on electric fences:* Joyce Poole, *Elephants*, p. 36.

122 *Burma hoisted a log:* "Elephant Escapes after Dropping Log on Electric Fence," *New Zealand Herald*, January 23, 2004; also Peter Calder, "One Morning Out Walking an Elephant Crosses My Path," *New Zealand Herald*, January 24, 2004.

122 *testing every aspect of their new lives:* Author interviews with Brian French and Steve Lefave.

123 *crash on the cot in the hall:* Author interviews with Brian French.

123 *didn't act like circus elephants:* This account of the elephants' behaviors and personalities is based on the author's interviews with Brian French and Steve Lefave.

124 *anatomy of an elephant's face:* Interpretation of elephant expressions provided by Murray E. Fowler and R. Eric Miller, *Zoo and Wild Animal Medicine*, p. 44.

126 *ominously named Elephant Restraint Device:* Author witnessed the keepers using the ERD to draw blood and exfoliate the elephants' skin.

127 *rehearsed, so she wouldn't be startled:* Author interviews with Brian French.

128 *English, German, French, and Hindi:* Ibid.

128 *"She was my elephant.":* Ibid.

128 *the sacred and the scientific:* The artificial insemination scene is reconstructed from the author's interviews with Brian French and Steve Lefave, and a phone interview and e-mail exchange with Dr. Thomas Hildebrandt, as well as numerous papers and articles explaining elephant AI, including "Successful Artificial Insemination of an Asian Elephant at the National Zoological Park," published in *Zoo Biology*, volume 23, pp. 45–63.

129 *a technique originally developed to allow paraplegic men:* Vicki Croke, *The Modern Ark*, p. 167.

129   *just another day in a remarkable career:* Gretchen Vogel, "A Fertile Mind on Wildlife Conservation's Front Lines," *Science*, November 9, 2001, pp. 1271–1272.

129   *"He'll ultrasound just about anything":* Ibid.

130   *mechanics of elephant reproduction:* Author interview with Thomas Hildebrandt, also "Aspects of the Reproductive Biology and Breeding Management of Asian and African Elephants," an article written by Hildebrandt, Göritz, and others for *International Zoo Yearbook*, 2006.

131   *"It's for the best for Ellie":* Author's phone interview with Hildebrandt.

9   MATING

132   *In the darkness beyond the edge of the sky:* The opening section describing the satellite tracking the manatee is based on author interviews with Monica Ross and on information from NOAA and from CLS America, the company that tracks the manatees using NOAA's satellites.

133   *attempting to capture him one last time.:* The author accompanied Monica Ross, Virginia Edmonds, David Murphy, and other manatee researchers as they searched for Stormy on the St. Johns River.

135   *newborn male, still connected by the umbilical:* Author interviews with Kevin McKay and Lee Ann Rottman.

136   *trying to mark the entire zoo:* Author interviews with McKay, Rottman, and Andrea Schuch.

136   *first meeting did not go well:* Author interviews with Carie Peterson and Pam Noel.

136   *joined forces to clean the moat:* Author witnessed this scene after climbing into the lemur moat with the keepers.

138 *They had to make it fun:* This section describing the lives of the keepers is based on the author's interviews with many members of Lowry Park's staff.

138 *bustled through their morning workload:* The author was following Carie Peterson on her rounds that day.

139 *"He wants her so bad":* The author witnessed the tiger mating ritual while sitting beside Peterson under the boardwalk.

10 THE HUMAN EXHIBIT

143 *Another sexual request from Herman:* Details of the chimp's sexual habits and of the keeper reactions were based on author interviews with Andrea Schuch, Angela Belcher, and Lee Ann Rottman.

143 *"It makes me crazy":* The author witnessed this exchange between the female keepers.

144 *Rukiya was easily the most intelligent:* This description of the female chimp's behavior and personality is based on the author's interviews with Lee Ann Rottman.

145 *deception and counter-deception:* Anne E. Russon, "Exploiting the Expertise of Others," a chapter in *Machiavellian Intelligence II*, edited by Andrew Whiten and Richard W. Byrne, pp. 193–194.

146 *the chimp would listen:* Author interview with Lee Ann Rottman.

146 *who was really in charge:* The author witnessed this moment between Herman and Lex Salisbury.

146 *he could identify every bird and every gecko:* This scene is based on a tour Salisbury gave to the author.

147 *how to woo mayors and governors.:* This section describing Salisbury's history and management style is based on the author's observations of the CEO during years of reporting, plus several

of the author's interviews with Salisbury, as well as with many people who worked for him over the years.

148 *complaints were almost always whispered:* Author interviews with multiple members of Lowry Park staff, past and present.

149 *"a benevolent dictatorship":* Author interview with Salisbury.

149 *Diamonds sparkled inside augmented cleavage:* The author attended Karamu and witnessed these scenes firsthand, including the late-night visit to the elephant building.

150 *"just kick me in the balls":* Overheard at the table where the author was seated.

153 *surveyed his creation:* The author followed Brian Morrow through the construction site that day, interviewing him as they walked.

155 *a deep crimson form stirring:* This section is based on the author's firsthand reporting and on interviews with Kelly Ryder and other members of the aviary staff.

156 *the magazine saluted:* Maureen P. Sangiorio, "The 10 Best Zoos for Kids," *Child*, June–July 2004, pp. 112–122.

156 *The lucky guest:* Author witnessed this scene.

156 *"Because God made us":* Andrea Schuch recounted this moment to the author.

157 *final days before the debut:* Author witnessed these scenes, as well as the unveiling ceremony with the mayor and then the grand opening of Safari Africa.

11 CITY AND FOREST

159 *news of Ellie's pregnancy:* Author interviews with Brian French and Steve Lefave.

160 *a hybrid of* The Odyssey *and* Wild Kingdom: Author interviews with Jeff Ewelt, Melinda Mendolusky, and Heather Mackin.

161   *an unexpected obstacle:* The author reported firsthand on these experiences inside the basement at Rockefeller Center and outside and inside the studio of *Late Night With Conan O'Brien.*

164   *a lethal fungus known as chytrid:* Author interviews with Kevin Zippel and Dustin Smith, also information from Project Golden Frog's Web site, http://www.ranadorada.org/.

164   *they had to decide:* Author interview with Kevin Zippel.

164   *their first two weeks in the forest:* Author interviews with Kevin Zippel, Dustin Smith, and other members of the research team.

165   *the Thousand-Frog Stream:* The author joined the research team in Panama and accompanied them on this journey into the gorge by the water's edge.

166   *Jeff and Melinda saw it:* Author interviews with Jeff Ewelt and Melinda Mendolusky.

166   *Dustin had to devote almost three weeks:* Author interviews with Dustin Smith and Lee Ann Rottman.

166   *Lowry Park's conservation fund had donated:* Figure supplied by the zoo.

167   *He and Brian French were disagreeing:* Author interviews with Lex Salisbury and Brian French.

168   *Lex's big push:* Interviews with multiple members of Lowry Park's staff, past and present.

168   *One of the doubters was Carie Peterson:* Author interviews and e-mail exchanges with Peterson.

168   *Lamaze class was under way:* Author interviews with Brian French, Steve Lefave, and Heather Mackin.

169   *a newborn calf ran forward:* The scene describing the discovery of the baby elephant's birth is reconstructed from the author's interviews with Brian French, Steve Lefave, and Lee Ann Rottman.

12 UNDERTOW

172 *In those first days after the virgin birth:* Based on the zoo's media releases and on press conference statements made by David Murphy and Lex Salisbury.

172 *the marketing team knew how to capitalize:* "Ellie's Big Bundle of Joy," by Alexandra Zayas, *St. Petersburg Times*, November 11, 2005.

173 *the clear winner, suggested by a second-grade class:* "Elephant Calf Christened at Lowry Park," by Alexandra Zayas, *St. Petersburg Times*, December 22, 2005.

173 *Ellie, now reigning as the unquestioned matriarch:* Author interviews with Brian French and Steve Lefave.

173 *unmistakable signs of an undertow:* Based on the author's interviews with multiple members of the staff, past and present, as well as the author's observations while reporting at the zoo in that period.

174 *Brian, always camera shy:* Author interviews with Brian French.

174 *the zoo was letting him go:* Author interviews with Brian French and Lee Ann Rottman.

174 *"It's a personnel matter":* Author interview with Rachel Nelson.

174 *Brian and Lex confirmed:* Author interviews with Brian French and Lex Salisbury.

175 *"You could get fired at any time for any reason":* Author email exchange with a former keeper.

175 *Carie Peterson debated:* Author interviews with Carie Peterson.

175 *The two Sumatran tigers:* Author interviews with Carie Peterson and Pam Noel.

175 *Dr. Murphy was preparing:* Based on statements Dr. Murphy made at a press conference on August 23, 2006.

176   *"That's my son":* Author witnessed this scene.

176   *he had never forgotten Herman:* Author observations and interviews with Ed Schultz.

177   *The young female's name was Sasha:* Details on the baby chimp's gradual introductions are based on author interviews with Lee Ann Rottman and Angela Belcher.

177   *she would immediately raise her arms:* Sasha did this for the author, who held her.

178   *Herman and Bamboo had tangled:* Author interviews with Lee Ann Rottman.

178   *Lee Ann noticed something odd:* Ibid.

178   *The chimps were fighting:* This section is based on author interviews with Lee Ann Rottman, David Murphy, and Jeff Kremer.

180   *He looked at peace:* Scene based on author interviews with Ed Schultz and Lee Ann Rottman.

13   FREEDOM

181   *Noting Herman's prominence:* Rebecca Catalanello, "Fight Kills Lowry Park Chimp," *St. Petersburg Times,* June 9, 2006.

181   *primate males are often viewed as inherently violent:* The author was present at a meeting of *St. Petersburg Times* editors the day after Herman's death and watched as one editor made this assumption explicit, theorizing that Rukiya had "tried to help" and stop the fight because females are more nurturing.

182   *"Everybody considered them buddies":* Author interview with David Murphy.

182   *rumors circulated, both inside and outside the zoo:* Based on author interviews at Lowry Park and on theories raised in Rebecca

Catalanello's article "Bringing Up Babies, Bringing in Dollars," *St. Petersburg Times*, July 9, 2006.

183   *some wondered out loud if Bamboo should be punished:* The author heard this issue debated several times, including during a conversation at a meeting of *St. Petersburg Times* editors the day after Herman's death.

183   *He refused to look at them:* Author interviews with Ed Schultz.

184   *Bamboo was suffering as well:* Author interviews with Lee Ann Rottman.

184   *a quest to identify the caller:* Author interviews with Carie Peterson, Brian Czarnik, and Jeff Kremer. The campaign to track down the tipster was confirmed and defended in author interviews with Lex Salisbury and Rachel Nelson.

184   *Carie finally quit:* Author interviews with Carie Peterson.

185   *fired only a few days:* Author interviews with Brain Czarnik and Carie Peterson. The firing was confirmed by author interviews with Lex Salisbury, Lee Ann Rottman, and Rachel Nelson. Salisbury also discussed the firing in a press conference on August 24, 2006.

185   *the zoo hired a new keeper:* Statements made by Lex Salisbury and Lee Ann Rottman at the press conference in August 2006.

185   *the new keeper found himself alone with the tigers:* The description of Enshalla's escape and shooting is based on author interviews with Lex Salisbury, Lee Ann Rottman, Virginia Edmonds, and Pam Noel, as well as a written statement Chris Lennon made for investigators, as well as statements made by Salisbury, Rottman, and David Murphy at the press conference the next day.

14 CONSPIRACY THEORY

189   *"What's wrong?" Carie asked:* Author interviews with Carie Peterson.

189   *a good draw at the front gate:* Author witnessed the ticket line the day after Enshalla's shooting.

190   *Chris was so devastated:* Author interviews with Lex Salisbury and Lee Ann Rottman, as well as statements made at the 8/24/06 press conference by Lt. Steve De Lacure, a Fish and Wildlife Conservation Commission inspector.

190   *Lex had no choice:* Author interviews with multiple staff members, past and present.

191   *the zoo had been stretched:* Author interviews with Brian Czarnik.

191   *Lex was asked about Czarnik's firing:* Salisbury statements made at the 8/24/06 press conference.

191   *"We don't call them unless we need them":* Ibid.

192   *Lee Ann was stunned:* Author interviews with Lee Ann Rottman.

192   *Lex guided two reporters to the boardwalk:* The author was one of those reporters.

193   *talk of a statue:* Author interviews with Lee Ann Rottman and Rachel Nelson.

193   *The surviving chimps . . . had not fully recovered:* This section, including the theory on what could have motivated Rukiya to instigate a coup, is based on the author's interviews with Lee Ann Rottman.

195   *former staff members stepped forward:* Author interviews with Jeff and Coleen Kremer; also, their Web site, TampasZoo Advocates.com.

196   *The zoo fired back:* These rebuttals are based on the author's interviews with Lex Salisbury, Lee Ann Rottman, and Greg Stoppelmoor.

197   *he gave a triumphant speech:* The author reported the speech firsthand.

15 WINNING

198 *The critics pounded away:* Author interviews with Jeff and Coleen Kremer; also, their Web site.

199 *something had gone deeply wrong:* Author interviews and e-mails with Carie Peterson.

199 *Lex had learned not to worry:* Author interviews with Lex Salisbury.

199 *filling Lowry Park with more species:* Author interview with Larry Killmar.

200 *Detroit officials questioned the practice:* The quote was excerpted from a discussion on the Detroit Zoo's Web site, http://www .detroitzoo.org/News%10Events/In_the_News/Elephants_ Questions_and_Answers/, but it has since apparently been removed from the site.

200 *warmer temperatures of Florida were well suited:* This update on the elephants' progress and on Sdudla's transfer to the Montgomery Zoo is based on the author's interviews with Steve Lefave, Lee Ann Rottman, Brian French, Lex Salisbury, and Rachel Nelson.

200 *"among the best in the country":* Author interview with Steve Feldman.

200 *stemming the tide of extinction:* Author interviews with Dan Costell.

201 *situation with the tigers:* The update on Eric and the white tigers is based on author interviews with Lee Ann Rottman and Rachel Nelson.

201 *no conservation value to them:* The case against exhibiting white tigers has been made in many interviews and articles. The most damning criticisms have come from Ronald Tilson, director of conservation at the Minnesota Zoo and one of the world's acknowledged experts on various tiger subspecies.

201   *Lex did not agree:* Author interview with Lex Salisbury.

202   *his will never seemed to waver:* This section is based on the author's observations and interviews with Salisbury over several years, as well as multiple interviews he has given to other journalists.

202   *posed for the cover:* Bob Andelman, "A Wild Thing: How Lowry Park Zoo Scratched Its Way from Worst to First," *Maddux Business Report*, October 2008.

203   *Lex invited a* St. Petersburg Times *reporter:* The author was the journalist who toured Safari Wild that day in December 2007 with Salisbury and his wife and Larry Killmar.

206   *memorandum of understanding:* The memo was first publicly reported by the author in "Zoo Story," *St. Petersburg Times*, December 16, 2007. Over the following year, the memo was dissected at length in further coverage of the zoo and of Safari Wild in the *St. Petersburg Times* and the *Tampa Tribune*, as well as in multiple reports from several media outlets.

16 NOT WINNING

209   *The real trouble began:* The account of the monkeys' escape and miscellaneous adventures is based on numerous news articles published in the *St. Petersburg Times*, the *Tampa Tribune*, and the *Lakeland Ledger*. It would require pages, literally, to list them all. In addition, Lex Salisbury and Elena Sheppa discussed the escape in an interview with the author in February 2010.

209   *people had warned him the species could swim:* Author interview with Salisbury.

210   *patas monkeys appear somewhat comical:* Tom Lake, "Fastest Monkeys on Earth Won't Be Easy to Capture," *St. Petersburg Times*, April 24, 2008.

210 *sometimes called dancing monkeys:* Herb Clement, *Zoo Man*, p. 144.

210 *the males typically weigh:* patas monkey fact sheet available online from the University of Wisconsin's Primate Info Net, http://pin.primate.wisc.edu/factsheets/entry/patas_monkey.

210 *they rely on evasive tactics:* Kelley Benham and Don Morris, "Escape from Monkey Island," *St. Petersburg Times*, February 1, 2009.

210 *None of this deterred Lex:* Benham and Morris, "Escape from Monkey Island."

211 *"I have monkeys in my yard":* Erin Sullivan, "Seeing Monkeys? You're Not Bananas," *St. Petersburg Times*, August 30, 2008.

211 *They snuck onto a ranch:* Baird Helgeson, "Escaped Monkeys Make Mischief on Ranch," *Tampa Tribune*, October 25, 2008.

212 *Revelations tumbled forth with dizzying speed:* This section summarizing the exposés into Lex Salisbury's business affairs is based on numerous news reports, but the lion's share of the investigative work was pieced together by Alexandra Zayas of the *St. Petersburg Times*, Baird Helgeson of the *Tampa Tribune*, and Steve Andrews of News Channel 8.

213 *"I should have had better political instincts":* Alexandra Zayas, "Iorio Says Zoo Didn't Keep City Informed," *St. Petersburg Times*, September 16, 2008.

213 *board had reviewed the memo:* These details on the controversy are based on the city of Tampa's audit of the zoo, released to the public in its final form in March 2009. The document is available online at http://www.tampagov.net/dept_Internal_Audit/files/09/0901.pdf. In addition, the audit's contents were reported and discussed extensively in numerous news articles in the *St. Petersburg Times*, the *Tampa Tribune*, and other media outlets.

214 *a three-day trip to Paris:* The city audit, pg 45.

214 *"Mr. Salisbury appeared to treat the operation":* p. 61 of the audit.

215 *"Plead for mercy":* Alexandra Zayas, "Zoo Leader Takes Issue with Audit," *St. Petersburg Times*, December 16, 2008.

216 *many of the audit's findings about Lex should not have shocked anyone:* Numerous difficulties at Lowry Park were publicly disclosed many times in the two years before Lex Salisbury was forced out. Alex Pickett at Creative Loafing repeatedly sounded an alarm about conditions at the zoo, most prominently in "Endangered Species: How Safe Is Lowry Park Zoo?" a lengthy exposé that appeared on the magazine's cover on October 25, 2006. Jeff and Coleen Kremer gave interviews to several reporters at different media outlets and documented problems at the zoo on their group's Web site, tampaszooadvocates.com, long before the scandal exploded. The author, meanwhile, detailed Herman's and Enshalla's deaths in "Elegy for the King and Queen," published in the *St. Petersburg Times* on October 1, 2006, and chronicled Salisbury's fiery management style and morale issues at the zoo, as well as the potential for conflicts of interest at Safari Wild, in "Zoo Story," a nine-part series published in December 2007.

216 *the staff routinely saw him driving a trailer:* The author observed this repeatedly and heard zoo staffers talking about it as a matter of course, including at a docents meeting he attended in October 2003, where Lee Ann Rottman announced that four of the zoo's zebras had come from Salisbury's ranch.

216 The Mayor's Hour: Alexandra Zayas, "City of Tampa TV Showed Rhinos' Delivery to Private Zoo," *St. Petersburg Times*, October 23, 2008. As of this writing, photos of the two rhinos being transported to Safari Wild—and of Lowry Park employees observing the move—can still be viewed on the city of Tampa's Web site, http://tampafl.gov/dept_Cable_Communication/programs_ and_services/city_of_tampa_television/_behind_the_scenes/ behind_the_scenes37.asp.

217 *Trent Meador thought maybe it was a coyote:* This account of Meador's shooting of one of the escaped monkeys is closely based on Ben Montgomery's remarkable article, "The Real Fate of Monkey No. 15," *St. Petersburg Times*, January 30, 2009.

219 *"You're not going to catch those monkeys":* This account of Lex and Deana Brown's experiences trapping the final four monkeys is based on an award-winning multimedia project written by Kelley Benham and illustrated by Don Morris, titled "Escape from Monkey Island" and published in the *St. Petersburg Times* on February 1, 2009. An interactive version of the story, featuring animation by John Corbitt and Desiree Perry, can be viewed on the *Times'* Web site at http://www.tampabay.com/specials/2009/reports/monkey-island/. Additional information from the original interviews with the Browns was also shared with the author, courtesy of Benham, and was woven into this account.

17 CULL

222 *That Thursday broke bright and clear:* This chapter is based on numerous news articles on the board meeting, especially Alexandra Zayas's "Lowry Park's Longtime Chief Forced to Resign," *St. Petersburg Times*, and Baird Helgeson's "Lowry Park Zoo Director Announces Resignation," *Tampa Tribune*, both published on December 19, 2008. The author also relied on Web updates that these reporters and others filed even before the meeting was over. The account is also based on the author's interviews with Salisbury and Sheppa and with two members of the Lowry Park board who voted that day.

224 *the nothingness of the hotel corridors:* The descriptions of how the day felt to the reporters are based on the author's interview with Alexandra Zayas.

225 *"You can't possibly be serious":* Author interview with Marti Ryan, spokeswoman for Hillsborough County's Animal Services.

225 *"in a car with the windows cracked?"*: This scene is based on the author's interviews with Elena Sheppa, Marti Ryan, and Corporal Denise Brewer, the animal services officer who cited Sheppa, as well as photos that Brewer took of the Pathfinder that day in the parking lot as part of her investigation. The author also relied on an article by Dennis Joyce, "Wife of Ex-Zoo Director Charged with Animal Cruelty," *Tampa Tribune*, December 18, 2008.

226 *details trickled out:* This account of the board meeting is based on the author's interviews with Salisbury, with former board member Bob Jordan, and with another board member who wished to remain anonymous.

227 *board chairman went to the room:* Based on the author's interview with Lex Salisbury and on statements made by Robert Merritt, the chairman, during a press conference immediately after the board meeting.

Epilogue   DUSK

228 *search for a new executive director:* Baird Helgeson, "Tampa Zoo Uses Vague Ad to Seek New CEO," *Tampa Tribune*, September 30, 2009.

229 *"A business with two brands":* Quoted from a Lowry Park media release.

229 *"the number one zoo in America":* Heard by author repeatedly during calls to the zoo in the fall of 2009 and spring of 2010.

229 *Lee Ann remembered:* This section, including the details of Bamboo's and Sasha's deaths, is based on the author's interview with Rottman in early 2010.

231 *El Diablo Blanco stared into the flames:* This section is based on the author's interview with Salisbury and Sheppa at their ranch in Pasco County on February 28, 2010.

232 *clearly weary of the whole affair:* Alexandra Zayas, "Tampa's Lowry Park Zoo and Former President Lex Salisbury Negotiate a Financial Settlement," *St. Petersburg Times*, August 22, 2009.

232 *further prosecution is not warranted:* Salisbury supplied the author with a copy of the letter.

235 *"the serial killer of the biosphere":* E. O. Wilson, *The Future of Life*, p. 94.

235 *golden frogs have all but vanished:* Author interview with Kevin Zippel.

236 *a toddler, staring down a rhino:* The author saw the poster during a visit to Mick Reilly's home.

236 *"Nature . . . plays no favorites":* The author reported these scenes in Mkhaya, including the closing conversation at the watering hole, during an April 2007 trip to Swaziland.

··· Bibliography ···

Baratay, Eric, and Elisabeth Hardouin-Fugier. *Zoo: A History of Zoological Gardens in the West.* English translation. Reaktion Books, 2002.

Bartlett, R. D. *Poison Dart Frogs: Facts & Advice on Care and Breeding.* Barron's Educational Series, Inc., 2003.

Beard, Peter. *The End of the Game: The Last Word From Paradise.* Updated edition. Taschen, 2008.

Biology, Medicine, and Surgery of Elephants. Edited by Murray E. Fowler and Susan K. Mikota. Blackwell Publishing, 2006.

The Care and Management of Captive Chimpanzees. Edited by Linda Brent. The American Society of Primatologists, 1997.

Chadwick, Douglas H. *The Fate of the Elephant.* Sierra Club Books, 1994.

Clement, Herb. *Zoo Man.* Macmillan, 1969.

Cognitive Development in Chimpanzees. Edited by T. Matsuzawa, M. Tomonaga, and M. Tanaka. Springer, 2006.

Crandall, Lee S., in collaboration with William Bridges. *A Zoo Man's Notebook.* University of Chicago Press, 1975.

Croke, Vicki. *The Modern Ark: The Story of Zoos: Past, Present and Future.* Scribner, 1997.

A Cultural History of Animals. Volumes One through Six. Edited by Linda Kalof and Brigitte Resl. English edition by Berg, 2007.

de Waal, Frans. *Chimpanzee Politics: Power and Sex among Apes.* Revised edition, Johns Hopkins University Press, 2000.

Donahue, Jesse, and Erik Trump. *The Politics of Zoos: Exotic Animals and Their Protectors.* Northern Illinois University Press, 2006.

Douglas-Hamilton, Iain and Oria. *Battle for the Elephants.*
First American edition, Viking Penguin, 1992.

*An Elephant in the Room: The Science and Well-Being of Elephants in
Captivity.* Edited by Debra L. Forthman, Lisa F. Kane, David
Hancocks, and Paul F. Waldau. From a 2006 symposium at Tufts
University's Center for Animals and Public Policy, since posted
online at elephantsincaptivity.com.

Elephant Management: A Scientific Assessment for South Africa.
Edited by R. J. Scholes and K. G. Mennell. Witwatersrand
University Press, Johannesburg, 2008.

Elephants and Ethics: Toward a Morality of Coexistence. Edited by
Christen Wemmer and Catherine A. Christen. The Johns Hopkins
University Press, 2008.

The Encylopedia of Mammals. Edited by David Macdonald. Second
edition. The Brown Reference Group, 2001.

Ethics on the Ark: Zoos, Animal Welfare, and Wildlife Conservation.
Edited by Bryan G. Norton, Michael Hutchins, Elizabeth F.
Stevens, and Terry L. Maple. Smithsonian Institution Press, 1996.

Fowler, Murray. *Restraint and Handling of Wild and Domestic
Animals.* Third edition. Wiley-Blackwell, 2008.

Friend, Tim. *Animal Talk: Breaking the Codes of Animal Language.*
Free Press, 2004.

Goodall, Jane. *In the Shadow of Man.* First Mariners Books edition,
2000.

Goodall, Jane. *Through a Window: My Thirty Years with the
Chimpanzees of Gombe.* First Mariners Books edition, 2000.

Grandin, Temple, and Catherine Johnson. *Animals in Translation.*
Paperback edition by Harcourt Books, 2006.

Hancocks, David. *A Different Nature: The Paradoxical World of Zoos
and Their Uncertain Future.* University of California Press, 2001.

Hanson, Elizabeth. *Animal Attractions: Nature on Display in American Zoos.* Princeton University Press, 2002.

Hediger, H. *The Psychology and Behaviour of Animals in Zoos and Circuses.* English translation. Dover Publications, Inc., 1969.

Hediger, H. *Wild Animals in Captivity: An Outline of the Biology of Zoological Gardens.* English translation. Dover Publications, Inc., 1964.

Hill, Peggy S. M. *Vibrational Communication in Animals.* Harvard University Press, 2008.

Hosey, Geoff, Vicky Melfi, and Sheila Pankurst. *Zoo Animals: Behaviour, Management, and Welfare.* Oxford University Press, 2009.

Human Zoos: Science and Spectacle in the Age of Colonial Empires. Edited by Pascal Blanchard, Nicolas Bancel, Gilles Boetsch, Eric Deroo, Sandrine Lemaire, and Charles Forsdick. English translation by Liverpool University Press, 2009.

Jamison, Kay Redfield. *Night Falls Fast: Understanding Suicide.* Alfred A. Knopf, 1999.

Joubert, Salomon. *The Kruger National Park: A History.* Volumes One and Two. High Branching, 2007.

Kessler, Cristina. *All the King's Animals: The Return of Endangered Wildlife to Swaziland.* Boyds Mills Press, 2001.

The Kruger Experience: Ecology and Management of Savanna Heterogeneity. Edited by Johan T. du Toit, Kevin H. Rogers, and Harry C. Biggs. Island Press, 2003.

Linden, Eugene. *The Octopus and the Orangutan: New Tales of Animal Intrigue, Intelligence, and Ingenuity.* Dutton, 2002.

Lotters, Stefan, Karl-Heinz Jungfer, Friedrich Wilhelm Henkel, and Wolfgang Schmidt. *Poison Frogs: Biology, Species & Captive Husbandry.* Chimaira, 2007.

Machiavellian Intelligence II: Extensions and Evaluations. Edited by Andrew Whiten and Richard W. Byrne. Cambridge University Press, 1997.

Malamud, Randy. *Reading Zoos: Representations of Animals and Captivity.* New York University Press, 1998.

Maple, Terry L., and Erika F. Archibald. *Zoo Man: Inside the Zoo Revolution.* Longstreet Press, 1993.

Moss, Cynthia. *Elephant Memories: Thirteen Years in the Life of an Elephant Family.* Ballantine Books, 1989.

Mullan, Bob, and Garry Marvin. *Zoo Culture.* University of Illinois Press, 1999.

O'Connell, Caitlin. *The Elephant's Secret Sense: The Hidden Life of the Wild Herds of Africa.* Free Press, 2007.

Payne, Katharine. *Elephants Calling.* Crown Publishers Inc., 1992.

Payne, Katy. *Silent Thunder: The Hidden Voice of Elephants.* Paperback edition. Orion, 1999.

Peterson, Dale. *Elephant Reflections.* Photographs by Karl Ammann. University of California Press, 2009.

Poole, Joyce. *Coming of Age With Elephants: A Memoir.* Hyperion, 1996.

Poole, Joyce. *Elephants.* Voyageur Press Inc., 1997.

Robinson, Phillip T. *Life at the Zoo: Behind the Scenes with the Animal Doctors.* Columbia University Press, 2004.

Rothfels, Nigel. *Savages and Beasts: The Birth of the Modern Zoo.* The Johns Hopkins University Press, 2002.

Ryan, R. J. *Keepers of the Ark: An Elephants' (sic) View of Captivity.* Self-published by Xlibiris Corporation, 1999.

Scigliano, Eric. *Love, War, and Circuses: The Age-Old Relationship Between Elephants and Humans.* Houghton Mifflin Company, 2002.

Sihler, Amanda and Greg. *Poison Dart Frogs: A Complete Guide to Dendrobatidae.* T. F. H. Publications, 2007.

Sukumar, Raman. *The Living Elephants: Evolutionary Ecology, Behavior, and Conservation.* Oxford University Press, 2003.

Sutherland, Amy. *Kicked, Bitten, and Scratched: Life and Lessons at the World's Premier School for Exotic Animal Trainers.* Viking Penguin, 2006.

Tigers of the World: The Biology, Biopolitics, Management, and Conservation of an Endangered Species. Edited by Ronald L. Tilson and Ulysses S. Seal. Noyes Publications, 1989.

Turner, Alan. *The Big Cats and Their Fossil Relatives.* Columbia University Press, 1997.

Wild Mammals in Captivity: Principles and Techniques. Edited by Devra G. Kleiman, Mary E. Allen, Katerina V. Thompson, Susan Lumpkin, and Holly Harris. The University of Chicago Press, 1996.

The Wildlife of Southern Africa: The Larger Illustrated Guide to the Animals and Plants of the Region, edited by Vincent Carruthers. Larger format edition. Struik Publishers, 2008.

Wittgenstein, Ludwig. *Philosophical Investigations.* Revised English translation, 50th Anniversary Commemorative Edition, published in 2001 by Blackwell Publishing.

Wrangham, Richard, and Dale Peterson. *Demonic Males: Apes and the Origins of Human Violence.* Mariner Books, 1997.

Wright, Lawrence. *The Looming Tower: Al-Qaeda and the Road to 9/11.* Alfred A. Knopf, 2006.

Wylie, Dan. *Elephant.* Reaktion Books Ltd, 2008.

Zoo and Aquarium History: Ancient Animal Collections to Zoological Gardens. Edited by Vernon N. Kisling, Jr. CRC Press LLC, 2001.

SCIENTIFIC PAPERS

"The Effects of Early Experience on Adult Copulatory Behavior in Zoo-Born Chimpanzees (*Pantroglodytes*)," Nancy E. King and Jill D. Mellen, *Zoo Biology* 13: 1 (1994); 51–59.

"African Elephant Vocal Communication I: Antiphonal Calling Behaviour among Affiliated Females," Joseph Soltis, Kirsten Leong, and Anne Savage, *Animal Behaviour* 70: 3 (2005); 579–587.

"Anatomy of the Reproductive Tract of the Female African Elephant (*Loxodonta africana*) with Reference to Development of Techniques for Artificial Breeding," J. M. E. Balke, W. J. Boever, M. R. Ellersieck, U. S. Seal, and D. A. Smith, *Journal of Reproduction & Fertility* 84 (1988); 485–492.

"Aspects of the Reproductive Biology and Breeding Management of Asian and African Elephants *Elephas maximus* and *Loxodonta africana*," T. B. Hildebrandt, F. Göritz, R. Hermes, C. Reid, M. Dehnhard, and J. L. Brown, *International Zoo Yearbook* 40: 1 (2006); 20–40.

"Assessment of Elephant Management in South Africa"—powerpoint presentation delivered on February 25, 2008—authored by Bob Schole and 62 other elephant researchers.

"Electroejaculation, Semen Characteristics and Serum Testosterone Concentrations of Free-Ranging African Elephants (*Loxodonta africana*)," JoGayle Howard, M. Bush, V. de Vos, and D. E. Wildt, *Journal of Reproduction & Fertility* 72 (1984); 187–195.

"Elephant Communication," W. R. Langbauer, Jr., *Zoo Biology* 19: 5 (2000); 425–455.

"Elephant Culling's Cruel and Gory Past," article posted on International Fund for Animal Welfare's Web site, http//www.ifaw .org/ifaw/general/default.aspx?oid=155902.

"Liquid Storage of Asian Elephant (*Elephas maximus*) Sperm at 4°C," L. H. Graham, J. Bando, C. Gray, M. M. Buhr, *Animal Reproduction Science* 80: 4 (2004); 329–340.

"Managing Multiple Elephants Using Protected Contact at San Diego's Wild Animal Park," by Gary Priest, Jennine Antrim, Jane Gilbert, and Valerie Hare, *Soundings* 23: 1 (1998); 20–24.

"Manual Collection and Characterization of Semen from Asian Elephants (*Elephas maximus*)," D. L. Schmitt, T. B. Hildebrandt, *Animal Reproduction Science* 53: 1 (1998); 309–314.

"A Review of Injuries Caused by Elephants in Captivity: An Examination of Predominant Factors," M. Gore, M. Hutchins, and J. Ray, *International Zoo Yearbook* 40: 1 (2006); 51–62.

"Reproductive Evaluation in Wild African Elephants Prior to Translocation," Thomas B. Hildebrandt, Robert Hermes, Donald L. Janssen, James E. Oosterhuis, David Murphy, and Frank Göritz—from the proceedings of a 2004 joint conference of the American Association of Zoo Veterinarians, the American Association of Wildlife Veterinarians, and the Wildlife Disease Association, pp. 76–77.

"Responses of Captive African Elephants to Playback of Low-Frequency Calls," William R. Langbauer, Jr., Katharine B. Payne, Russell A. Charif, and Elizabeth M. Thomas, *Canadian Journal of Zoology* 67: 10 (1989); 2604–2607.

"Rumble Vocalizations Mediate Interpartner Distance in African Elephants, *Loxodonta africana*," Katherine A. Leighty, Joseph Soltis, Christina M. Wesolek, and Anne Savage, *Animal Behaviour* 76: 5 (2008); 1601–1608.

"Semen Collection in an Asian Elephant (*Elephas maximus*) Under Combined Physical and Chemical Restraint," T. J. Portas, B. R. Bryant, F. Göritz, R. Hermes, T. Keeley, G. Evans, W. M. C. Maxwell, and T. B. Hildebrandt, *Australian Veterinary Journal* 85: 10 (2007); 425–427.

"Social Interactions in Captive Female Florida Manatees," Jennifer Young Harper and Bruce A. Schulte, *Zoo Biology* 24: 2 (2005); 135–144.

"Successful Cryopreservation of Asian Elephant (*Elephas maximus*) Spermatozoa," Joseph Saragusty, Thomas B. Hildebrandt, Britta Behr, Andreas Knieriem, Jurgen Kruse, Robert Hermes, *Animal Reproduction Science* article in press, doi:10.1016/j.anireprosci .2008.11.010.

"There's No Place Like Home—'The Swazi 11,' a Case Study in the Global Trade in Live Elephants," Adam M. Roberts and Will Travers, presented at the XIXth International Congress of Zoology, August 2004, Beijing.

"The Use of Low-Frequency Vocalizations in African Elephant (*Loxodonta africana*) Reproductive Strategies," by K. M. Leong, A. Ortolani, L. H. Graham, and A. Savage, *Hormones and Behavior* 43: 4 (2003); 433–443.

"Unusually Extensive Networks of Vocal Recognition in African Elephants," Karen McComb, Cynthia Moss, Soila Sayialel, and Lucy Baker, *Animal Behaviour* 59: 6 (2000); 1103–1109.

West African Chimpanzees: Status Survey and Conservation Action Plan, edited by Rebecca Kormos, Christophe Boesch, Mohamed I. Bakarr, and Thomas M. Butynski, published in 2003 by the International Union for Conservation of Nature and Natural Resources.